S0-CBB-058

The *Paulines*, publishers, receved financial support from the Canadian Religious Conference (CRC) and the Corporation of Capuchin Friars for the publishing of this book.

5610 Beaubien East St.
Montreal QC H1T 1X5

Cover: *Diane Lanteigne*
ISBN: 2-920912-25-9

Légal deposit 1998
Bibliothèque nationale du Québec 1998
National Library of Canada 1998

STONE SOUP

REFLECTIONS ON ECONOMIC INJUSTICE

Gregory Baum, Michel Beaudin, Mary Boyd,
Leonard Desroches, Vivian Labrie, Guy Paiement, sj,
André Myre, Richard Renshaw, csc, Priscilla Solomon, csj,
Kevin Arsenault

Preface by Betty Berrigan, csj

Paulines

Canadian Religious Conference / Jesuit Centre for Social Faith and Justice - Toronto

ACKNOWLEDGEMENTS

The Canadian Religious Conference would like to thank all those who contributed to this publication project, including, very especially, Diane Marleau who coordinated the whole process with patience and careful attention. The Jesuit Centre for Social Faith and Justice was our co-partner in the process and generously collaborated from the very beginning. We thank also Sister Ann Miller csj, who edited the final version of our English text. Special thanks go to the authors of each chapter who dedicated their time and talents, to our editorial committee (Diane Marleau, Monique Thériault snjm, Kevin Arsenault, Barbara Paleczny ssnd and Richard Renshaw csc), to Betty Berrigan csj who wrote the preface, to our translator Ursula Desmarteau and other collaborators, Helena Kelly, Patricia Leahy, Patricia Sherlock. And finally, to the team of the *Paulines* publishing house for their marvellous collaboration in this publishing venture.

Hélène Robitaille, fdls,
General Secretary
Canadian Religious Conference

CONTENTS

ABBREVIATIONS

AFB: Alternative Federal Budget
AFN: Assembly of First Nations
ANC: African National Congress
APEC: Asia Pacific Economic Cooperation Forum
APGM: Autonomous Precision Guided Munition
ARC: Aboriginal Rights Coalition (Project North)
ASP: All-weather Smart Projectile
BCNI: Business Council on National Issues
CAPMO: Carrefour de pastorale en monde ouvrier
CAP: Canada Assistance Plan
CBD: Civilian-Based Defence
CCCB: Canadian Conference of Catholic Bishops
CCF: Cooperative Commonwealth Federation
CED: Community Economic Development
CEO: Chief Executive Officer
CHC: Canadian Health Coalition
CHST: Canada Health and Social Transfer
DND: Department of National Defence
ECEJ: Ecumenical Coalition for Economic Justice
FTA: Free Trade Agreement
GDP: Gross Domestic Product
IMF: International Monetary Fund
MAI: Multilateral Agreement on Investment
NAFTA: North American Free Trade Agreement
OECD: Organization for Economic Development and Cooperation
TNC: Transnational Corporation
UK: United Kingdom
WB: World Bank

Preface

For years, I have been struggling in my own life, as have we, in our Congregation, to know how best to respond as Christians to the increasing dilemma of the marginalization and poverty of our people in this our Canadian culture. Having been raised and having lived mainly in rural settings, I have come to believe strongly in the responses to crises of the ordinary local people and especially of small faith communities.

On a more global level, a few events stand out for me in which everyday people took their lives into their own hands and forced the changes that they deemed necessary for their dignity and destiny. The example of others can urge us on. The scene of the people of the Philippines, arm-in-arm facing the military, has left an indelible mark in my memory. And change resulted.

I continue to admire the peaceful resistance of the Chiapas native peoples. Under the leadership of Bishop Samuel Ruiz, the Mexicans of the diocese have finally succeeded in getting the attention of the government so that it would consider including them in decisions made about them and their land. At our Latin-American Conference of Sisters of St. Joseph, in Mexico City in 1996, Bishop Ruiz, a quiet, joyful, unassuming man, received a standing ovation when he stated, "The only way to be bishop in my diocese is to be one with the people."

I watch the changing face of Haiti and hope that the faith and courage of the people will eventually, and soon, bring the transformation this nation needs if the people are to live with dignity and true democracy. And so, I ended my reflection eager to read the articles that make up this book and to preface them.

I think there would be agreement among many people today that one of the signs of our times is the increasing economic disparity between the rich and the poor of our country and indeed of most other developed countries. How do we dialogue with our faith and the signs of the times? As religious leaders of Congregations, leaders in the Church and those close to the oppressed, the hungry and the poor, we have a responsibility to put our expertise and resources at the service of those seeking solutions to the obvious struggles of our people. We are less than what we say we are if we are not missionaries, that is, if we are not reaching out beyond ourselves to help liberate others. Was this not Jesus' mission as he himself so clearly stated in Luke's Gospel, "The spirit of the Lord . . . has sent me to proclaim liberty to captives, give sight to the blind, to let the oppressed go free" (4:18). It is the mission of every Christian.

Another sign of our times, as several of the authors state in their submissions, is the fact that today we are living in a new historical situation. It has been with us since the 1980s and is often referred to as neoliberalism. The articles presented in this book explain very well how the market governs, while the government, whose mandate is to do just that, does not govern but manages. What appears to be growth and over-production of wealth in our society paradoxically causes a scarcity of employment, a deterioration of working conditions and serious cuts to social services. As Christians, we have a responsibility to become better informed so as to act in solidarity with our struggling sisters and brothers to effect solutions to the strife of our day.

The scope of this book is such that a serious reading will do much to educate, inform and incite action. Because of the method used—see, judge, act—the authors give insightful reflections on various aspects of our culture that touch the pulse of our day. At the same time, we are left with realistic hope that change will be effected. Because Jesus never promoted fatalism, our faith urges us to continue the dialogue with our present situations in the light of the Gospel and Church teachings, so as to know how to act.

This book is an excellent place to begin.

Betty Berrigan, csj

INTRODUCTION

The Title

Vivian Labrie tells us a wonderful story about "stone soup" in her chapter in this book. It is an old Russian folktale that has been often edited as a "children's" book. The images in the story came to have special meaning for the editorial committee and ended up inspiring the title of the book. The story of the stone soup is set in a context of oppression, hunger and economic hardship. Nevertheless, the actual making of the soup is an expression of solidarity, creativity and empowerment to meet shared needs in a way that overcomes the hardship. Soup nourishes and gives energy; it can also bring us together around the same table. In the case of our story, making soup built a community of solidarity. All the authors you will read here reaffirm the challenge we have today to make "stone soup." We are convinced that, as responsible and thinking adults, there is a great deal we can do to improve the economic climate in the world. However, we need to understand how to do that and to have the courage to act.

The Process

This book is the result of a dialogue among its authors and is being published simultaneously in both English and French. The project grew out of a concern expressed by the Administrative Council of the Canadian Religious Conference (CRC) meeting in Pierrefonds in 1995. They wanted to know how vowed religious could continue today to exercise the leadership they have had historically in Canada's past. To provide some direction for dealing with that concern, the National Secretariat of the CRC, along with the Jesuit Centre for Social Faith and Justice, sponsored a consultation with eight Roman Catholic thinkers. We selected the participants on the basis of their history of reflection but also because of their commitment to issues at a grassroots level.

While each author is responsible for her or his own thoughts, the book results from long hours of discussion about the perspectives represented here. The participants came from Quebec, Ontario and Prince Edward Island, from university, worker and native circles. We are particularly happy to have initiated a dialogue between English and French-speaking thinkers. Such a dialogue needs to continue. In this respect you may find some phrases in our "soup" a bit spicy. We have made no effort to soften the discourse.

Besides the English-French dimension there are several others of importance in our collection. The contribution of Priscilla Solomon offers a distinctly Aboriginal perspective that is also valuable in this context. Among the authors are men and women, celibate religious and parents of young children, serious academics and manual labourers. We think this multidimensionality has enriched the reflections. The result is thus distinctly Canadian in a number of ways.

The Question

What leadership do we as Christians offer in face of the injustices of our globalized economy? While this question was raised initially by a group of Major Superiors, we have tried to address only one small part of their larger concern. The concern about a response to economic injustice has taken on a life of its own and become for us a question that can (and should!) be addressed to the entire faith community in Canada, to all the Churches, to Church leaders and to everyone who takes his or her faith commitment seriously. It is a question many people in the Americas and elsewhere have agonized over in recent years. The old responses are no longer adequate or even appropriate. What God calls us to today is not very clear. Here you will find eight authors who have reflected together and offer their views, not as a definitive solution—we are far from that—but at least as an incentive to move the question along, an encouragement to believe that it can be approached and that a vision can be developed from our Christian tradition.

In order to address our question, we asked each author to keep a *see-judge-act* methodology [1] in mind. We then divided the book into three parts, largely to help the reader find readable "sips." Each part carries the name of a vegetable that is native to the American continents. Together the chapters form a kind of "recipe" for what is, ultimately, our very own "soup"—stone soup! The chapters move from a variety of perspectives and with different styles that we think can be juxtaposed creatively. There is no other logic to the order. Readers will certainly benefit just as well by reading the chapters in whatever order suits them.

* * *

The book opens with a chapter by Gregory Baum. In it he explores our tradition as Roman Catholics on social issues and the economic transformations during these last decades. That history can provide us with a clearer understanding of our strengths and our weaknesses. He offers us some pointers on where, in our tradition, we might look for guidance into the future.

Vivian Labrie tells a story that reminds us that we cannot expect to develop a popular movement for transformation if we do not courageously open the space for that to happen. Her lively account of the "Relay Fast" in Quebec City is full of hope that we are not alone and that we can make a difference.

Michel Beaudin, analyses models of Church and society. This provides an important tool for understanding how each of us assesses the relationship between a faith commitment and social questions. Not all of us are in the same place. After examining his models we may better understand why we (and others) see the questions in the way we do. We can also review critically whether our starting point and the resulting conundrums are appropriate. Like Gregory Baum, Michel Beaudin also provides a critical review of the ideological dimensions of neoliberal economics.[2] His contrast of the "religious" dimensions of neoliberalism with the biblical tradition is particularly striking.

* * *

Priscilla Solomon and Len Desroches, like Vivian Labrie, are concerned with those experiences that expose the consequences of neoliberal ideology. They too challenge us to action. In their stories we discover other local contributions that Christians can make. Priscilla Solomon, speaking from traditional aboriginal wisdom challenges us to think in a very different way about our relationship to the world around us. More and more aboriginal and non-native people alike are finding that their traditional wisdom deeply enriches their Christian faith. As we begin to notice the first visible signs of climate change, Priscilla points to a way to help salvage humanity from its own self-destruction.

Len Desroches is concerned about self-destruction from another viewpoint. He has struggled against the military economy in Canada for many years. It has cost him personally in important ways. His reflections cut deeply and personally. They call to conversion on a variety of levels.

* * *

André Myre complements Michel Beaudin's contribution with an exploration of the political-economic context of Jesus' times and the impact of his ministry in that context. This is a cutting edge of biblical research today, one that is offering fresh perspectives on Jesus' human identity, his ministry and the impact of his teaching. At the same time, this knowledge can contribute a great deal to orienting our response, as followers of Jesus, to the issues that plague us today.

Mary Boyd helps us appreciate some of the dynamics at work in the world today that crush the most vulnerable in society as well as pointing to the *kairos,* moment of grace hidden in these events. Her contribution to a discussion of economic injustice is sharp and full of outrage.

Guy Paiement offers a final set of reflections and, in very Jesuit fashion, invites us to a discernment of neoliberal ideology. Drawing from the apocalyptic tradition in the Bible he offers a powerful image that can guide us through a review of neoliberal ideology and a discernment of the "signs of the times."

Hope

There is also a second question implicit in all these chapters: How important is the leadership Christians can offer? The book is meant to address a rich diversity of faith communities from one end of the country to the other. We hope many people from a variety of faith traditions will find here encouragement in the chaos that characterizes this change of epoch. We certainly don't have all the answers but we do want to contribute to an important dialogue and to offer some perspectives that will stimulate the intense energy we felt as we prepared these texts. After reading all the chapters, I think you will agree that there is much room for hope that Christians can provide significant leadership to the dilemmas of our time. To accomplish this will require much reflection, dialogue and consensus building. We hope our book contributes to that process.

Finally, it is also my personal hope that the men and women committed to vowed religious life in Canada will consider this book, conceived out of their concerns, to be of special interest for them. Geraldine Lancaster, sc, in a recent article in the *CRC Bulletin,*[3] reported on an international summit on microcredit she attended in Washington. The invitation she received to that event stated that "Religious Congregations could play an important role because of their experience in poverty-stricken areas and because of the integrity of their work." We concur.

Richard Renshaw, csc

Richard Renshaw, csc, Assistant General Secretary of the Canadian Religious Conference. He studied at the University of Notre Dame (B.A.), Gregorian University (S.T.L.), University of Toronto (M.A.). He is a former editor of Connexions as well as Latin American Documentation (LADOC). He has been lecturer at St. Thomas University (N.B.), the Catholic University of Peru and the John XXIII Institute of Theological Studies (Lima).

NOTES

1. See-Judge-Act is a methodology originally developed for the Young Catholic Workers (YCW) and extended to most of the organizations of Catholic Action in the 1940s and 1950s. Later it underlay the final documents of the Medellin Conference of Latin American Bishops in 1968. After that it became the underlying methodology of the other Latin American Bishops' Conferences at Puebla and Santo Domingo as well as much of liberation theology. In the methodology there are three movements. In very summary and simplified terms, *See* refers to the concrete reality as experienced by the participants. In the case of the YCW, it meant looking at what was happening in the specific factory where the participants were working. In the case of Latin American theology, it meant examining the social, economic and political reality of the Latin American poor. *Judge* on the other hand referred to the examination of the underlying values that guide decision-making in these areas. In Catholic Action, in the Latin American bishops' conferences as well as in the case of liberation theology, it meant examining whatever aspects of the Gospel message might shed light on the reality exposed in the *See* part of the methodology. Finally, the *Act* part of the methodology involves a search for alternatives and options in light of the previous two steps. It leads to decisive action to transform the situation exposed in the first step so that it conforms more to the values uncovered in the second step.

2. Some of the terms used in this book may not be familiar to all readers; others are frequently used in widely divergent ways. At the end of this book you will find a short Glossary of terms with a brief explanation of how they are being used here.

3. *CRC Bulletin,* Vol. XXXVII, No. 2, pp. 14-15.

1

"potatoes"

Thickening the soup

ARE WE IN A NEW HISTORICAL SITUATION?

MUST WE RETHINK WHAT JUSTICE AND SOLIDARITY MEAN TODAY?

GREGORY BAUM

Gregory Baum, during Vatican Council II a theologian "peritus" at the Christian Unity Secretariat, was a professor of theology at St. Michael's College (1959-1986) and, later, at McGill University (1986-1995), member of the editing staff of the Relations *review. He recently published,* Karl Polanyi on Ethics and Economics *(McGill-Queen's University Press) and* The Church for Others: Protestant Theology in Communist East Germany *(Eerdmans).*

At the time of Vatican Council II, I was a theological liberal: I believed that the redemptive work of Jesus Christ granted us personal transformation, rescue from sin, greatness of heart, love of neighbour, and openness to outsiders. Since I paid little attention to the sinful and oppressive structures that cause human misery, I did not ask myself whether Christ's redemptive work also promised to rescue humans from unjust structures.

Later in the early seventies, I was deeply affected by the Conclusions of the Medellin Conference, Latin American liberation theology, and the prolonged encounter with two theologians, Johannes Baptist Metz and Rosemary Radford Ruether. I was now willing to look at the world, no longer from the perspective of my own rather comfortable situation, but rather from the perspective of the poor and oppressed. I was touched by the pastoral statements of the Canadian bishops published during the seventies. As a theologian and an activist, I began to participate in the groups and networks of the Catholic Left, now deeply convinced that Christ is the saviour of the world, intent upon saving us from sin, injustice and every form of oppression.

In this article I wish to reply to the two questions posed in the title. To do this I have to discuss a number of issues. First I want to show that the hopeful social vision entertained by Vatican Council II reflected, in part at least, the cultural optimism of the sixties. Even the hope for social revolution found in the Medellin Conference and liberation theology were carried by a cultural optimism that pervaded Latin America in the late sixties and seventies. The cultural optimism in the NATO countries, I shall then show, was related to the success of the welfare state and the idea that economic expansion could be extended to the whole world, making poverty a phenomenon of the past. After that I shall turn to more recent events: the growing power of transnational corporations, the invention of computer technology, the globalization of the free market economy, the decline of the welfare state and the appearance of chronic massive unemployment. This is not a time for optimism. In this new historical phase growing sectors of the population, in Canada and in other parts, find themselves excluded from work and the necessities of life. Finally I shall ask how people who love justice, and Christians in particular, are responding to this situation? Christian hope never dies.

The Vatican Council

At Vatican Council II the Catholic Church, responding to lay movements all over the world, adopted a critical openness to modern society and encouraged all Catholics to engage themselves in the defence of human rights and the promotion of social justice. In the past, we used to make a neat distinction between the Church's supernatural mission to offer people faith, hope and love and the Church's temporal mission to support peace and justice in society. In neo-scholasticism, charity was seen as a supernatural virtue while justice was simply a natural virtue. At Vatican Council II, especially in *Gaudium et spes*, the Church recognized that faith, hope and love summoned people to participate in society and involve themselves in cultural, social or political movements that promote freedom, justice and peace. The Council criticized the individualistic ethics contained in the manuals used in Catholic schools and seminaries. (*GS* 30). The famous first sentence of *Gaudium et spes* was a declaration of love and solidarity addressed by the Church to the whole human family, beginning with the poor and the weak.

There was an optimistic tone in *Gaudium et spes*. We find in it repeated expressions of the conviction that, if the people of good will in the world acted together, the economic order of the wealthy nations could be reformed, and with their help the poverty of the masses in the less fortunate countries could be overcome. "For the first time in human history, we read, all people are convinced that the benefits of culture ought to be and can be extended to everyone." (*GS* 9). But are we certain that "all people" are really convinced of this? The Council held that because God is graciously present to the sinful world, there is reason to hope that the liberal ideals of modern society, freedom, equality and fraternity—though at one time rejected by the Church—will come to be realized in all parts of the globe.

It is possible, I think, to speak of the Council's social democratic confidence that capitalism can be tamed and made to serve the common good of society. We find the same confidence in papal social teaching, beginning with John XXIII. An interventionist government, a strong labour movement and an ethical culture of solidarity should be able to guide and restrain the free market system so that the wealth produced will be distributed in accordance with the norms of justice. As late as 1987, Pope John Paul II, writing his encyclical *Sollicitudo rei socialis* still believed that Western capitalism and Eastern European communism could be reformed, the former by strengthening the government's redistributive function and the latter by granting more civic and economic freedoms.[1]

The Medellin Conference

In 1968, three years after the end of the Council, the Latin American Bishops Conference held its meeting at Medellin, Colombia. Looking at the expanding liberal world system from the margins, i.e from the perspective of their impoverished continent, the Latin American bishops did not share the optimistic interpretation of the Council. With the emerging liberation theology, they feared that the spread of western-style capitalism on their continent enriched a relatively small elite while pushing the majority of the population, the poor, into greater deprivation and dependency. The bishops, urged and supported by the base communities, declared themselves in solidarity with the poor and their struggle for greater justice.[2]

A principle emerged at Medellin that received a more precise formulation only at the Latin American Bishops Conference of 1979, held at Puebla, Mexico. The preferential option for the poor, as presented by Puebla, involves two dimensions, the hermeneutic dimension of reading society from the perspective of the poor and the activist dimension of giving public witness of solidarity with their struggle for justice.[3]

Medellin pointed in a direction that was sustained and further explored by base communities and associated with them, by liberation theologians. Western-style economic development, they recognized, depended on capital from the wealthy centre, made use of sophisticated technology, created jobs only for the few, and produced goods, not to satisfy people's needs but for export to Western markets. The poor, and those in solidarity with them, demanded liberation from this system. They wanted an economic system that used local skills, employed a simple technology, involved everyone in production, and produced the goods and services needed by the people. These Christians applied a Marxist sociology of oppression without endorsing Marxist philosophical presuppositions. Their judgement upon the oppressive society and their hope for social transformation were drawn from Scripture, the Exodus event of liberation recorded in the Old Testament and the Resurrection of the humiliated Christ, in whom all the victims of society were rehabilitated. While the Latin American bishops and theologians were ill at ease with the liberal optimism of Vatican II, they were, in their own way, optimistic: they shared the expectation widely spread on their continent that the seventies were a *kairos*, a special historical moment, when a revolution for greater justice had become an historical possibility.

In the late sixties and the early seventies, liberation movements spread in Latin America and on other continents. People wanted a socialist economy, not the centralized economy of the communist countries, but a community-based economy adaptable to various forms of ownership. It was at this time that Pope Paul VI acknowledged that this sort of socialism was attractive to Catholics. While in the past socialism had been condemned by the Church, Paul VI now distinguished between different kinds of socialism, some based on principles at odds with Christian faith while others were in conformity with Christian teaching.[4] Equally remarkable was the impact of Third World liberation theology on the 1971 World Synod of Bishops which recognized that "a network of domination, oppression and abuses is being built up around the world which stifle freedom and which keep the greater part of humanity from sharing in the enjoyment of a more just world." The Synod also declared that the redemption Christ has brought includes "the liberation of people from every oppressive condition" and that "action on behalf of justice is a constitutive dimension of the Church's proclamation of the gospel."[5]

As a result of these developments, faith-and-justice Catholics in Canada and Quebec (and other developed countries) understood their engagement in two different ways: one group, following a reformist vision, supported social democracy or democratic socialism, while the other, following a radical perspective—this happened especially in Quebec—struggled with their secular comrades for a revolutionary transformation of society. The bold social teaching of the Canadian bishops, influenced by the Latin American Bishops and the World Synod of Bishops, can be read both in a reformist and a radical manner. Some Catholics supported the perfecting of social democracy in Canada while others struggled for the creation of an alternative society.

The Canadian bishops also proposed the idea (to which we shall return further on) that it may be more realistic to think of the struggle for greater justice in social, rather then political terms.[6] According to social scientists of the period, the foundation for radical social change will most likely be laid by social movements, the old ones such as the labour movement, and especially the more recent ones, such as the women's movement, the peace movement, the ecological movement, the cooperative movement, and the movement against free trade.

Welfare Capitalism

The optimism of Vatican II was not unrelated to the achievement of welfare capitalism which had reached its high point in the sixties. The industrialized countries were enjoying economic growth, full employment, and welfare for the needy. The middle-class societies of north-western Europe—France, Germany, Belgium and Holland—were the home of the most influential bishops and theologians of the Vatican Council. The present system, these men were inclined to believe, could be perfected and spread throughout the world.

What was the origin of the welfare state? We recall that unrestrained capitalism had revealed its failure in the great depression of the thirties. Unemployment and poverty prevailed in the Western nations. No wonder that in those years many people turned to radical forms of socialism. In Canada, a new political party, the Cooperative Commonwealth Federation (CCF) was founded in 1933, the socialist policy of which was expressed in the Regina Manifesto. "No CCF government will rest," it said, "until it has eradicated capitalism." The thirties also saw the growth in Canada of the Communist Party—at odds with the CCF because of the latter's democratic style. Canada's future was uncertain.

It was only during World War II that countries like Britain and Canada recovered from the economic slump and solved their problem of unemployment. Because of the war, the government, now exercising greater power, was able to tell the national bank to assume the public debt and to tell the industries to produce the tools and goods the country needed to pursue the war effort. Government intervention here made the capitalist system operate more efficiently.

The economic elites supported the interventionist policies of the government also for other reasons. Since many of the soldiers who were risking their lives on the battlefield had been unemployed before the war, the governments of Britain and Canada now felt obliged to promise these men that returning to their country they would find employment. A certain national solidarity made the economic elites support this policy. The owning classes, moreover, were greatly afraid of socialism, whether democratic or revolutionary. They were therefore ready to enter into an unwritten social contract with the government that respected labour organizations and their right to collective bargaining, supported full employment and provided a safety net for people who, for one reason or another, were excluded from the market. What took place was the birth of the welfare state.

In Canada, these social democratic policies had been advocated in the thirties by the CCF and the labour movement, but they were realized only after the war thanks to the emergence of a new consensus. The welfare state eventually became part of the electoral platform of every political party. While their rhetoric was reassuring, in actual fact the traditional parties were slow in implementing these reforms when they were in power.

The economic thinking behind this political development is attributed to the British economist and political thinker, John Maynard Keynes. He was not the only one who had new ideas. After all, Roosevelt's *New Deal*, initiated in the thirties, was based on ideas that were to be fully developed by Lord Keynes. As a thinker, Keynes was greatly aware of the destructive forces in the world and hence regarded as absurd the idea of Adam Smith that the self-regulating market was steered by "a hidden hand" to serve the well-being of society. In the twenties and thirties, Keynes observed these destructive forces operating in varying degrees in the Soviet dictatorship, belligerent Nazi Germany and the unrestrained drive for the maximization of profit that had produced the great depression. Keynes agreed with Marx that capitalism was an essentially unstable economic system oscillating between boom and bust. According to Keynes, the task of national governments was to protect their citizens from these destructive forces and create a region of security and social peace. He argued that to assure greater stability, governments should intervene in the economy, sustain the industries in periods of slackness (by grants, loans, tax breaks, etc.), and redistribute the wealth of society through a fair system of taxation. Keynes also wanted government to foster the loyalty of the labour force by putting in place a set of laws that protected the formation of labour unions and gave them the right to collective bargaining. In the long run, Keynes argued, these policies are economically advantageous. The rich shall not lose but win.

Keynesian capitalism was supported by a development in democratic theory. Political thinkers became convinced that equality in the sense of equal opportunity must be secured for all. To assure that people have the opportunity to develop their careers and, at the same time, become responsible citizens, a democratic government must guarantee not only their civil rights but also their social rights, such as the right to work and to housing, health care and education. These services strengthened democracy, the argument went, but they were also good for business. To foster production and commerce on any level, health and adequate training are of the essence. The political thinker often associated with this interpretation of democracy was William Beveridge, the author of the Beveridge Report submitted to the British government in 1942. This Report provided the basis for the welfare legislation introduced by the Labour government after the war. These ideas were brought to Canada by the British political scientist, Leonard Marsh, who wrote the Report on Social Security which oriented the social policies of the Canadian government.

Welfare capitalism was enormously successful. Some economists speak of the three "glorious decades" (1950-1980) in which the Western nations produced great wealth and distributed more of this wealth to the labouring classes than ever before. At the same time, one should not idealize the welfare state. It also had its dark side. Society did not recognize that much of its wealth resulted from the production of arms. Militarism served the interests of the economic elites. Nor did society recognize how much of its wealth was derived from natural resources bought at exploitative prices from the poorer continents. Nor did exploitation of labour disappear within Western society, despite its social democratic orientation. In Canada, the dependency on American capital steadily increased. The welfare state, moreover, became heavily bureaucratized so that it acquired oppressive features. Nor did society in the three glorious decades recognize that its growth orientation was a threat to the natural environment. While the movements challenging the racist and sexist character of society became very strong in the sixties, they were in fact unable to free society from these evils. The Native Peoples remained excluded and forgotten. Still, the three decades of economic growth generated a cultural optimism which affected not only those who wanted to reform the existing society, but even the youth movement and other radicals who dreamt of replacing the realm of necessity by the realm of freedom.

Keynesian Economics Replaced by Monetarism

In the eighties it appeared that Keynesian capitalism did not work any more. Government investment in the industries increased inflation and did not overcome unemployment. The public debt was beginning to rise. Economists are still arguing about exactly what happened. Was the crisis due to the sudden increase in the price of oil? Or was it the enormous expense of the arms race and the Vietnam War? Was it because wages were too high or social welfare demanded too much money? Did we live beyond our means? Was the growing unemployment the result of the new, electronic technology which succeeded in replacing more and more workers? Or was the crisis a propaganda victory engineered by the economic elites to increase their profit?

Whatever the complex causes, a new breed of economists, the so-called "monetarists," now advocated a return to the *laisser-faire* capitalism of the last century.[7] The monetarists opposed government intervention in the economy; they criticized state policies that protected the national economy; they demanded the privatization of publicly owned institutions; they favoured the deregulation of services and industries that had been regulated for the good of society; they opposed labour unions as obstacles to the free labour market; they revived the nineteenth-century idea that unrestrained competition was the natural "engine" that produced wealth, raised the standard of living and eventually improved the well-being of society as a whole. Ronald Reagan and Margaret Thatcher were the first political leaders who introduced the monetarist policies in their respective countries, the US and Britain. Mr. Brian Mulroney was soon to follow.

The unwritten contract between capital and society made during and after WW II was unravelling. The corporations severed their loyalty to the society in which they were founded, whose working people had created their wealth and whose government had sustained them in slack times. As governments introduced legislation in support of free trade, many corporations became transnational: they expanded, moved to other countries, and produced their goods in parts of the world where labour was cheap, unions were weak or illegal, and environmental restrictions were minimal or non-existent. In this process, many transnational corporations became major powers. The national governments that had allowed them to grow were now beholden to them. Governments had to persuade major industries to remain in the country and woo others to come into the country, promising them favourable conditions, such as building part of their installations, constructing new highways for transportation, and offering tax exemptions and other privileges. Thanks to their power, supported in each country by a strong business lobby (in Canada, the Business Council on National Issues), the government made laws that served the interests of the economic elites.

The monetarist policies first introduced by Mr. Reagan and Mrs. Thatcher were called "neo-conservative" because they first appeared in Conservative parties. Yet they were at odds with traditional political conservatism in Britain and Canada, which had defended community values and protectionist economic policies. John A. McDonald, the Conservative premier of the newly founded Canadian state, set up the National Policy that introduced tariffs in support of the Canadian economy. Conservative politicians in Britain and Canada recognized that however important markets are, there are some concerns of society that markets are unable to serve and that must be dealt with by government. In Canada, it was the Liberal party that, from the beginning, trusted the self-regulating power of the market and supported free trade with the USA. The "neo-conservative" policies are in fact a return to the original, laissez-faire liberalism of the nineteenth century. That is why in Quebec, in Latin America and on the European continent, the policies calling for minimal government and unregulated capitalism are called "neoliberal." Neoliberalism, as we shall see, is both an economic policy and a social project.

Since many people are confused by the terms "neo-conservative" and "neoliberal," let me say a few more words about them. The word "liberal," we note, is used in different ways. At the end of the eighteenth and in the nineteenth century, liberalism was used in two senses. "Economic liberalism" opposed mercantilism (the economy controlled by the king), advocated the freedom of merchants to buy and to sell as they wished, and thus fostered the growth of industrial capitalism. "Political liberalism" in its own way also opposed the aristocratic order: it advocated popular sovereignty and democratic government, promoted liberty, equality and fraternity, and fostered the idea of responsible citizenship. While these two expressions of liberalism have a certain affinity, they also contain an inner tension. Why? Because economic liberalism stands for the free market and non-interference by government, while political liberalism stands for equality and the responsibility of the government to promote peoples' well-being. It is therefore possible to call monetarist policies "liberal," in fact, a return to the original economic liberalism, while also designating as "liberal" movements that oppose unregulated capitalism in the name of equal opportunity and social responsibility.

The prefix "neo" means that the adoption of monetarist policies is a switch from policies that both the Conservative and the Liberal Parties held in the past. Both of them, even if on different theoretical grounds, had come to advocate the welfare state. In addition to unrestrained free trade, the term "neo-conservative" also suggests an emphasis on conservative social values such as law and order, women in their place, capital punishment, opposition to gun control, etc. Yet when speaking about the free market economy on the world scale, even English-speaking authors begin to prefer the term "neoliberal." It is used by the Canadian bishops in their recent pastoral letter on the eradication of poverty.

The Globalization of the Economy

The globalization of the liberal economy is, as we have seen, a creation of governments and not, as its advocates claim, a spontaneous development. Governments created the global economy by making free trade agreements with other nations and by making laws that allowed corporations to escape their social responsibility. This fact is disguised by the neoliberal rhetoric about "getting the government off our backs." Despite this insincere discourse, governments are expected to remain involved in the economy. To make the industries in their countries more competitive—the new "categorical imperative"—governments lower their taxes, sustain them financially if necessary, weaken labour unions and put the burden of the public debt on the weakest members of society.

One condition for the globalization of the economy we have not yet mentioned is the new, electronic technology. There are authors who attribute great power to the technology of production and communication. They claim that just as the steam engine and later forms of mechanical technology produced the industrial age and the nation-state, so will the new electronic technology produce a global economic system in which the nation-state will become weak and ineffectual. I fail to be convinced by such a deterministic theory, even though I recognize the powerful impact of the new technology on culture and society. Worldwide communication has become almost instantaneous. This means, among other things, that the financial market has become truly global. Money crosses national borders without control and without paying taxes. Speculation has become a universal phenomenon. The new technologies of communication, automation and transportation have allowed corporations to acquire a new flexibility, move from one continent to another and even decentralize the process of production, having certain parts produced in one country and other parts in another. Flexible capital and flexible industries call for a flexible work force. Hence the war against labour.

The new computer technology and various forms of automation derived from it, allow corporations greatly to reduce their staff. It is convenient for neoliberalism to make the government's high public debt the primary worry in people's minds. Let me explain why this is so. The public debt is undoubtedly a problem. Yet there is little discussion of why the debt has become so large. Was it produced by high interest rates, by the arms race, by lowering the fiscal contribution of corporations, by incompetent management, or by financing the social programmes? The economists who assign primacy to public debt reduction usually assume, without proof, that the debt is due to the excessive costs of health care, education and public welfare. The Canadian federal and provincial governments have successfully persuaded the electorate that for the sake of rapidly paying the public debt, great sacrifices are required: reducing the health care system, weakening educational institutions, eliminating support for cultural activities and pushing people on welfare into destitution. Governments also drastically "downsize" their own administrative offices. In the public rhetoric "downsizing" has become the theme song of the nineties. In this climate corporations, banks and insurance companies have also decided to "downsize" their staff. Even when their profits are very high, they decide to automate their factories and offices and lay off large numbers of their employees. Millions upon millions of workers and employees have lost their jobs in the nineties. Some governments have the nerve to brag about how many jobs they have created, without mentioning the enormous numbers of jobs that have been lost.

Because of the new computer technology, we are not likely ever to see full employment again. Even if there should be an economic recovery, it promises to be jobless. We shall return to this topic further on.

The Three-Sector-Society

What is taking place at present in Canada and other western capitalist countries is the creation of a hierarchical three-sector-society. The first sector is made up of the economic and political elites and the professionals in their service. The second sector consists of people with secure employment or owners of a small business, enjoying a reasonably good income. This sector, we note, includes unionized workers protected, for the time being, by a collective agreement. The growing third sector is made up of "the excluded," embracing the unemployed, the working poor (fully employed women and men whose low wages leave them in poverty), people precariously employed or in part-time jobs, and people too old or too weak to look after themselves. The sector of the excluded is not only growing in Canada and the other industrial societies, it also promises to be a permanent feature of society. We note that the percentage of women and children in this sector is very high.

Karl Marx, we remember, saw society divided between two antagonistic classes, the ruling class and the working class, and only mentioned in passing, and with a certain contempt, the few at the bottom, the "Lumpen" as he called them, i.e., the vagrants and good-for-nothings. Marx did not anticipate the present situation where the excluded constitute a growing sector of society.

What happens to a society with a permanent class of the excluded men, women and children? John Maynard Keynes and many other social thinkers have argued that to do well and thrive, a society must avoid widening the gap between rich and poor and do its utmost to allow all men—in his day, married women did not look for a job—to participate in the production of wealth. Otherwise society would become unstable and decline. Abandoned at this time is not only the Keynesian perspective but also the democratic theory of Beveridge and thinkers like him, who argued that a society that wants its members to be active and responsible citizens must support their health and their education. Betrayed at this time is also the Universal Declaration of Human Rights, promulgated in 1948 by the United Nations, which included among the human rights (see Articles 22 and 23), the right to work and the right to social security. What we are experiencing is a far-reaching decline of democracy. The important decisions affecting society and its citizens are made today by transnational corporations and international financial institutions such as the World Bank and the International Monetary Fund. People who have not been elected shape the fate of our society, while the elected government claims to have no power to protect and promote the well-being of its citizens.

Political leaders in Canada and Quebec openly admit that in response to international market forces, they are obliged to introduce social adjustment policies: support free trade, offer natural resources and produce commodities for export, and for the sake of enhancing the competitivity of the industries, reduce their taxes, weaken the power of labour and cut social programmes, health care and education. In a recent statement, the United Church of Canada described what is happening as "a war against the poor." Our political leaders claim that in doing so, they bow to necessity, i.e., to impersonal international market forces. In actual fact, behind these forces stand powerful actors and their institutions.

The structural adjustment policies, which our governments seem to introduce voluntarily, are imposed in much harsher ways upon the countries of the poorer continents by the World Bank and the International Monetary Fund. In addition to this, the governments of Canada and most other Western countries have reduced their support for Third World development and withdrawn part of the funding for non-governmental organizations that sponsor social and economic projects in these regions. Western society is deserting the poorer countries.

There is a growing literature written by important, nonconformist economists that analyses the brave new world that is being created at this time. Well-known are Philippe Engelhard, *L'Homme mondial* (Paris, 1996), Robert Heilbroner, *The Crisis of Vision in Modern Economic Thought* (New York, 1995), David Korten, *When Corporations Rule the World* (New York, 1995), and Lester Thurow, *The Future of Capitalism* (New York, 1996). *Le Monde diplomatique*, a prestigious journal published in Paris, brought out several issues in 1996 that analyse the new world in the making. These studies predict a bleak future, unless a radical change of orientation takes place. Some of these authors believe that there are already signs that a strong reaction against the neoliberal orthodoxy is in the making.

The first question posed in the title of this essay was whether we find ourselves living in a new historical situation. It follows from the preceding analysis that the answer to this question is Yes.

The neoliberal world project is not imposed upon unwilling Western nations. People vote for governments whose policies are frankly neoliberal. People have been made to believe that we are forced by the public debt and global competitivity to pursue the present course. There is no choice, they are told. Alternatives do not exist. Neoliberalism is grounded in a social philosophy, an updated version of nineteenth-century Social Darwinism, and supported by an appropriate culture that legitimates the public indifference to solidarity. It would be worthwhile to study this legitimating culture in detail. Allow me to name three cultural currents that presently undermine social solidarity. First, there is the self-serving individualism generated by universal competitivity that tends to reduce all values to economic utility and makes people dream of enjoying more power and seeking ever more satisfying material gratifications. Secondly, there is the neo-conservative moralism, supported by many conservative Christian groups, that stresses private virtue yet fosters hard-hearted indifference to social injustices and the soul-destroying suffering they produce. Thirdly, post-modern currents with their emphasis on the particular and the different, and their consequent rejection of universal values, legitimate people's preoccupation with the small circle to which they belong and thus effectively undermine universal social solidarity. Added to this is the fictional violence in films and on television that hardens our moral sensibilities and reinforces our indifference to the suffering of others.

This solidarity-denying culture is communicated by the mass media that are increasingly controlled by powerful capitalists and their corporations. The Canadian government has not resisted this trend. On the contrary, it has reduced the support of the CBC and the assistance given to Canadian publishers, cultural organizations and research institutes that promote an alternative vision of society. The political space where public policies are being debated is becoming smaller and smaller.

Christian Responses to the New Situation

The cultural optimism that has characterized progressive people, reformist and radical, since World War II has disappeared. The political and cultural Left have been decimated. While people of the Left had, for the most part, little sympathy for Soviet-style communism and strongly disapproved of its totalitarian style, they saw in the socialist economy at least an historical alternative to Western capitalism. Since its collapse, the world is caught in a single economic system. China is presently opening its doors to industrial capitalism. Apart from a few mavericks, even Marxists admit that the command economy in the Soviet-bloc countries was a complete failure. Markets are necessary. Yet social democracy that favoured regulated markets and a mixed economy also seems to have lost its appeal. When social democratic parties are elected to form the government, they are forced by international market forces—so they claim—to introduce neoliberal policies.

There are two valid reasons, it seems to me, why there is no going back to Keynesian welfare capitalism. First, Keynesianism wanted the government to protect and promote the national economy. But today a national economy no longer exists: it has been, to a great extent, integrated into the global economy. A national economy as a more or less unified system has disappeared. Until recently, progressive people in Quebec believed that because of its strong sense of national identity and social solidarity, Quebec had the chance to protect and enhance its national economy. They thought that nationalism could have progressive economic consequences and make possible, even in today's world, fidelity to the idea of social democracy. Yet more recently, there are signs that the government of Quebec is committed to neoliberal policies and no longer defines Quebec's future in social democratic terms.

Secondly, because of the new computer technology, full employment has become a thing of the past. Governments, labour unions, and some Catholic pastoral letters still speak of full employment as a realistic goal, yet the evidence suggests that industries and offices increasingly rely on electronically steered automation. Because of ever more sophisticated computers, a large sector of the population has become economically useless. They are no longer needed as workers; and being poor they do not invigorate the economy as customers. We stand here before an intractable problem. In the present situation the traditional Left offers few new ideas. Nobody, at this time, has all the answers, nobody is able to offer a blueprint for a more just and more humane alternative society that should and could replace the present order.

How do Christians respond to this new situation? This is the second question posed in the title of this essay? The articles collected in this book wrestle with this question.

In 1996, the year dedicated by the United Nations to the elimination of poverty, the Catholic bishops of Canada, Britain and France have published pastoral letters in which they lament the growing gap between the rich and the poor and denounce the neoliberal policies adopted by their governments. They make an important doctrinal point. It is wrong for governments, their counsellors and their apologists, to justify the neoliberal policies by invoking "necessity" as if the market were a natural force, like forces in chemistry or biology that simply follow the law of nature. We are free human beings, the bishops insist. Humans are the subjects of the economy, they are capable of making choices, they cannot hide behind necessity, they must not evade their moral responsibility.

The present demise of cultural optimism does not rob Christians of their hope. Their faith in the divine promises continues to nourish hope and love. Christians believe that since God is graciously active in human history, good things always emerge in the midst of social and cultural crises, even if they at first touch only a minority. I have never forgotten a paragraph written at the turn of the century by the Catholic philosopher, Maurice Blondel, which claims that because of God's redemptive immanence, humanity is, in every period, in labour giving birth to the new. Blondel spoke of "the stirrings of parturition."[8] Christians, he wrote, must listen to the new ideas and practices, testing them with the gospel, and learn from them if they are compatible with it. In the same vein, the political economist, Karl Polanyi, also a Christian, has shown that when society has been threatened by economic forces, social movements emerge among ordinary people that try to protect the community and its environment from disintegration.[9]

That God is redemptively at work in the world and sustains people struggling to create a more just and humane society was, we recall, the teaching of Vatican Council II. This Council, we noted, was carried by a certain cultural optimism which it passed on both to reformist Christians hoping to improve social democracy and to radical Christians hoping for revolutionary change and the creation of an alternative society. In the present situation this optimism has dissolved. Yet the collapse of optimism does not mean that Christians give up hope. Believing that God is graciously at work in the world, Christians scan society to detect "the stirrings of parturition" occurring in it. The drama of redemption, revealed in Jesus Christ, continues to be operative in the history of nations.

Let me say a few more words on Christian hope. The Gospel that calls us to believe and to love, also summons us to have hope. In today's world we have to protect ourselves against depression and despair by spiritual practices, such as prayer, meditation on the divine promises, and participation in groups or networks of engaged Christians who, relying on God's solidarity with the poor, continue to believe that society can be changed. God is at work in the world ever summoning forth the new.

What then, I wish to ask, are some of the good things happening in Canada and Quebec and how can we, as Christians, offer our support for them? The essays in this collection deal with these questions. I join my colleagues in offering my own proposals. I suggest three areas in which I see new things happening.

1. Neoliberalism, as we saw above, is a socio-economic project and a cultural enterprise. The success of the socio-economic project depends on the ability to gain the approval of the majority of the

population. Serving this interest is a public culture that fosters success-oriented individualism, short-term utilitarianism, ethical relativism and indifference to the suffering of others.

Yet there are also counter-currents in society that promote a culture of cooperation and solidarity. We find these currents in the social movements, old and new, such as the labour movement, the women's movement, the ecological movement, the peace movement, the cooperative movement, and the movement against free trade. We also find these currents in the Christian Churches as well as among humanists, artists, teachers and other professionals serving the community. Christians committed to justice want to cooperate with these groups and, in this context, emphasize the spiritual dimension. Christians want to help to bring the different currents together in a single movement, and give this movement greater visibility in society and thus increase its moral power. These Christians urge their bishops and church leaders to speak out in public in the name of the Gospel, revealing the false set of values implicit in neoliberalism, thereby delegitimating present government policies. These Christians use a variety of means—meetings, associations, discussion groups, lectures, newsletters, newspapers, reviews, books, etc.—to raise the consciousness of parishes, congregations and the wider community, to which they belong.

A few years ago, Kenneth Galbraith published the book *The Culture of Contentment*, in which he showed that the present economic orientation satisfied the needs of 70 per cent of the American population and left 30 per cent in dire straits. Since in democratic societies the majority has the power to define public policy, he continued, the present monetarist orientation will not change. But what will happen, I ask myself, when over 50 per cent of the people recognize the social disintegration and the human suffering caused by neoliberalism? To create such a majority is the aim of the cultural struggle to raise people's political awareness and promote the values of cooperation and solidarity.

2. Since the taming of the transnational corporations and the international financial institutions can only occur on the international level, national politics does not, at this time, offer many opportunities for resisting neoliberal economics. Yet the guidance and control of these transnational institutions could be achieved on

the global level through such world organizations as the United Nations. Groups of lawyers and political scientists are working out many useful proposals. As the United Nations Organization has, in the past, composed human rights charters that have acquired the force of law, the same organization could create charters laying down conditions for transnational economic actors that aim at protecting the public good. It has been suggested, for instance, to create an effective Economic Security Council in the UN to which the World Bank and the International Monetary Fund are responsible, rather then, as is presently the case, to the G-7 nations. A universal charter protecting the environment and demanding a living wage for workers and employees would prevent transnational corporations from making decisions with the sole intention of maximizing their profit. To contain short-term speculation by moving capital across national borders to the detriment of these countries, some political thinkers have proposed that these operations be taxed, while others favour the creation of an international agency with the power to monitor and control these operations. These kinds of proposals are being followed by church groups, in Canada by the *Taskforce of the Churches and Corporate Responsibility*. While the realization of such projects lies in the future, it is important to have people talking and thinking about them now.

3. New on the community level is the sudden expansion of social endeavours that have existed for a long time. The endeavours of which I speak are taking place especially in "the third sector," the sector of the excluded. These endeavours include local self-help groups such as common kitchens, joint backyard gardening, house repair teams, lobby groups to protect the neighbourhood, refugee committees, centres of popular education and storefront counselling of immigrants and the unemployed. While most of the work of these self-help groups is done by activists who volunteer their services, the groups do depend on some financial support from external sources. The social endeavours of which I speak also include community economic development (CED)—in Quebec, this is called "l'économie sociale"—which is made up of non-profit enterprises, cooperatives, and other economic projects that involve democratic participation. CED is active in many different fields: health services (uncovered by government programmes), education, housing, rotating loan funds, agriculture, forestry, publication, restaurants,

commodity production, and so forth. While some of the work of CED is done by activists (or volunteers, as they used to be called), CED also creates salaried jobs. Yet in most cases CED is in need of some financial support from external sources, at least at the beginning.

Self-help groups and CED constitute important movements in Canada and many, if not most, other countries.[10] There seems to be a new vitality in "the third sector." The financial support on which these groups and organizations are, in varying degrees, dependent is made available by public and private institutions. They are supported by small grants offered by the federal, provincial or municipal governments, by banks and large corporations, and by chartered foundations and benevolent institutions such as churches and religious congregations.

The most important point is that these projects not only relieve people's economic needs, but that they also serve social ends: they create community, rescue people from isolation and passivity, and offer them active participation. They create a culture of cooperation and solidarity, at odds with the dominant culture. The participants in these endeavours become critics of society. While in the past "volunteering" was regarded as a work of charity that did not question the existing order, in self-help groups and community economic development "volunteering" is a form of activism sustaining a society-transforming social movement.

Political scientists and social activists are presently engaged in an interesting debate as to whether or not CED is the bearer of something new that teaches us a lesson about linking economic and social goals and reveals the new direction in which the society of the future should move. The enthusiastic supporters of CED think that it may eventually replace the social services planned in an impersonal way by the government bureaucracy and generate a new understanding of social citizenship that will prompt people actively to involve themselves in the well-being of their community. This vision offers a realistic goal, it seems to me, only if the government decides, under increasing public pressure, to introduce a minimum guaranteed income for all citizens. But even observers of CED who do not have such high expectations recognize that it creates a new *ethos,* a culture of cooperation and solidarity, and hence deserves admiration and support.

Christians will want to support this movement. They will want to find out what community development projects exist in their neighbourhood, ask their parish or religious congregation whether it wants to support them, and ask themselves if they have some free time and energy to volunteer their services, even if it only once or twice a week.

In this essay I have tried to answer the two questions mentioned in the title "Are We In a New Historical Situation? Do We Have to Rethink What Justice and Solidary Mean Today?" My answer to the first question was that we are indeed in a new situation created by the globalization of the free-market economy, the regime of the trans-national corporations, the decline of the welfare state, the discovery of a new computer economy, chronic permanent unemployment and the growing third sector of the excluded.

The answer to the second question is treated in the articles of this volume. In my essay I have attached great importance to the cultural struggle against the oppressive system, a struggle which for Christians is grounded in God's revelation in Jesus Christ. And I attach great importance to the movement of self-help groups and community economic development that extends help to thousands upon thousands of people in need and, more than that, produces a culture of cooperation and solidarity that is full of promises for the future.

Notes

1. Gregory Baum and Robert Ellsberg (eds.), *The Logic of Solidarity: Commentaries on Pope John Paul's Encyclical "On Social Concern"* (Maryknoll, NY: Orbis Books, 1989).

2. For the Medellin Conclusions see Joseph Gremillion (ed.), *The Gospel of Peace and Justice* (Maryknoll, NY: Orbis Books, 1976), pp. 445-476.

3. See John Eagelson and Philip Scharper (eds.), *Puebla and Beyond* (Maryknoll, NY: Orbis Books, 1979), p. 264.

4. *Octogesima adveniens,* No. 31; *The Gospel of Peace and Justice,* p. 499.

5. *Justitia in mundo*, No. 3-5; *The Gospel of Peace and Justice*, p. 514.

6. Gregory Baum, "Toward a Canadian Catholic Social Theory," *Theology and Society* (Mahwah, NJ: Paulist Press, 1987), pp. 66-87.

7. For a history of economic theory written for non-specialists, see Kenneth Galbraith, *The Age of Uncertainty* (Boston, 1977) and *A History of Economics* (Boston, 1987).

8. Maurice Blondel, *The Letter on Apologetics, and History and Dogma*, translated by A. Dru and I. Trethowan (London, 1964), p. 147.

9. See Gregory Baum, *Karl Polanyi on Ethics and Economics* (Montreal: McGill-Queen's University Press, 1996).

10. There exists a growing literature on this topic. For the USA: Harry Boyte, *The Backyard Revolution* (Philadelphia: Temple University Press, 1980); Severyn Bruins and James Meehen, *Beyond the Market and the State: New Directions in Community Development*, 1987; Meredith Ramsey, *Community, Culture and Economic Development: The Social Roots of Local Action* (New York: SUNY Press, 1996). For Canada: David Ross and Peter Usher, *From the Roots Up: Economic Development as if Community Mattered* (Toronto: Lorimer, 1986). For Quebec: Louis Favreau et Benoît Lévesque, *Développement économique communautaire* (Presses de l'Université du Québec, 1996); Juan-Luis Klein, dir., *Économie et solidarité* (revue du CIRIEC, Canada), Vol. 28, No. 1, 1996.

LET'S DO IT AND IT WILL GET DONE

Vivian Labrie

Vivian Labrie, researcher and activist, PhD in Social Science, received her Doctorat d'état ès Lettres et Sciences humaines, Paris, Sorbonne, in 1979. She works at the Pastoral Crossroads for Working Class People (CAPMO). She is also a researcher in the field of oral traditions and folklore. As a member of the Comité externe de réforme de la sécurité du revenu *(External Committee for Income Security Reform) in Quebec in 1995 and 1996, she signed this Committee's majority report entitled* Chacun sa part *(To Each His Own) with Camil Bouchard and Alain Noël.*

People around me tease me at times because of the "we" that I use in texts and articles, remarking that it is a distinctive feature of my writing style. In fact, when "we" work for a group, the line between "I" and "we" becomes blurred because one of the responsibilities is to speak and act on behalf of the group. To say "we" means identifying with a community, it also means being able to identify what is being said with this community. To write "we" is an attempt to create a space for words that members of the community will recognize as their own and through which they will feel that they have spoken. I have been with Pastoral Crossroads for Working Class People (CAPMO) since 1988. What constitutes the "we" at this crossroads changes with the people involved. As for me, I learn from what is happening and marvel at it when people decide to merge spirituality and militancy, which, I believe, is what characterizes CAPMO. The issue of social justice seems to me to be inscribed in time immemorial. In my limited experience, I have noticed that strict militancy is not sufficient: days of celebration are often followed by periods of disenchantment; the words "progress" and "gain" are not automatically synonymous with the word justice. What I am wondering about these days is how to address this issue of social justice during the course of our lives of "I" and "we"; in other words, in the long term for us, which represents but a moment in the long history of humanity. What is the part of this inscription that we are called upon to bake as if were our daily bread?

I. Illegal Immigrants

In September 1996, Jacques Gaillot was the long-awaited guest speaker at the *Congrès de l'Entraide missionnaire* (Missionary Exchange Conference) which was focusing that year on exclusion. Yet, when it was his turn to speak on Sunday morning, he talked about the previous summer. He and all sorts of people—militants, intellectuals, families—occupied the churches and empty warehouses to prevent the French government from sending illegal immigrants back to their country of origin. He told us all the little details, about how they lived in the church and the problems it caused, their fear of eviction, the families' daily lives, the relations between the occupation and parish life, the visitors, the way they organized themselves for sleeping and for reacting quickly in case of problems. He talked about the importance of the choice of places because places have a symbolic dimension. He ended his speech with a sentence, paraphrased, from the Gospel, "Do it and it will get done."

A number of my co-workers from *Carrefour de pastorale en monde ouvrier* (CAPMO—Pastoral Crossroads for Working Class People) were there. Madone, for example, asked him to explain what he meant by a symbolic place. As for me, I was intrigued. As a bishop who had been expelled from his diocese for supporting those who are marginalized by society, Jacques Gaillot could have been expected to deliver a sort of synthetizing essay on exclusion. But no, he talked very simply about what they had done that summer as he might have related events to a group at the corner pub.

II. Prehistory and Sacred Fire

What if we really have only a few stories and symbols with which to make a stand against neoliberalism? What if these stories and symbols, like the prehistoric nomads' bags of moss, could transport the sacred fire needed to breathe new life into other times, other humans, other places?

I was a researcher before coming to CAPMO. I had spent several years among Acadian storytellers and was impressed by the vigour of the oral tradition. Hilaire told *Le sabre de lumière et de vertu de sagesse* (The Sword of Light and the Virtue of Justice) and we were all deeply moved; Honoré recited *Merlin* and transported us by word of mouth far back through the ages; Alvina, who couldn't read, delighted us with her stories of Ti-Jack; Dina, who was nearly one hundred years old, had a wonderful time telling us the adventures of comrade Wolf and comrade Fox and as for us, well, we had learned *Le roman de Renart* in our medieval literature course.

Even communities that have nothing—and the region where Hilaire, Honoré, Alvina and Dina lived was very poor—are still richer than the richest if they have their memories. They can survive and pass on their knowledge.

I was aware of that when I arrived at CAPMO, but I had not yet made the interconnections with the militant work we were doing; between reflection and action at the crossroads of people's lives; with the society project and solidarity and spirituality. Recently, this connection had been made through populist education, because of the need to find ways of developing and transmitting knowledge compatible with the principle of inclusion.

Of course, it eventually becomes clear that working at the bottom of the social scale means refusing to exclude because when we evict a person, the bottom of the ladder moves a little lower and we have to start all over again. It is in this sense that we can understand the preferential treatment for the poor; always opting for ways to ensure that the poorest among us feel included in the gathering.

It is not only with money that we erect barriers between us. We also establish many barriers with words and language. Since school became compulsory, and literacy is taken for granted, except in practice, ordinary words have had a tendency to lengthen. They have become high-tech and loaded with initials. Universities have greatly contributed to this phenomenon. At times, words begin to resemble registered trademarks marking off our territory. As a result, language becomes stereotyped, formal and inaccessible unless we possess the key to the words. The more words lengthen, the more they succeed in excluding people.

Even the work of solidarity has been complicated by this problem. Take a simple concept like the struggle against neoliberalism. Elizabeth, an Ursuline, and far from illiterate, has been living in the neighbourhood for some time and is being initiated into the community and the working-class milieu. A few days ago, before an information session on social economics, she asked me gently, "Can you tell me what this neoliberalism is all about?"

She was right to ask. We use words very carelessly. Take, for example, *La seconde déclaration de La Realidad pour l'humanité et contre le néolibéralisme* (La Realidad's Second Declaration for Humanity and against Neoliberalism) which we are called upon to support as part of an intercontinental network of resistance to neoliberalism. It grew out of the Zapatista movement in Chiapas, Mexico. Considering what is happening in our societies, we have a good mind to say with the Zapatistas, "*Ya basta!* That's enough! We long to become a part of a universal community that declares: 'That's enough!' As far as we are concerned, we are going to try to look after one another. We will fight against what causes us harm and together we will try to advance the cause of life." When we ask ourselves how many people would understand the text of the Declaration, words fail us suddenly. If Elizabeth needs to have neoliberalism explained to her, how many of the words in the first paragraph of the Declaration would have to be explained to Anna, André, or Louise in the literacy group, who, poor and unemployed as they are, should be the first to hear these words? See for yourself:

> Whereas we are against the globalization of war and arms, against dictatorship, against authoritarianism, against repression, against the policies of economic liberalization, against hunger, against poverty, against theft, against corruption, against patriarchy, against xenophobia, against discrimination, against racism, against crime, against the destruction of the environment, against militarism, against stupidity, against untruthfulness, against ignorance, against slavery, against intolerance, against injustice, against marginalization, against forgetfulness, against neoliberalism. . . .

How long they are, these words that describe what eats away at us. Perhaps Jacques Gaillot, Hilaire, Alvina, Honoré and Dina were right. When the words get too long, we should perhaps make a point of telling the stories as well, so that they can continue to transport the sacred fire.

And why would it not be the actions of people like Elizabeth, Anna, André or Louise that might supply us with the words we are seeking?

Our first meeting for this book was held in Ottawa. At the same time, in my group and in my neighbourhood, we were about to begin a *Jeûne à relais du refus de la misère* (Relay Fast for the Rejection of Poverty). A few months later, I reflect again on the objective that we established for this book, "to react to neoliberalism," and the task that Kevin and Richard subsequently assigned to me in the minutes of the meeting.

> Development of the community that takes responsibility for itself. Contribution of human and/or Christian creativity in a society that leaves large segments of the population without recourse. Occasionally we refer to the emergence of a new form of citizenship, not in political terms where one supports a party but in terms of a social understanding that encourages people to become involved in the community and to share their talents and aptitudes.

How am I to write about this? In the minutes, Guy insisted on the fact that we must tell our stories. Michel talked a great deal about the "house" and had quoted Isaiah 58:12 that day: "You will be called Repairer of broken walls."

So yes, I will tell you a story about a house. After all, we not only fasted by turns but we also slept for thirteen days on recycled mattresses in a very strange dwelling filled with paintings and gilt, a stone's throw from the altar, in the glimmer of votive lights under a very high ceiling.

As I look back at these events, it is really there that I catch a glimpse of the sacred fire. So I may as well tell you a little about it since we did what we set out to do.

III. Ernesto's Fantasy

"Development of the community that takes responsibility for itself . . . "

After the Missionary Benefit Conference, Jacques Gaillot returned to France, and we went back to Quebec City. I was a member of a small group preparing a symposium on social economics for the following Saturday, and we were trying to devise a slogan that would lead to action. During one of our meetings I mentioned, "Do it and it will be done." We changed the wording a little and it became "Let's do it and it will get done!"

CAPMO's monthly meeting was held on the Thursday of that week. At news time, we told the others about the happenings at the conference, including the Sunday morning spent with Jacques Gaillot. Then as we usually do at the start of the new season, we went on to an analysis of the overall economic climate.

The situation was tense. We were between the two socio-economic summits[1] that the Premier had convened, haunted by his zero-deficit objective. For our part, in our brief to the Commission on Taxation, we had retorted: no zero deficit without a zero impoverishment clause for the poorest one-fifth of the population. It should be remembered that all sorts of measures leading to increased impoverishment had been announced in the preceding months. People now had to empty their bank accounts down to the very last cent before they could obtain welfare; even the common share at the *Caisse populaire* (Credit Union) was calculated in the total. Many people were having a very difficult time and seemed to be imploding from the pressure. To illustrate the situation, we drew ourselves on a tightrope between two summits with a safety net underneath us, but a net that had more and more holes through which people were falling. Yet here we were in the middle of the International Year for the Eradication of Poverty. And as a matter of fact, the next summit was to take place fourteen days after October 17, the International Day for the Eradication of Poverty. We tried to determine how we could disrupt this second summit a little, a summit indifferent to poverty and oblivious to any thought of eradicating it. We knew that the solidarity would have to be effective and that we would have to generate it ourselves. Yves felt that the highest stake was solidarity itself. We told Yves that solidarity is not a question of stakes but of means. Yorick said that what is at stake is people talking about their social contract. That prompted some renewed doubts. So perhaps Yves was right. Solidarity is more than a means, it is the stake.

Jean-Yves explained, "The stake is our development in relation to different visions, the process of development and its control."

"It is seeing others as human beings," Doris added.

And Bernard said, "Democracy itself is at stake."

We wondered what we could do this year to make some progress in this area? Yves came back with his effective solidarity. Yorick talked about a tool for spreading hope, "Our utopia needs to be defused."

"And we need to see ourselves as brothers and sisters," Raymond added.

Stop living by proxy, by delegation, and begin shouldering the suffering that prevails in Quebec; counter the implosion of the welfare recipients; convert violence into love; take back our institutions; disrupt the summit. Someone said, "We have to put some humanity into the picture."

We felt that we had reached the point of reinventing and transmitting hope and that a latent energy was there just waiting for some pivotal action. But, what could we do? For the past few days, Ernesto had been fantasizing about a relay fast that would create a bridge between October 17 and the start of the Montreal Summit, a fast to oppose the routine and the indifference, because the second half of the month is when people suffer most.

The further we advanced in the discussion, the more this idea seemed to respond to what we had just glimpsed in our analysis of the economic climate. It would not be a hunger strike but a fast, relayed every twenty-four hours from one person to the next, like solidarity that must be passed from one person to the next. In that way, we would not blackmail ourselves and there would be no danger to anyone's health. We were affirming a rejection, declaring that enough is enough, and clarifying something as well—this would not be a religious event but a gesture of civil protest.

So we checked. Who agrees that CAPMO should be involved in this action? All hands were raised one after another; such action is important. Yves said, "Yes, but who is ready to be committed, to take part in this?"

All the hands were raised again, one after another. It was impressive. We felt both determined and a little humble as we considered this undertaking. And if it didn't get off the ground, if we only had a few people? Then we would live a spiritual protest experience. We settled on five people a day as the minimum number needed to go ahead. With five we could do it. Let's do it and it will get done!

IV. Stone Soup

" . . . Contribution of creativity . . . "

Jean-Yves, our wise man, added another condition: that other groups should become involved in the event. In the following days we contacted a number of associations. Eight groups would participate in the organization: CAPMO; four combinations of groups and unions, namely, the *Coalition DROIT* (RIGHTS Coalition), the *Carrefour de relance de l'économie et de l'emploi du centre du Québec* (CRIECQ—Central Quebec Crossroads for Stimulation of the Economy and Employment), the *Regroupement des organismes communautaires de la région 03* (Region 03 Community Organizations Group), the *Table de concertation Pauvreté Limoilou* (Limoilou Poverty Consultation Committee), *Solidarité Régionale Québec* (Quebec Regional Solidarity), and two unions, the *Conseil central des syndicats nationaux, section Québec-Chaudière-Appalaches* (CSN—Central Council for National Unions, Quebec-Chaudière-Appalaches Chapter) and the *Syndicat de la fonction publique du Québec* (SFPQ—Quebec Public Service Union). "We proceeded with support from everywhere!" as the handout would say. We then contacted some of the national popular movements and they in turn decided to go along with the idea.

The concept took shape during the discussions. The headquarters for the fast would be in Quebec City, but anyone living anywhere could participate as long as the individual was registered. Four demands were put forward in relation to the Montreal Summit: 1. commitment to zero impoverishment toward the poorest one-fifth of the population, notably welfare recipients and the working poor; 2. significant investment in new money for the creation of lasting, well-paying jobs in a supportive economy; 3. tax reform to halt the growth of the gap between rich and poor and to initiate narrowing this gap; 4. public debate on welfare reform with significant input from welfare recipients.

We found a logo and printed a two-sided sheet that would be passed from hand to hand and reproduced by the fax machines that were becoming the nerve centre of the event. All those who registered subscribed to the following declaration:

> We too reject poverty. We have had enough. At the Montreal Summit on the social and economic future of Quebec, we are calling for an end to the impoverishment of the poorest members of this society and for a genuine rectification of exclusion through job creation, tax reform to stop widening the gap between rich and poor and to start closing it, and a public debate on welfare reform with significant input from welfare recipients.
>
> For this reason, we are committed to fasting for 24 hours between October 17 and 30, 1996 (day indicated below). We will fast in solidarity with all Quebecers who are obliged to struggle each month for their survival. We will fast because we ourselves are impoverished or because we believe that poverty is not someone else's business, it is ours too. We want to reweave the fabric of a Quebec that shows solidarity, as it should, for the people and with the people.

Little by little the event was organized. CAPMO lent its office and the CSN offered its big hall to launch the event. The SFPQ covered the cost of a soup kitchen for the launching and *De la bouffe pas des bombes* (Bread, not Bombs) prepared it. The civil servants assigned to serve the soup were stunned to learn that the persons beside them with the rings in their noses were not the beneficiaries but the cooks. The CRIECQ was a drop-off point for registrations, with Bernard entering the data as it arrived. A bakery that wished to remain anonymous supplied the bread. (We would never run short.) A number of groups volunteered their services to develop a programme for each day. Themes and projects were being proposed as well. Marie-Christine offered to organize a Tuesday focusing on the issue of women and poverty. Françoise, who is president of the *Fédération des femmes du Québec* (Quebec Women's Federation), would come and fast in Quebec City on that day. Diane, the member of the Quebec Assembly for the region, promised to participate in the first day of the fast with the president of the CSN and the president of the *Front Commun des personnes assistées sociales* (Welfare Recipients Coalition).

The telephone never stopped ringing. Jean-Yves ran around looking for mattresses; Mark took care of public relations; Mario, the parish priest, assumed the responsibility for the cultural programme. Recitals and short concerts would be held in the evenings. Louis invited some artists to come and paint on the first Saturday. Our lives were turned completely upside down and moving too fast for us to fully realize that we were involved in an uncommon event which allowed each one of us to contribute according to our means. The fast was like the stone in the story of the stone soup that we had been using over the past months to illustrate the kind of solidarity that we wanted to live by. The Stone Soup was the subject of our third press release:

PRESS RELEASE NUMBER THREE

It is possible to make a world with all sorts of people, or "The Stone Soup Story"

Dated October 18. At 17:00, 767 persons were registered for the Relay Fast for the Rejection of Poverty. Many are amazed at the support this seemingly paradoxical activity is receiving. In fact, the question asked is: why fast when it is precisely the want of everything, or the reason for this want, that is being denounced?

When the people participating in the fast gathered on October 18 to review the situation, they asked how the members of the organizing committee were organizing this event. A little story provided a partial answer:

Once upon a time there was a man who was hungry. He took his pot and sat at the side of the road. He then lit a fire and put water and a stone into the pot.

A passer-by asked him what he was making.

"Stone soup, but it would be even better with a cabbage."

The passer-by went and got a cabbage and put it in the soup. Another person passed along and asked the same question.

"It's stone soup but it would be better with a piece of bacon."

Each person who passed by added something, so that finally the soup began to smell delicious with carrots, beans, pasta, meat. The cook then removed the small stone and kept it for the next time. Everyone had a wonderful meal.

This fast is like the stone. It is inedible but it is the starting point to which nourishing, appetizing elements can be added. Within it there is a common cause: the rejection of poverty and the conviction that it is possible to call on all sorts of people to make a world. So everyone, Léopold, Pierrette, Juliette, Roger, Denis, Lise, Louise-Anne, Jean-Marie, Madone, and François are all doing their share instead of having everything supplied in advance. This is how it is when you start with nothing because you need everything.

Could it be that Quebec needs to find a common appetite for a good soup for everyone instead of continuing to divide the cake unequally, instead of pulling up the smaller carrots in the garden so that the others can grow even bigger?

– 30 –

V. A Church?

" . . . human and /or Christian . . . "

Around midnight on October 17, following the soup kitchen and an opening night with more than 450 participants, the scene is strange. About twenty people are stretched out on makeshift mattresses in the nave and the chancel of Notre-Dame-de-Jacques-Cartier church in the very centre of our poverty-stricken downtown area. After preparing and sending the daily press release that we are committed to distributing, I am assessing the strangeness of this day that is drawing to a close.

For the first time in my life, I am sleeping in a church, and, to tell the truth, I am finding the atmosphere rather pleasant. Living a civil protest experience in a church is not something to be taken for granted. Not because of the parish—Mario, the parish priest, was in agreement from the beginning and so were the members of the parish team. No, it is because of the inherited heaviness of the church with which we no longer want to be associated; because of the sexism in the Church. We do not much care for the idea of camping in a branch of the only remaining institution in which women are excluded from carrying out certain functions. The domination of the past remains in our memories and blinds us to the life that is beginning to take root among the stones. But in the end, the practical and symbolic aspects of the place, to which Madone had been attentive, prevailed. This church is located in the very centre of a street affected by a biker war. A few months ago, a man was gunned down two steps away. At the same time, people are attempting to revitalize this once flourishing thoroughfare and the surrounding neighbourhood. In the church, a former chapel has been transformed into a headquarters for groups working on the North-South development perspective. Since one of the groups, ROC-03, is also one of our organizing groups, we have access to very important resources such as the telephone and photocopier. The church has other advantages as well. It offers a large, open space allowing all kinds of activities to take place at once. It can be occupied twenty-three hours out of twenty-four without causing any problems. The agreement is that the parish will be able to continue its usual liturgical activities, namely, a daily Mass.

The site constantly reminds us of the ambiguity of the human and/or Christian nature of our various motivations. Our society no longer knows how to deal with what is human and/or Christian, or with its spirituality that it wants to see unrestrained, fulfilled, open to others and to diversity. On the first night, Yves arrived directly from Colombia, where he had been attending a meeting of the Assembly of the People of God, a macro-ecumenical movement that is trying to rally groups fighting for and in the name of life by enhancing their religious, ethnic and cultural diversity. He brought us back a message of support, a rare message of solidarity from the South to the North! He also brought back a small sculpture given to each participating country as a symbol of union and of communion in defending and celebrating life: two cupped hands holding two doves with a ear of wheat topped by a sun.

Without these gestures being confessional or intentional, the fact of sharing bread and water, listening to the news, reading texts, discussing our concerns or simply being silent together in this place, will have, I believe, the effect of giving us all a sense of community. Something spiritual will have taken place in this church. It will have nothing to do with the church itself, but everything to do with the people inside.

The people inside it will teach us tolerance in living together, as on the Sunday when: the Coalition Y students in the side benches read Marx for their course on historical materialism; while the White Berets, [2] whose visit we were not expecting, say their monthly prayers at the front of the church; and at the back, Camil, a researcher, discusses a recent survey on poverty with welfare recipients. The press release for that Sunday is prepared by the students.

Press Release Number Four

One day

The presence yesterday of young Coalition Y students highlighted the concerns of youth on poverty-related issues and allowed them to share these concerns with those present, people of all ages and social conditions, notably during an evening discussion period that proved to be a learning experience. At the end of the day, the Coalition youth wrote the following Declaration:

Declaration by the Youth of Coalition Y

On this third day of the Relay Fast for the Rejection of Poverty, having eaten only bread during the entire day, during an exchange we had with about forty people, a participant improvised the following story:

There was a basket of bread in our midst. One of the individuals used force to take more than he needed. He gave his surplus only to those who applauded him and served him coffee. With empty stomachs, the majority united to organize themselves and to impose a new way to share the bread.

One day, young and old, men and women, the poor and the not so poor, will cease seeing each other only in their differences and understand each other in their solidarity.

One day, we will no longer live under the threat of exclusion.

One day, we will be able to share our knowledge and combat ignorance.

One day, social programmes will no longer be viewed as variables in the economic equation, but as essential factors of a just society.

One day, we will once again have free, accessible and quality education.

One day, the new generation will be on its feet and not on its knees.

And when this great day arrives then privilege will cease. Equality will be permitted for one and all!

Coalition Y

The Last Word

Maybe we lived a little bit of that day today. On our lists, beside the name of a participant who had spent the night here, under the heading "address," we found the word "hom lus."

– 30 –

VI. Albert

" . . . in a society that leaves large segments of the population without recourse . . . "

Albert, pock-marked and homeless, drove us to the limits of our patience. Drunk, frozen, injured and violent, it could be said that the totality of human misery had found a refuge in one human being. He arrived on the third night. We were afraid for him and for ourselves, but he stayed, thanks to the young people who were there that night and who strongly objected to calling the police, sending him to the hospital against his wishes or returning him to the street. During those days of confusion, he was able to talk and cry as much as he wished and even mellow a little, if only for a moment of relief. Because life is still hard outside, as it is for the past accumulated on the inside—and "on the inside" the hard life quickly re-imposes its law. We set conditions. He participated in the discussions, accepting little by little the rule of raising his hand to intervene . . . and then raising it solemnly! He slept there, several nights, huddled up in a little corner two steps away from the altar and I thought about the wolf from Gubbio in the story of St. Francis.

Through his presence, Albert raised a very important question: how do we disarm without letting others do harm? Throughout this fast, the question was there beneath the surface at the personal and collective levels: what neoliberalism makes us live is violent, the legacy of unshared wealth is violent; the legacy of unrelieved poverty is violent; the legacy of exclusion is violent; the legacy of the misunderstood, of the unseen, of the unspoken, is violent; violence is violent. How can we avoid entering this spiral of violent relationships, how do we disarm, how do we defuse, and at the same time energize the relations that are both rich in humanity and radical as far as justice is concerned?

A few months later, the question remains. Once we realize that if we leave our isolation there will be great numbers of us, and that far from being without recourse we can choose to act, we will discover that we also have a choice of recourse and the choice of rejecting certain options. We are free to choose one kind of action or another. This choice is not uniquely strategic or tactical. Is it more advisable, for example, to present a brief before a parliamentary review, organize a demonstration, personally meet decision makers, or all of the above, even if it means overtaxing our strength? The choice is also ethical: we could break a few windows, but is that what we want to do? We could portray some people as monsters, but is that our goal? How do we practise justice while firmly rejecting unjust regulations? How do we deal with the law when it becomes an accomplice to suffering? How far should we take over disorder to shake up an established order that supports social inequalities? The day that we discover that we have recourse, we also discover that we are responsible for the recourse that we choose to exercise.

As an example, the following spring the Coalition Y youths chose to hold a sit-in at a bank, to protest peaceably but determinedly against an economic system that allows banks and financial institutions to make large profits while social protection and funding for essential needs are being cut. Forty-two of them were arrested. They explained that this minor infraction which did no harm to anyone, permitted a serious and legal infraction of justice to be highlighted. They were given conditions of release out of all proportion to the offence. So a number of unions and groups, including our own, protested that "it is better to be young and sit in a bank than to be rich and sit on humanity."

How far do we go in withdrawing assent and how do we discern that the means chosen does not divert from the original purpose? In April, after a year of unprecedented cuts and immediately following a budget speech in which the Minister of Finance announced that he expected shortly to lighten the burden of the taxpayers, welfare benefits were cut by $10 a month. How are we to understand a government that lightens the obligations of those who have a little too much while putting a greater burden on those who have neither employment nor income? As the food bank becomes the principal source of groceries for a growing number of households, how should we interpret the action of a committee of unemployed persons in Montreal, whose members entered a supermarket to buy some food, and recommended to welfare recipients that in the future, they should serve themselves without paying, thus breaking an agreement that is central to the functioning of society. Some militants would have approved, others would not. I think that a question could help in our discernment: do we reject the notion of law as such or do we attempt to make the law evolve?

Ethical problems arise in one sense as in the other. We had decided on bread and water for the Relay Fast. Although this was a choice that had been made by poor people, some groups were critical, alleging that it was contradictory to ask persons constantly living in want knowingly to deprive themselves. This type of discussion also takes place regularly when the idea of a silent demonstration is proposed. Why, some ask, deprive ourselves of speech when we are precisely in need of the right to speak? To which others reply that dignified silence can be very eloquent, even more than shouts and slogans. Those in charge of some organizations did not feel comfortable proposing this action to their members who were living in poverty and did not want to be associated with the Relay Fast. Others, on the contrary, appreciated the fact that this gesture was within their reach because it cost nothing and did not require any particular ability, except willpower. They appreciated the fact that it was a true recourse, feasible, capturing the imagination, credible, demonstrating our solidarity, with a nobility of soul and a capacity for putting the collective interest above our own when necessary.

And then Albert and others like him made us understand that when the alternative is "nothing," eating bread alone could not be fasting, but eating. This common place was not a place of privation but a place of abundance of the goods that are missing outside in the street: time, others, listening, content, goodness, beauty, hope, the opportunity to do something, to find one's place, to live for a moment removed from money, a forum for once, a place with open doors and the opportunity to speak and be heard.

VII. A Place For Speech

" . . . Occasionally we refer to a new form of citizenship . . . "

Nearly every night during this fast, we gathered together for discussions, anywhere from twenty to forty of us. We were deeply moved one Monday night when people from the *Mouvement personnes d'abord* (People First Movement) explained to us how difficult it is to be understood and respected when you are living with a disability, with an intellectual impairment.

Excerpt: Press Release Number Six

"We need each other"

[. . .]

Lucie

The small choir that came to the Jacques Cartier church tonight to support those who are fasting were not able to have their piano accompanist with them. Lucie, from the Mouvement personnes d'abord, accompanied them. Instead of knowing her through her disability, it is because of her providential expertise that we met her. It just shows how much we need each other. [. . .]

Serge

"I was working eight hours a day, five days a week, at a drug store. After three years, they just let me go."

"Your training period was finished?"

"Yes, it was a paid training period."

"How much were you making a week, Serge?"

"$25."

Question: if people with disabilities can be given years of work on training periods, it is because there are jobs and because these people are able to do the work. So why are they not given real jobs?

Madeleine

Madeleine was there as well. She arrived at the church after reading an article on the Relay Fast in a daily. Tonight we understood that she rejects her son's poverty with every fibre of her being. He is energetic, wants to work, is still looking for work. Doesn't he have a right to a job too? "They ask us to tighten our belts . . . poor people are at the last notch. Couldn't we at least have a guaranteed minimum wage until everyone can get a job?"

On Tuesday, the women spent the day in a discussion group to consider what is on their own table in comparison to what is expected to be on the table at the upcoming Socio-Economic Summit in Montreal.

EXCERPT: PRESS RELEASE NUMBER SEVEN

"There will be bread and roses on the table at the Summit... and afterwards!"

[. . .] The stakes at the Summit, however, are not a game. They are vital. Because they are accustomed to social interaction, women perceive them much more clearly and they will attempt to make sure that they are at the forefront of the discussion. Despite the temptation to forget roses in order to guarantee bread, they are determined that both will be on the table. Neither the bread nor the roses, however, will be left to the decision-makers—the women intend to be responsible for them from now on. Since they were so rarely listened to in the past, they have learned to prove themselves through their actions. The Women's March was a great collective gesture. The Vigil at the Parliament last June was another, and today, throughout Quebec, this fast is being carried out for the most part by women. In this Relay Fast for the Rejection of Poverty, in a mixed context where all are invited, men and women, young and old, rich and poor, many are now recognizing the extension of an irreversible will to persist until we can truly affix the concept of solidarity to the society project.

Will they succeed? The Summit is a gamble, but it is the aftermath that interests women, and they will be there for the aftermath. They have not exhausted all their possibilities; on the contrary, they are only beginning to use their imagination. And besides, in the future as they see the bread and roses constantly falling off the table because the tablecloth gets torn, they will weary of mending the tablecloth and putting everything back in order. They will be more interested in taking control of the sewing machine and the management of the banquet hall. The economy and politics will henceforth be on their menu. Just watch us go.

On Wednesday, we will go to the National Assembly with the people from *ATD-Quart Monde* (ATD Fourth World) to present rolls and a letter to each Member, inviting them to participate in the fast and to follow through on four demands.

Excerpt: Press Release Number Eight

"You can no longer do without us!"

Yesterday, as part of the Relay Fast for the Rejection of Poverty, people from Quebec City and Montreal met with the Members of the National Assembly to give them bread that they had made themselves. "We have chosen to give you bread because nobody can live with crumbs of income, training, participation and especially crumbs of dignity," they told Diane Barbeau, André Gaulin, Nicole Loiselle, Claire Vaive and Geoffrey Kelley who had come to receive the bread on behalf of the Members of the National Assembly. Among those present were Françoise David, President of the Womens' Federaton, and Ruth Rose, a member of the Commission on Taxation, who were concluding their day of fasting.

After their return, the members of the group gathered to discuss the experience. This gesture symbolizes their pride in their everyday work, the dignity of participating in their own development and their willingness to share. The bread represents the efforts involved in training, the steps taken to find a job, working in an employability programme. It is distributed as the sharing they would like to see in society: sharing knowledge, experiences, working time, sharing the wealth that is created. Those who have joined forces in the *ATD-Quart Monde* movement and the Relay Fast for the Rejection of Poverty are in agreement in declaring that governments do not take their experience and knowledge into account but that they should do so nonetheless. As Phillip Hamel of *ATD-Quart Monde* put it, "Economists are consulted when the economy is concerned. Why not consult people living in poverty when it is a question of the fight against poverty?" "Instead of businessmen!" another added. By offering bread to the decision-makers in our society, we are offering them our experience and knowledge that is essential to them. People on welfare learn how to be inventive, to hang on, to fight against poverty. How can anyone do anything in this area without their expertise? [. . .]

Thursday was a wonderful day. *Atout-Lire*, a literacy group, arrived with freshly-baked bread, followed by the minister for social services and the archbishop of the diocese. With Hon. Louise Harel and archbishop Maurice Couture, the discussion was direct, without concessions of any kind. Instead of seeking his comments on the employment situation, those who were present questioned the pastor, Maurice Couture, about an issue which concerns him directly.

EXCERPT: PRESS RELEASE NUMBER NINE

"Do we have to fast now to get a job?"

[. . .] Let us leave the *Atout-Lire* group to its mural and go to the other end of the church where the other fasters are having an impassioned conversation with Maurice Couture [archbishop of Quebec City], who has come to offer his support. Louise-Anne, after a week in a church with open doors, asks: "Bishop, can you tell me why the doors of the churches are locked?"

"It's paradoxical but it is because there is too much wealth in the churches," he replies. "It is to avoid robberies."

"But then churches become safes," retorts another faster.

At that point, the mother of Javier, eighteen months, who had arrived during the conversation, makes a heartfelt remark, "A church with so much wealth is beautiful but what use is it if there is no one inside?"

To the bishop and the parish priest, who likes having his church open, we propose that jobs for security guards could be created and ways found to open the churches and allow people to come in and rub shoulders with each other without putting the wealth of the churches in danger.

So too for the temples of debt? What is the point of cleaning up our collective wealth if we find ourselves excluded from it? On the *Atout-Lire* mural, there is a picture of a baby. A participant has written underneath it: "If things don't change, I will grow up in poverty."

Following this intervention, Mario, the parish priest, decided that henceforth the doors of Jacques Cartier church would remain open. And then the next day was Friday, that unforgettable day when from one side of the counter to the other, the welfare recipients and welfare officers exchanged their perceptions about each other, even going so far as to issue a common press release.

Excerpt: Press Release Number Ten

"Hands reach out from either side of the counter"

[. . .] "If what you're saying is true, I think I'll have to change my opinion about you," a welfare recipient says to the officers. The group agreed that "since we're all human, it is easy to be prejudiced." We talked about ignorance, thoughtlessness. "We can settle these things by talking to each other and getting to know each other." That is why everyone on both sides is unanimous in recommending that welfare strategies be developed to allow those receiving benefits and officers to get to know each other better. "I've been dreaming for years about this kind of meeting," Alain Fortin of ADDS revealed. Édith Bédard, the regional director of *Réseau Travail Québec* (Quebec Work Network) confirmed her interest in having these meetings continue on a voluntary basis. "We came here on a sort of blind date and we're leaving very happy. We found the time too short and we're hoping to take it up again another time." Paul Pelletier of the *Syndicat de la fonction publique* declared that in his opinion, "Today was a preliminary meeting and we couldn't take anything for granted. Well, it went beyond my expectations. We have to continue and spread the good news around!"

The last word here can go to a welfare officer. "We were looking for mutual respect. I heard the word 'tolerance.' It should be banned, because when we use this word it can also mean that, although we are not in agreement with something, we let it go on anyway. From now on, we have to talk in terms of changes."

In fact, everyone left here changed in some way: through the refusal to tolerate the intolerable; through the recognition of each other's abilities, notably the animation method proposed by the ADDS; and finally, through a first gesture where hands reached out to each other from either side of the counter.

In the days that followed, we felt an indefinable nostalgia sweep over us as we saw this interlude of full citizenship coming to an end. During the last press conference Alain, a journalist, was as impressed as we were by the turn of events and declared in an article entitled *Les matelas dans l'église* (Mattresses in the Church):

> The poor did not collect only mattresses at Jacques Cartier church last week. They collected something else as well, something that is perhaps difficult to define in words, but nonetheless easily perceptible, in terms of energy. [3]

At this point the question is how can we use the interlude to inspire us to change the reality? When we live through an extraordinary experience we would like to be able to erect a tent and stay there indefinitely. But once we reach the top of a mountain, we must come down again, and the value of the mattresses at the church is precisely because they are not usually there. We could not have maintained this intensity forever. And Lisette and Gérard must have secretly longed to rediscover their normal routine of secretary and sacristan without continuously running the risk of finding some crank soaping himself in the priest's shower. So how do we continue to gather and circulate the indefinable energy rather than reverting to the indefinable nostalgia?

VIII. The Real Opposition to the Summit

" . . . not in political terms as in supporting a party, but in terms of social understanding . . . "

The sequence of events led us to the foot of another mountain where we rejoined groups and unions that in recent weeks had agreed on a similar objective. Five thousand of us called for "Zero Impoverishment!" at the entrance to the Socio-Economic Summit that began on the evening of October 20 at a large Montreal hotel. This time the doors were not open but tightly guarded. Identification was requested everywhere. That night, after the meeting of the delegates and advisors for the socio-economic sector (Françoise, the delegate for the Federation of Women had asked me to be an advisor), I stayed in a hotel room as impersonal as it was comfortable. I missed the recycled mattresses, the glow of the votive lights and the ceiling decorated with the last Judgement, and vaguely reflected before dropping off that the modern-day missions may very well be located somewhere on the upper floors of skyscrapers.

Be that as it may, it was the socio-economic movement that constituted the real opposition to the Summit. There had been no plan to discuss poverty at this Summit that focused on fabricating a consensus without any true public debate. Despite appearances and the carefully timed interventions, the true stakes had been negotiated without us, in the corridors and in the suites. Françoise and the others succeeded however, in getting some time included in the Thursday morning session on taxes to propose the clause dealing with Zero Impoverishment for the poorest one-fifth of the population. During the preceding hours, we undertook to discuss it with the greatest possible number of participants.

For my part, immediately on the first night, I had inched my way forward to the Premier after his opening speech and gave him the register of the Fast with all the names of the participants, letters to those taking part in the summit, press releases and other documents. A copy of this same register, placed at the entrance to the Summit, was consulted often in the days that followed. Each letter written by a person participating in the fast provided an opportunity to approach one person or another. Some letters addressed to the delegates in general were very harsh. To whom could we deliver them without creating a counter-effect? I decided to approach Pauline Marois, the Minister of Education and to explain everything to her, letting her see that as Minister of Education, she should be able to understand the cry for help expressed in these letters. After a surprised look, she replied that I had done right in speaking to her and that, yes, she would read them carefully. She revealed her sensitivity a few weeks later by sending each writer a hand-written reply.

What is the weight of such gestures by which we try to reach others person to person while stakes are played out from function to function or from interest to interest? When it is received, the "hand-written" letter from the Minister will appear disassociated from the threats of cuts to education and difficult to "understand" for students who, during these same weeks, are occupying their institutions to establish a balance of power.

With the zero impoverishment clause, we will have travelled only a part of the way leading to social understanding, to the translation of a convention expressing a qualitative leap in solidarity and concern for real equality into a social and fiscal pact. As I see it, a part of the way is a great deal, nothing, and worse, all at the same time. It is a great deal because most of the delegates finally declared themselves in favour of examining the possibility of such a clause, with the notable exception of those earning $55,000 or more! It is nothing because it was not approved and consequently there is no subsequent way to impose a review of the political decisions in the light of this criterion. It is worse because the government appropriated and distorted the underlying principle of the clause of solidarity with the poorest one-fifth of the population by presenting a counter-proposal limiting the guarantee of non-impoverishment only to those severely restricted in their ability to work, among the poorest one-fifth of the population. This counter-proposal, unacceptable to three groups that withdrew including the Federation of Women, clearly indicated the scapegoat in the positions the government would adopt, a scapegoat quite in line with the neoliberal credo: unemployed persons who are fit to work are thus designated as guilty of being absent without reason from the national activity.

IX. Two Thousand Five Hundred

“... that encourages people to become involved in the community...”

We had told each other that we would need at least five people a day to hold a fast. If we could get five persons, we would go ahead. We stopped counting at 2500. Registrations came from more than 130 different locations. Something about this adventure had persuaded people to become involved. Some technical conditions probably: a specific task, within their reach, that did not force people to travel to a central location and even allowed a gesture of protest to be integrated into everyday life; an economic climate and political actions from which we wanted to disassociate ourselves, and here was the opportunity to do it; key persons who took on responsibilities, like Alfreda who worked so hard so that 100 people from Chibougamau would relay each other during these two weeks; a “human and/or Christian” heritage too, probably, that perceived the fast as a noble and radical means of resistance and of personal and collective transformation.

All throughout the year that followed, this experience that encouraged so many to become involved has presented us with a multitude of questions. And one of the questions is, “How do we make room?” On its own, a successful crowd event is like a fire in straw. It glows briefly, then everything goes out. The fight against exclusion entails preparing the place for those who will come. It implies making it possible for them to stay, to notice a place, to take it and live there, to be at home.

We have met the challenge of continuing to act as a church without a church. We encountered growing pains, just as children do when their bones grow and they feel pain in their legs. Growing pains are very different from the pain of illness but they still cannot be ignored. What do we do when there are forty at the monthly meetings now instead of twenty, when people want to initiate new actions while the permanent staff are out of breath, and other groups with whom we work need a break and some time for their own initiatives, when new people joining the group arrive with different needs from those of the old brigade? What can we do when everyone wants to be on a committee, when there are more requests than ways to respond, when being even more conscious of the stakes, we want to be even better informed and take part in the decisions, when days only have twenty-four hours and meetings last only one night?

We do what we can, realizing that we have to focus more closely on what is essential in order to continue progressing without running in all directions, and to develop ourselves without losing our way. In February, we had two opportunities in the world of the living to review the situation. There was the concern about moving on from utopia to organization that had been expressed by Don Pedro Casaldaliga and Don Samuel Ruiz during the annual meeting of the *Secrétariat international chrétien de solidarité avec l'Amérique latine*—Oscar A. Romero (SICSAL) (International Christian Secretariat for Solidarity with Latin America) in Panama. I was intrigued by this phrase that was so perfectly timed after the joyful hope contained in "Let's do it and it will get done!" and presented Daniel, a Mexican, with the following problem: "The theological trends in Latin America have included a sort of wave of liberation, next a wave of utopia, and now the wave of organization. The wave of liberation found a great deal of its inspiration at the biblical level from the Book of Exodus; the wave of utopia, the changes to the system, refers, among others, to the book of the Apocalypse. With which biblical inspiration would you associate this concern about moving on to organization?" He did not hesitate—with the Last Judgement or Matthew 25 for the initiated: I was hungry, did you give me food? I was thirsty, did you give me drink? I was alone, did you visit me?

At the same time, the bishops asked us to work with them in preparing the message for the first of May. In the abundance of availability that marked this year, about a dozen people from the group formed a committee with this mandate, and several others gravitated around it in one way or another. In our reflection on the economy that Claude Béland, the President of Desjardins Movement, had described as putting the house in order, we saw these times of exclusion as the temptation of a gilded, empty house, inhabited by some and excluding others. We looked for ways to find a house that would be good for all and that would really make us feel like celebrating, as we should, on the first of May in years to come. Beyond the criticism of neoliberalism and its logic, we asked ourselves what could be strong enough in our human condition to transcend this logic. And then this little passage came to mind, inspired by Daniel and his comment on the Last Judgement, inspired by Matthew, inspired by . . .

At the end of our lives no one will ask us, "How much money did you make?" Will we be able to reply, however, to this simple question that must be considered and that will be asked, "I was there, did you make room for me?" [4]

X. The Reproduction Factors of Solidarity

" . . . and to share their talents and skills . . . "

I am coming to the end of this narrative. We used this last question as a basis for working on our text. In real life, we still do not know how to succeed in organizing ourselves sufficiently to construct dwellings in which there is room in abundance for everyone; dwellings responding to the needs of individuals in our groups and in our surroundings but also responding to the need for a true and good social and fiscal pact. How do we arrange things so that the talents and skills of each one of us can be united to make a better world, rather than engaging in competition and repeating the never-ending underhanded tactics that so easily succeed in dividing us?

We—and each time, "we" means an organizing committee with several groups—have returned a few times to Jacques Cartier church during the past months: once to assess the Fast; once for the Romero event that we hold each year in solidarity with the Latin American communities who commemorate together the assassination of Oscar Romero and his rebirth in the struggle of a people for more humanity for humanity. Over 250 of us spent a Night of the Stinging Horseflies (I'll refrain from explaining that name to you because if I do I'll have to tell you yet another story) reviewing the economy, jobs and public finances, and making a bridge between April 30, the last day to submit the income tax return, and May 1, International Workers' Day. Early in the morning on the first of May, we brought a message to the Premier and succeeded in meeting him as he came out of the pool. He promised us an appointment, and subsequently advised us that he would not be meeting with us. As for this meeting—we'll see. The game is not over yet.

A few days ago, just before the holidays, we decided to end the year once again at the church with a day focusing on Spirituality and Militancy. We asked ourselves, "What is this breath that carries us forward?" On the threshold of mystery at the crossroads of our different denominations, philosophies, spiritualities, with or without religion, without being able to give a name to Life other than the All Other as Gabrielle said, or the Unknown Spirit, as André with his Montagnais culture would say, we sense that beyond the words, we want to celebrate this life and defend it together.

One of the workshops was about loving. What does loving mean in a context of militant action for social justice? Are we fighting with love? Groups that could be united in the same struggle sometimes do more harm to each other than to their adversary. And must we love this adversary? We talked about an intelligence of the heart. Loving is not being soppy or lukewarm or insipid. We can love and be firm. Loving could perhaps be recognizing and appealing to the humanity in others. Jean-Paul said that what could characterize the action of Christian militants is pardon, the ability to recognize the errors, the lapses, the false moves and to use them to advance rather than to exclude the culprits. I felt very moved when he said that perhaps because to act is to be always, unavoidably, a little mistaken, and to act is inevitably to be judged. In this, there is something quite unforgiving that is accumulated over the days and through the actions. Jean-Paul's simple words cured something in me.

Tia Rita, a Brazilian over eighty years old and a member of a *Fraternité du serviteur souffrant* (Fraternity of the Suffering Servant), also explained to us that in her opinion love dilates the senses. Love makes us see, hear and notice more clearly. If this is the case then we are going to need a great deal of love to continue changing the world and to discover the skills we need to change it for the greatest good of all.

In ending this story, this is the grace that I wish for us: that love will dilate our senses more and more each day forever and ever . . .

Oh yes, I nearly forgot. Just before the beginning of our fast, feeling very humble about the decision we had taken, I sent an e-mail to Jacques Gaillot to tell him what we were preparing and to ask for his advice. He replied, sending us his congratulations. And what advice do you think he gave us? "You asked me for advice. Concerning the occupation of the church, the parish priest and the parish council must be in agreement." Of course they were in agreement. It was the first thing we had checked! Mario, the parish priest had a good laugh when he heard it. He must have found Jacques Gaillot to be a man after his own heart.

The big things are often small things—that ask to be told so that they can be reincarnated.

Notes

1. In 1996, the Premier of Quebec convened two socio-economic summits, one in March and the other in October, on public finance, the economy and employment, and invited representatives from the business community, the unions, and socio-community groups. These summits were to be used to create a consensus which the Premier would subsequently rely on to advance his intentions with regard to the issues presented.

2. A group associated with a certain period in Social Credit and advocating traditional religious and political values.

3. See Alain Bouchard, "Les matelas dans l'église," *Le Soleil*, 4 November, p. A7.

4. Comité des affaires sociales de l'Assemblée des évêques du Québec and Carrefour de pastorale en monde ouvrier, *J'étais là, m'as-tu fait de la place?* Montreal, Assemblée des évêques du Québec, 1997, par. 16.

"YOU WILL BE CALLED BREACH-MENDER, RESTORER OF RUINED HOUSES" (ISAIAH 58:12)

Michel Beaudin

Michel Beaudin, a theologian and economic sociologist, PhD in Theology, has been a Professor of Social Ethics, Faculty of Theology, University of Montreal since 1985. His publications include Obéissance et solidarité, Essai sur la christologie de Hans Urs von Balthasar *(Obedience and Solidarity, Essay on the Christology of Hans Urs von Balthasar, 1989). He is presently writing a book on the subject of a theology of solidarity.*

As outlined in greater detail in the introduction to the text that follows, my sensitization to injustice, as well as to social solidarity, goes back to my childhood, following the bends and curves of my family's history. Subsequent experiences nourished and energized the seeds that had already been planted. A stay in Latin America at the age of nineteen, studies in theology and economic sociology; then a series of commitments, first to Development and Peace, from 1974 to 1985; to the Organisation populaire des droits sociaux *(O.P.D.S., Montreal) (Community Social Rights Association); to the* Groupe de théologie contextuelle québécoise *(Contextual Quebec Theology Group); to the* Journées sociales du Québec *(Quebec Social Action Days); to the Faculty of Theology, etc. I am indebted to all my companions in these groups for having given me a passion for social justice, in opposition to an economic system intent on normalizing anti-solidarity in our society. And even more, I am indebted to them for having opened my eyes to the face of a God that this system will never succeed in subjugating.*

Introduction

In a recent article entitled *Comment le Canada tourne le dos à l'état providence* (How Canada is turning its back on the welfare state), journalist Michel Venne discussed some publications dealing with the meaning of the shift that is taking place in the country. [1] This diagnosis refers not only to a new orientation in the economy but also to a new orientation in the majority of governments, even the traditionally moderate ones, in which the most conservative ministers seem to have seized power in their respective cabinets, as well as in the Liberal Party of Canada and the *Parti Québécois*. The fight against the deficit is giving rise to a frenzy of cuts that are in the process of causing irreversible harm to society.

But the most disturbing aspect, according to a book by pollster Angus Reid, [2] is that neoliberals have succeeded in winning over large areas of public opinion to their thesis and values. The most destitute have every reason to feel abandoned: the State, and even a large segment of society, is siding with a market that has become stateless, allowed free rein, and left to the sole blind logic of the accumulation of capital. Thus, Angus Reid writes, "Canada is entering an era dominated by mean-spirited individualism encouraged by the new economy and the globalization of markets ('Sink-or-Swim Era')." [3] He is also concerned by the new radicalism "of divisions based on income" [4] and by the fact that "there is far more willingness to ascribe blame to the poor . . . even though it's getting much easier to sink into poverty." [5] A recent survey confirmed moreover "that a majority of Canadians were opposed to programs of economic support for poor regions and that a large proportion of the population was more than ever determined to restrict the social security net before too many can benefit from it." [6]

The depth of the disturbance in societies is forcing Christian communities into decisive reappraisals of faith. I would like to contribute in a modest way, in four sections, to this examination: (1) by clarifying the imaginary or the conception of the relationships between faith and social structuring that make a commitment against the tide of neoliberalism [7] Christianly conceivable and even urgent; (2) by proposing a systematic analysis, at various levels, of neoliberalism as a structural obstacle to the exercise of citizenship and to the community's ability to live the Gospel; (3) by confronting these dynamics of sacrificial anti-solidarity with the movement launched by the God of Jesus and the meaning of a Church seeking to "follow Jesus" and persistent in its desire to be a "community" in a society that is "de-communitizing"; (4) finally, by sketching out the paths to a societal alternative that "prepares the way of the Lord." The theme of the "house," to which the Greek etymology of the word "economy" refers (*oikos*-house, *nomos*-management), will serve as the main thread for this reflection. But before I set out on this journey, I would like to recall the personal background that inspired it and that still spurs my research.

Looking back over the past, I realize that for nearly twenty-five years my social commitment and theological work have not ceased to plough the furrow of solidarity. Vatican II invited us to read the "signs of the times" as a setting to listen to the appeals of the Lord of history. We practised this reading at Development and Peace where I worked from 1974 to 1985. As we sought to understand the logic that was forever widening the gap between North and South, we began to discern, in the very heart of the western world, the dynamics of an anti-solidarity that would now leave its mark on historical relationships with Third World peoples as well. Because of these dynamics of anti-solidarity, they were already suffering the effects of neoliberalism in the seventies. Beginning in the eighties, the savage prescriptions of this same phenomenon would be applied to our own societies as well. Rereading the Gospel on the basis of this "sign of the times," according to the approach proposed by liberation theology and by the Synod on Justice in the World, [8] subsequently led me to rediscover God and His project from a perspective of solidarity, as witnessed in so many Third World communities, and to work for the development of a theology and an ethic of solidarity.

But I have to return to my childhood to rediscover the primary roots of these two threads of anti-solidarity and solidarity. For me, the theme of solidarity has always been linked to the theme of the "house". I spent my first years in the ancestral home that my father, the twenty-second child in his family, had bought from his own father. In addition, since my paternal grandparents had about a hundred or so children and grandchildren, the feeling of belonging to a large "household" was forever present. This vast network, nourished by visits, celebrations and mutual help, created a hospitable world where we felt secure despite a poverty that although common at the time, was unaccompanied by the pain of social exclusion.

I also lived an unforgettable experience of economic solidarity that went beyond the circle of relatives and reflected the tightly-woven character of the era's social fabric. For years, the village grocer had given us credit, knowing that my parents would repay him as soon as they were able. But he was especially aware that the needs of children warranted taking a few economic risks. I saw this man, by chance, about forty years later when he was working part-time as a service station attendant; I had never forgotten his goodness and offered him my heartfelt thanks.

But I also encountered the structural injustice and anti-solidarity of capitalism. After World War II, manufacturers who were trying to lure a plentiful supply of labour to the city convinced the provincial government to put an end to agricultural loans to young farmers. This policy, combined with two successive bad harvests due to rain, plunged us into poverty. The ploys of the foreign land speculators who prowled around vulnerable young owners almost made us lose the farm and the family home. My father finally resolved to rent his land and subsequently to sell it to one of his brothers. To ensure our survival, he took his "lunch-box" and "travelled" morning and evening to the "factory" in Montreal.

It was only much later that my parents understood the structural dimension of the change that had swept them along in its wake, when they understood that their poverty had nothing to do with the value of their efforts but rather with the precariousness that capital constantly creates in order to force people into its service. In the meantime, their health, their dignity and their self-image was affected. From this experience and even from the less turbulent decades that followed, I became convinced that the well-being and the education

I had enjoyed was not due to capitalism, but that it had been wrested by my parent's courage and their superhuman efforts, at the expense of a thousand sorrows and humiliations;[9] that they were also due to the solidarity of other sectors of the civil society such as educators in the primary school and later the classical college, whose generosity made education accessible even to the poorest.

Later, in 1967, a stay in Latin America allowed me to discover a capitalism that rendered the survival of family households radically impossible. This time I saw capitalism face to face and no longer from the back as we had viewed it in our societies from the 1940s to the 1970s. I resolved that I would never forget its characteristics, a resolution that led to my studies in theology and economic sociology and my commitment at Development and Peace.

Since the eighties, it is the spectre of this same capitalism, proposing a return to the utopia of the old, supposedly self-regulating market of the nineteenth century, that I see emerging even here in Canada as in all the western countries. In the future, Third World countries will no longer lag behind our "development," but they represent our common future if nothing is done to block the dynamics of neoliberalism. I see this return to precariousness, as a secular standard of capitalism, in my children's concern for their future, despite their sound education. Will they have a job? Will they be able to develop their talents?

I also read in the current economy that is in full overproduction of wealth and has no need of those it declares useless. It is this same economy that decides who can live in the societal house on the sole basis of the jobs available, jobs moreover, that it is eliminating on a grand scale. Neoliberalism is indeed creating a world in which it is no longer a good place to live, a world where citizens are seeing their right to be included restricted in the name of liberty, and where society appears to have the right to survive only through the chinks in the economic and political system. There must be an alternative! This is what we will try to glimpse at the end of this reflection. As a preliminary step, let us take the measure of the neoliberal threat to the societal "house" by determining, first of all, the implications within our faith, of a commitment to a new departure from "Egypt," and an appeal to our fellow citizens in this sense. For as the Book of Proverbs puts it, "For want of guidance a people falls" (Pr. 11:14). Therefore, let my words and this book in its entirety be read as an act of resistance, of summoning, and a rebuilding of hope. It matters little that we will not see all the results of our efforts during our lifetime. We are indebted, in this respect, to our children and grandchildren, through inter-generational solidarity. Let it suffice for us, as it did for our ancestors in the faith, to "see and to welcome in the far distance," at least, "he who had made the promise" and like Moses, to "persevere," "as if we were seeing the invisible" (Heb. 11:13,27).

I

THE "SIGNS OF THE TIMES" URGE US ON TO AN APPROACH THAT REVIVES THE GREAT PROPHETIC TRADITION

Sociologically, everything would appear to push the Church to the right, especially since ecclesial tradition contains a multitude of "ready-to-wear" models for adapting to the societal context. These models have so long appeared to be self-evident to the believing conscience that the recent approach may come as a surprise since it favours listening to the word of God in the "signs of the times" and integrating the struggle for justice as a fundamental constituent of the mission of evangelization. [10] It marks a true *departure* from the dominant concepts of the past fifteen centuries, but on the other hand, it *revives* the great biblical and patristical tradition that had faded since the fourth century of our era. Putting the Christian ideal of the relationship between faith and societal organization into historical perspective could constitute a useful reference point for the crucial choices of our time.

Let us define three models, the last of which has two versions, and specify a few implications for each of them. I will begin with those that differ most widely from our approach, namely, the models of "Christendom" and "modernity." Chart No. 2 below provides an overview of these models (p. 114).

The Christendom model or the Gospel subjugated

The period of Christendom that would soon make the frontiers of the Church and the empire coincide opened with the Edict of Milan (313). Later, it would be said that "outside the Church, there is no salvation." The logic of power eventually contaminated the structures of the Church. By attaching too much importance to the mediation of power as a method of societal integration, the Church lost all its capacity to contest a so-called "Christian" order. The Gospel became mired within it and the Church eventually came to regard the structural disparities it contained as sacred, as if "all authority comes from God." Justice was reduced to a matter of individual virtue and almsgiving, despite a generosity that would extend to founding religious orders to help the poor. It remained blind, however, to social "in-justices." It is not surprising that this model, which would endure without too much protest until the eighteenth century in France, and even until 1960 in Quebec, was a contemporary of the Crusades, the Inquisition, feudalism and royal absolutism, as well as the colonization/evangelization of the Third World.

The modernity model or the privatization of faith and ethics

From the eighteenth century onwards, a significant variant of this paralysis of Christian social criticism began to appear. Initially, capitalism and emerging modern states attempted to subjugate the Church because of its support for the Old Regime and because of the scourge of religious wars. But instead, the Church demanded an autonomy that was soon conceded to it on condition that it confine itself to the religious "domain" and remain within the fold of private life.

This marked the beginning of an accelerated privatization of Christian faith and ethics as well as a spiritualizing ejection of salvation outside of the stakes of history. "Walls" were thus erected between the Gospel on the one hand, and public affairs that professed different credos and ethics (e.g., competition or survival of the fittest) on the other. In this case, but for different reasons, justice was again limited to "good works" while the Church, in a context of poverty brought about by the industrial revolution, preached an attitude of submission with regard to the authorities and the established order. A letter to the internuncio, Bishop Garibaldi, from the French Secretariat of State contained the following observation: "It is obvious that as religion spreads throughout France, souls will become more docile and the people quieter." [11] It was not without good reason that the nineteenth century was called the century of the "alliance of the throne, the safe and the altar!"

Thus, fifteen centuries of an excessive *proximity* of the Church vis-à-vis the powers of society were followed in Europe by two centuries of *separation* between the Church and the social order, combined with an arm's length legitimization of the latter. Is this not the model that continues to give structure to the vision of faith of a large number of believers and determines the general attitude of our society's elite toward relations with the Church? [12] It produces Christians who can fervently practise both a privatized religion and a neoliberal religion. This is how we have been socialized, but do the demands of the Gospel not lead in another direction?

From 1891 to our day: an unexpected return to the great prophetic tradition

The final model restores the Church to the heart of society but in a new relationship composed of two versions.

The first version was inaugurated in 1891 by the encyclical *Rerum novarum*, a veritable thunderbolt in the serene sky of brute capitalism. Christians involved in the labour movement succeeded in bringing a new awareness of the demands of faith to the very head of the Church. By proclaiming the priority of work over capital, with all the resulting consequences, the Church rediscovered its subversive "memory" and once again made the economy and politics ground for evangelization. The movement continued to grow [13] and received new impetus from the Council that was more openly receptive to the modern world. Unlike preceding models, the Church no longer sought to dominate, but neither did it appear to be indifferent to the social stakes. The world was recognized as a place where God "is beckoning" to us and as a recipient of the salvation to which the Church must bear witness, even if it means contesting the social order. John Paul II summarized the rediscovery in this way: "Man is the path of the Church."

But this model needed to be extended even further because the optimism of the sixties prevented the churches of the North from realizing the full measure of societal conflictivity. Based on a more rigorous social analysis, liberation theology, the Synod on Justice, subsequent encyclicals, as well as the stand taken by various episcopates shed new light on the problematic aspects of the relationship between the Church and society. These interventions would make the transformation of social structures, based on recognition of the marginalized, the axis both of society's future and the Church's evangelizing mission. At the same time, it recognized that it contained the central perspective of the entire biblical tradition, from the God "who heard the appeals of His people" (Ex. 3:7) to Jesus who came "to bring the Good News to the poor . . . ," so that it "would be fulfilled today" (Lk. 4:18,21).

It is in this movement that the commitment of so many "Abrahamic minorities" (H. Camara) here at home, and elsewhere, can be found and which this book would like to echo. Rooted in this option for the "losers," let us attempt to put into practice this new approach that the Church is following, first by examining the forces "shaping" our societal house and subsequently by promoting a dialogue between these "signs of the times" and the founding references of our faith.

II

NEOLIBERALISM: A DESTRUCTIVE PROJECT OF THE SOCIETAL "HOUSE"

As a societal force, neoliberalism includes various levels that must be distinguished for analytical purposes. I will examine it successively as an economic and political project, as a process of marketization of society, and as ethics, ideology and "religion."

1. "The market governs, the government manages"

There is no need to provide a lengthy description here of the symptoms of the current dislocation of societies. They stare us in the face at every turn and the media provides us with a multitude of examples on a daily basis. They are apparent, for example, in regions that are losing droves of young people, in the massive layoffs and the proliferation of "McJobs," the crowds roaming through shopping malls in mid-week, the increase in the number of Food Banks, or again, the waiting lists and lineups at hospitals, etc. They prowl our streets and have likely already forced their way into our homes.

It is perhaps more important to understand that these ills and the distress they cause do not fall from heaven, but that they are the product of a specific type of organization of society called *neoliberalism* that has been rampant since the eighties. It is especially important to understand the logic of neoliberalism that makes growth and the overproduction of wealth coincide with the growing scarcity of employment, the deterioration of working conditions and serious cuts in social services budgets. In a word, in the neoliberal context, there is no paradox in the fact that the economy is going well at the same time that the population is suffering. This situation is reflected in various newspaper headlines such as, "Unemployment is increasing and economists believe that it is a sign of recovery," or "Who's afraid of growth? Why financiers, of course!" [14]

The uniqueness of the neoliberal model will become more readily apparent if we make a small historical detour and examine the two other economic-political models that have set the pace in the twentieth century. These successive restructurings must be understood in the light of the basic rule of capitalism, that is, an obsessive pursuit of increasing, if not continuous, profits, through the interaction, in a normally competitive context, of the supply and demand of products and services. Let us try to take an "x-ray" of each model from this perspective, and enumerate its social components. Therefore, I will limit myself to a structural approach, setting aside the intentions of individuals as well as the expressions of resistance that each model did not fail to provoke. Chart No. 1 provides a basis for this journey (p. 113).

Until the thirties: "brute" liberalism and insecurity

From the nineteenth century to the beginning of our century, the new technologically underdeveloped capitalist regime based its race for profits on the maximal exploitation of human work that was regarded as a simple commodity. Hence the origin of the miserable condition of workers who were, in the words of Leo XIII, left "isolated and defenceless . . . to the callousness of employers and the greed of unrestrained competition" as a result of "the concentration of so many branches of trade in the hands of a few individuals, so that a small number of very rich men have been able to lay upon the masses of the poor a yoke little better than slavery itself." [15]

In view of the market's so-called self-regulating ability, the State did not intervene; it was obliged to adopt a "laisser-faire" attitude. Economic policies remained confined to police and military spending, etc., and social policies to meagre grants for a few charitable institutions. As early as 1931, Pius XI denounced this leniency of the State that instead of "ruling in kingly fashion . . . intent only upon justice and the common good, has become instead a slave, bound over to the service of human passion and greed." [16] It sounds very much like a description of the current neoliberal State!

There was no recourse for the workers who lived in the greatest insecurity. At the time, living conditions in Montreal were compared to those in Calcutta. The sequel to this situation is well-known; it quite simply exploded in the faces of the capitalists themselves. The enormous poverty prevented creditworthy demand from following the rhythm of production, or the supply, made possible by recent technological developments. Profits dried up with this imbalance and panic-stricken shareholders trying to sell everything at once provoked the Crash of 1929 that was followed by the Great Depression of the thirties. Capitalism no longer "worked"; it needed crutches. Let us schematize the trend leading to this crisis in the following way: *S (supply) > D (demand).*

The decades from 1940 to 1970: the Fordist-Keynesian model, or economic growth linked to the welfare of populations

To clear a way for the return of profits, a "New Deal" (1936) was proposed to the angry populations: the promise of increasing well-being in return for definitive acceptance of the capitalist system. In an economy that was captive to a primarily national market, industrialists in the wake of Henry Ford understood that the level of employment and salaries would have to be raised to ensure an ever-increasing creditworthy demand or mass consumption that could keep pace with a mass production capacity or: $S = D$ *(balance in upward spiral).*

The other crutch was borrowed from the economist Keynes, who conceived an active role for the State as a prop for and regulator of the demand. This is the meaning of *economic policies* (interest rates, taxation, public works . . .) that allow unemployment or excessive inflation to be corrected by re-launching or slowing the economy, as needed. It is also the function of *social policies* that insure the security of the system by keeping the unemployed ("useless arms") and mothers of families at home, economically "useful mouths" or as "consumers."

This was the origin of the prosperity and the social security of the post-war years, a happy and exceptional parenthesis in the history of a capitalism that was obliged at that time to accede to the struggles and demands of organized labour in linking the growth of companies to employment and social security. No one can deny, however, that Third World populations paid a heavy portion of the cost of this prosperity, either because they were forced to provide raw materials at derisory prices and salaries, or because countries of the North and multinational companies prevented them from developing their own secondary industries. In western countries, during that period, capital strategically integrated an institutionalization of solidarity. But can the *mechanisms of solidarity* and their automaticity dispense with a forever active *spirit and culture of social solidarity*? Have we perhaps been too inclined to take these mechanisms for definitive acquisitions? Capitalism's recent change of course is now catching us unprepared. It has found us in a state of individualism and social dislocation that weakens our resistance to new onslaughts.

Toward the middle of the sixties, however, the model ran out of steam and profits once again began to decline under the combined effect of a number of factors: slowdown in a local market reduced to only replacing the most basic everyday equipment; pressure from the rising prices of raw materials from Third World countries (oil was still selling at 1907 prices); ageing of industrial plants, and finally, new competition from the European and Japanese economies that were now fully rebuilt.

From the seventies to the present: emergence and triumph of the neoliberal model or capital's revenge on labour and social entitlements

During the seventies, as they struck the hour of capital's revenge on the recent social entitlements, large companies started, hesitantly at first, to look for a solution to the crisis. They reduced their production costs (layoffs and casualization of employment, wage restraints, transferring production to more "welcoming" regions and blackmailing them into granting subsidies and other benefits, etc.) and raising their prices, prompting a spectacular rise in inflation. Governments supported them through a policy of loans for large public work projects and international aid linked to Canadian contracts, but the crisis worsened even further.

Neoliberal restructuring suddenly appeared on the threshold of the eighties. The economists F. A. Hayek (Vienna) and M. Friedman (Chicago School) had theorized about neoliberal restructuring and it was subsequently tested in Pinochet's Chile (1973). Whispers of it finally reached the ears of the Thatcher and Reagan governments and it then became widespread in the West. This model, proposed as the way of the future, merely marked a return to the old liberalism (and thus to an economy of supply as opposed to an economy of demand, as in the preceding model), but it was strengthened this time by more direct support from the State, hence the prefix "neo". It is still characterized by a "liberation" of capital from the national yoke and by a globalization of its "pastures" both in relation to production and to markets.

The above-mentioned governments are *changing the rules of the game* in favour of the large corporations. *Externally,* they force the liberalization of trade and investments by erasing economic borders (free-trade agreements, new policies of international financial and commercial institutions . . .) that protected national economies. *Internally,* they slow the economy and curb inflation by raising interest rates, thus favouring the reorganization of large capital: eliminating weaker competitors, mergers and acquisitions, new technology, "rationalization" of the production processes, management and sales on a global basis, layoffs, etc. Conscripted or *satellitized*, the State is making itself an accomplice in the "competitivity" race and adds other benefits for "winning" companies: supplying infrastructures and subsidies to attract investments, tax relief, privatization, deregulation, compression of social programmes, etc. The x-ray of the new model now appears thus: ***S*** *(s local + S global)* = ***D*** *(d local + D global).*

Independent financial markets are formed functioning at the rate of 3,000 billion transactions a day and are beyond any fiscal control. For their own financing, governments, entangled in their enormous deficits that are due more to their economic than to their social policies, are at the mercy of this capital that roves in search of relative maximal profitability and is always liable to perturb the economic balance because of its weight and the unpredictable mobility of its operations. In short, neoliberal governments have abolished their own power in favour of the market, so much so that a participant at the last summit in Davos in 1996 could say: "The authorities are at best, mere sub-contractors for business. The market governs, the government manages." [17] As for Mr. Hans Tietmeyer, the president of the *Bundesbank*, he warned any government that might be tempted to ignore the rules of competition that "the markets would punish it immediately, for the politicians are henceforth under the control of the financial markets." [18]

This new configuration makes the world a vast economic battlefield. On behalf of their own "war" and "conquest" desires, the new feudal lords take populations as hostages and pit them against each other. To survive in the short term, the latter must consent to a general mobilization and to all the "sacrifices" demanded by a globalized competition that is creating uncertainty in the order books on which jobs depend. Except for a fringe group of very qualified workers who are indispensable, and treated accordingly, a competitiveness race, with its corollary of uncertainty for employment, condemns a growing number of people throughout the world to the "revolving doors" of precarious employment - unemployment - welfare - "McJobs" - unemployment, etc., and thus to a continuous deterioration of their working and living conditions. It is what employers euphemistically call work "flexibility." The American economist, L. Throw, said it well, "to be competitive today, a country has to offer only two things: lower salaries and a skilled labor force. There is nothing else."

Since foreign markets can be freely conquered, demand no longer depends mainly on the local market. People's income from work is less important. The same applies to the economic usefulness of public social programmes. Employers view them as a burden; thus they advocate reductions in government deficits by first making cuts in social expenses that are responsible, for only 6 per cent of the increase in the national debt as compared with 50 per cent for the rise in interest rates and 44 per cent for tax shelters! [19] The "useless arms" (the unemployed, welfare recipients, the elderly, etc.) also become "useless mouths"! Therefore, the welfare state can be substituted for the business state, accompanied by a discourse on the responsibility and solidarity of citizens. Thus the impoverished are referred to voluntary public charity, whether this takes the form of volunteerism, telethons, Church "charities," or the latest fad, the "social economy," viewed as a sub-market of employment that permits exclusion but poses no threat to the system.

The dismantling of social programmes that the authorities prefer to transform into manpower training at the taxpayer's expense has yet another advantage for employers: it forces a surplus of labour into the employment market, creating downward pressure on salaries and working conditions and further enhancing the competitiveness of companies. Thus, in Canada, according to the National Health and Welfare Council, in 1976 an individual was obliged to work forty-one hours at minimum wage to earn the equivalent of the threshold of poverty. Today, the same person must work seventy-three hours at minimum wage to obtain similar earnings. [20]

Some of the stakes of neoliberalism

In conclusion, let us enumerate a few of the stakes raised by the advent of neoliberalism:

– Our living environment has changed; we have moved from an economy that was primarily national and regulated by a democratic State to a globalized economy, open and unprotected from competition, and beyond the control of elected governments. Economic policy makers are accountable only to shareholders (including our own pension funds!) who are motivated by the criteria of profitability and competitiveness. *Are we still in a democracy?*

– Neoliberalism *sets growth against employment and social development.* This is how AT&T's announcement of the dismissal of 45,000 wage-earners resulted in a sudden rise in the company stock; its value increased by $6 billion in forty-eight hours. [21] Similarly, the news that the employment picture is improving appals Wall Street and "makes it stumble" [22] because this indicator generates fear that demand will increase and the subsequent inflation could absorb a portion of their profits! Increased competitiveness seems to be very rigidly coupled with the massive off-loading of manpower. Such logic, disconnected from social reality, betrays the economy's vocation, as indicated by its previously mentioned etymology, to manage the basic necessities of society as in a fraternal household where no one is surplus, instead of the current jungle. [23] Neoliberalism is a project that destroys our common house. Is it not ideologically significant that, during the same period, businesses, whose purpose is in no way fraternal, retain their self-designation as a "house" to build confidence in their products (parents always provide the best for their children, do they not?), to generate consumer loyalty and to develop a sense of belonging in their employees?

– Finally, populations rightly feel that they are caught in a structural trap, abandoned by the market as well as by government. Employment, always inflexibly necessary, as the main means of access to income, is shrinking before our very eyes, while the other route, the "emergency exit" of welfare payments, is in the process of being closed off. People are not dupes. They may well be more inclined to heed the call to resistance rather than listening to the deceitful discourse of a neoliberalism that attempts to convince them of the unequalled benefits of its old remedies outside of which there is no salvation!

2. Neoliberalism, fast forward episode of the transformation of society into market

In a recent interview, Mr. Claude Béland, the President of Mouvement Desjardins wondered: "Are we still living in societies or in markets?" This apprehensive question refers to a fundamental aspect of neoliberalism. It is impossible to understand neoliberalism without seeing in it the acceleration and the most recent illustration of a quite singular historical process which started in the eighteenth century: the toppling over of socialization into the economy, establishing the latter as the social order's foundation, and the market, left to itself, as its orchestrating principle. Two aspects characterize this mutation of society into a market: first, the economic rationality escapes socio-political control; subsequently, it tends to invade every aspect of life. People and their needs, the earth, work, everything becomes a commodity. A sort of "transubstantiation" occurs as education, the arts, social relations or health lose their own substance to become businesses and, in this way, are subjected only to the rules of the market. Access to basic goods begins to depend exclusively on the ability to pay. Social integration and exclusion, and even life and death are economically decided. Are health budgets and other societal choices not determined by financial markets?

Our current vocabulary already strongly reflects the hold of this market logic: we no longer espouse a cause, we are "sold" on it; we no longer get an education, we "invest" in our future; we do not agree with someone's ideas, we "buy" them; a government does not fulfil a mandate, it "delivers the goods"; a mayor is judged on his ability to "sell" the municipality, etc. People themselves cease to be citizens; they become manpower, consumers, beneficiaries, taxpayers, human "resources," etc. Thus, before being reduced to simple statistics, they are strictly defined according to their function or economic relevance.

Furthermore, this represents the first social order in history to base the social bond on economic opposition or competition among the members. Anti-solidarity is engraved in the very fibre of the economy and society, thus concealing the responsibility for exclusions in a mechanism that coincides with the normal "course" of a society redefined as market. Again, in Davos, Nestlé's manager, Helmut Maucher, declared, "Whether you are an individual, a business or a country, to survive in this world, the important thing is to be more competitive than your neighbour." [24] In a remarkable investigation of the relationship between markets and the social formations within which they have existed throughout history, Hervé Defalvar singled out a permanent feature: from ancient Greece to the present day, the separation of the market from collective reference marks "indicated a time of crisis" and the economic domination over the lives of people is made possible through a weakening of the "we" and its expression in political authority. [25] The American Secretary of Labour, Robert Reich, made a direct reference to this thesis recently with regard to massive dismissals and the widening gap between rich and poor: "If we continue with our current approach," he said, "that is, separating the winners and the losers, it seems to me that we are losing *the moral authority . . . which has always linked us to one another.*" [26] In the final analysis, one question deals with the majority of the stakes that concern us: can we exist socially other than as a market? Mrs. Thatcher had already replied in the negative. For her, society did not exist. There were only individuals who related through contracts and, therefore, it was impossible to talk about the "*social*" responsibility of the State.

3. Neoliberalism as ethics, ideology and "religion": sacrificial anti-solidarity vis-à-vis the losers

Let us now consider the ethics, ideology, and the unavowed "religious" profile of neoliberalism through which it attempts to gain our support and subjugate our imagination.

The rules of the market as ethics

What is the source of the prestige, and the moral prestige even, of capitalism? For the most part, it comes to us from Scottish and English thinkers in the tradition of Adam Smith (1776), who argued that the pursuit of personal interest by each individual, regardless of his intentions, would automatically result in general well-being. For Smith, this allowed society to " . . . subsist among different men as among different merchants, from a sense of its utility, without any mutual love or affection..."[27] In other words, in the same way that the economy could replace politics by favouring the growth of wealth, and, therefore, social stability, the rules of the market could replace the traditional morality of love of neighbour. Solidarity and the common good did not have to be pursued directly, but became the guaranteed indirect effect of another objective. Selfishness, them, could be elevated to the rank of the highest form of altruism!

From that point on, nothing could stop capitalism and protect it from itself. This is why business people and governments feel no embarrassment about applying the strict rules of the market, even in the field of health. They perceive themselves as benefactors and saviours of society in direct proportion to their harshness and even brutality in some cases. Just think for a moment of the virtues of political courage and self-sacrifice attributed to those responsible for government cuts, whereas social solidarity is being devalued. And if the rules of the market are fair, so are the results, including the inequalities which seem so unfair to us. Each person deserves and is responsible for his or her own fate, losers and winners equally.

The ideology of the economically correct

An entire ideology that Alice Amsden has identified as the *economically correct*, [28] defines the *possible* (operating) and the *acceptable* (values). All that remains is to submit to the "reality," defined beforehand according to the parameters of the market, and which in this case becomes the norm. This is how the "gospel" of competitiveness (R. Petrella) leads the economy into a self-referential logic which prevents populations from transforming productivity gains into social progress, and demands instead that the gains be immediately reinvested in order to stay in the race. Similarly, work can be recognized only *as* employment, needs only *as* demand, persons and nature only *as* "resources," a business or a region can survive *only if* they are more competitive than their competitors; services to the population can be ensured *only* once financial markets have been reassured. In short, nothing can be recognized or valorized anywhere except in the logic of capital. This logic infiltrates our deepest reflexes like an enervating gas. It offers the illusion of freedom, somewhat like the carnivorous plant that attract insects inside itself by means of a secretion, and then closes up on them while giving them the impression, through the means of a translucent wall, that they are still on the outside. The victims eventually fall to the bottom where they are digested!

The discourse here is crucial. Through the media which they own or control, the big businesses have succeeded in imposing their agenda by successively and strategically advancing the following themes: free trade, national debt, zero deficit through a reduction in social expenditures. Carefully measured doses of a "narrative fiction" thus govern the globalization of markets that is presented as the benevolent and inescapable fate of societies. [29] Even vocabulary is called to the rescue to "naturalize" the neoliberal vision. Do we not refer to capitalism as the "natural state" of the economy? Major stock market manipulations are described as "storms on financial markets." Attacks against society and the welfare of populations are even presented as a process of recovery: for example, we wish to repair "social fractures," "remedy" the "ills of unemployment"; we talk about "cutting the fat" (who would not like to lose weight, but in reality, we dare not use the term "bone" which would be much more accurate!), to ensure "healthy" public finances, to apply a "drastic remedy" to the economy, etc. The cutbacks and the departure of 7,700 people from the health field in Quebec are called a "cure" or "treatment." [30]

And what of the mergers, the factory closures and layoffs absorbed in "rationalizations," a term specific to human beings, that is used against them in this case by impersonal powers? Here, capital bluntly reveals that it has never liked *workers*; it has always preferred their *work* instead. This explains why, in North America, it promptly substituted *Labour Day,* in early September, for International *Workers* Day, on May first. Capital appreciated labour as long as it found it useful, in other words, profitable. Today, it considers labour to be a *burden* or a *stain* which calls for "cleansing" of the production machinery. It views labour as a sort of "madness" and uses "rationalization" to get rid of it. And, after all, is it not capital that is "working" today? It is while they are asleep, that the holders of capital make a large share of their profits, thanks to the financial economy.

Neoliberalism as a sacrificial "religion," or the hard and the soft

At a final level of analysis, when discussing neoliberal capitalism we must also make reference to a sacrificial and fundamentalist "religion" in our consideration of what it makes absolute or sacred, and what it makes relative or sacrifices. Is this not what constitutes its most secret strength, enabling it to resist all criticism despite its devastating effects?

Capitalism not only "naturalizes" its institutions, mechanisms and rules and pretends that they conform to human nature, it goes so far as to make them sacred or "super-natural" as well. It is described as a "spontaneous order" (F. A. Hayek) and, therefore, equipped with superhuman wisdom, which disqualifies in advance any external intervention stemming from a design. Capitalism is also presented as the "end of history" (F. Fukuyama) in that it is chronologically and qualitatively impassable. This anti-utopian aspect of capitalism, particularly in its neoliberal version, completes its self-transcendence. It even finds high-profile Catholics to sing its praises. Michael Novak, a conservative theologian employed by the American Enterprise Institute, considers that "democratic capitalism" is the ultimate system, [31] once a clear separation has been established between God's kingdom and our world. The IMF's director general, Michel Camdessus, presents the market as a sort of proxy for the kingdom. [32] As the all-powerful and self-proclaimed supreme authority in the organization of the human city, capitalism transfers its own absolutization to enterprises (our salvation!), to goods ("total quality . . . "), to life's objectives (to enrich oneself, to earn . . .), and to the laws of the market themselves. This is the "divine" background that provides a foundation for the economically correct, and serves as a credo or a reference, for example, for governments' current budgetary harshness. This is the "hard," the accountant, and it is non-negotiable.

On the other hand, the remainder, everything that is not immediately profitable or competitive, must pay the penalty. This is the "soft," the human, forever taking a beating, the harmful effects of which can never be "calculated" as clearly as columns of figures. The financial "health" of the State or of Capital must be ensured, even if it means that we all become ill.

It is precisely through the mediation of establishing what is economically correct that the social logic is relativized and that losers are "sacrificed." Persons, populations, businesses or entire areas are judged to be less performing and deemed unworthy of salvation or the capitalist heaven because they have failed to follow to the letter the only acceptable path or "gospel," namely, competitiveness. As it is "normal" and deserved, their sacrifice is without appeal. Here, anti-solidarity changes into sacrificiality. Henceforth, in Canada's foreign affairs policy, business will take precedence over human rights. At the Quebec Socio-Economic Summit in the fall of 1996, employers and the government refused to commit themselves to putting an end to the impoverishment of the poorest 20 per cent of the population!

Adam Smith had already anticipated the cost of this race for profits: "For one very rich man, there must be at least five hundred poor; and the affluence of the few supposes the indigence of the many." [33] In interviews with twenty-four business men and women in Montreal, all of them, without exception, stated to me that the creation of victims is inherent to capitalism. F. A. Hayek, economist and father of neoliberalism, again confirmed it in his own way by declaring: "The only moral rules then, are those that relate to the calculation of lives: ownership and the contract." [34] A shift has occurred since the time of Adam Smith. From a tool and a step in the direction of improved general welfare, competition has become, in a circular way, its own end, occasionally integrating solidarity as an instrument. Should we not call neoliberalism an *elimination* system rather than a *competition* system, since the "game" has openly become one of sacrificing a multitude of "small carrots" to save a few "big ones?" [35] Neoliberal capitalism is the only system in modern society that allows and even encourages human sacrifices, but on condition that these be made according to the only legitimate rules, those of the economy! The sacrifice then acquires all the virtues, as illustrated in a recent vote in the American Senate on social welfare that was disparaged as the cause of poverty: "the poor are corrupted by welfare, the cutbacks will *purify* them!" [36]

When neoliberalism transforms itself in this way, into an inexorable fate, without recourse for present or future losers, it is not surprising to see a growing feeling of powerlessness and even a culture of despair in populations. How do we react to this situation as citizens, as Christians? Do we agree too readily with the logic of capitalist salvation? One thing is certain: the most vulnerable of our brothers and sisters represent the most revealing and extreme case of a general situation, namely, that we are all viewed as potential subjects for "sacrifice". If we make compromises in their regard, we will all be swept away.

At the end of this journey, I see the rise of a sacrificial anti-solidarity toward the weakest and the losers appearing as a great sign of the times in the neoliberal wave. It is the dominant, sombre face of the societal dynamics. But the latter also wears another face that I have left in the background in order to better define the first. It also beckons to us—the face of practices that resist this logic and reverse its course through having as a priority solidarity with society's "sacrificed." These perspectives confront each other in an often uneven battle. Where is the good right? These two types of signs "shout to the heavens." What can we learn from our biblical and ecclesial tradition when we interrogate it anew on the basis of such signs of the times? Can we rediscover its revolutionary nature? Enlightened by this detour, we will then be in a better position to do justice to the alternative dynamics already in progress by attempting to sketch the profile of utopia.

III

Collision between the neoliberal project and the dream of God whose Spirit "Renews the face of the earth"

We have observed that the economy is something more than the economy, that neoliberalism has transformed it into a project with totalitarian pretensions, into a perverse infinitude that undermines the social terrain and feeds on the sacrifice of the least of Jesus' brothers and sisters. Can those who defend them call on the authority of the God of the Judaeo-Christian faith? A battle of gods and faith(s) is occurring here.

The "gods" of the neoliberal economy appear to be headed for a collision with the God of the biblical experience and the patristic tradition. This is what we shall examine briefly from two perspectives: solidarity, in particular with regard to the weaker members of society, and sacrificiality.

1. The God of solidarity and life or the "Economist" God who jealously guards His "house" that is "humanity"

One feature seems to characterize the identity and behaviour of the God of our tradition: a constant concern for solidarity among God's people, which, in a conflictual world, passes for a position in favour of the least of its members, or the victims.

The Old Testament

The God of Israel was intensely concerned about social injustice. God's first manifestation did not occur primarily as a matter of doctrine but rather through a political event: contrary to the idols who "have mouths but never speak, eyes, but never see, ears, but never hear" (Ps. 115), Yahweh "hears the appeals [not the prayers!] of his people" (Ex. 3:8) oppressed in Egypt. God brings about their liberation and gives them a land so that they may live. In return for this gift, the people will be urged unceasingly to put into practice the rules of social solidarity as a sign of belonging to their God. Conversely, injustice toward one of their brothers will be an insult to Yahweh. It is this double equation that Jesus later confirmed in the unity of the commandment of the love of God and one's neighbour, namely, that injustice and idolatry are cut from the same cloth, and that faith demands putting society in supportive order, with God's help.

It is interesting to note how God objects to any possibility of an indefinite human subservience to the rules of a given social organization. Thus the institution of sabbatical and jubilee years (Lv. 25) relativizes the situations created through the play of socio-economic relations by giving back people their land, eliminating their debts and liberating them from the slavery resulting from indebtedness. The economic registers must be turned back to zero when they threaten the community. The justification is always the same: what has been given by God to all cannot be taken away from others (Lv. 25:55). It is also in the name of faith that the prophets thunder against those who rob their workers and exploit the poor and the widows in order to accumulate houses and land. The exile and other scourges would come to punish the weakening of the people swept along by this disregard for the relationship between faith and solidarity, whereas conversely, "Brother helped by brother is a fortress" (Pr. 18:19). To express God's dream of "new heavens" and a "new earth," Isaiah would speak of a society where people can build a house and plant a vineyard for themselves and their children rather than doing it for the sole benefit of their masters and at the price of resigning themselves to the death of their children (65:17-25).

The New Testament

In the New Testament, the same logic is amplified with Jesus who is the "Life" that he gives "in full" (Jn. 10:10). During his first public appearance, Jesus read a text from the prophet Isaiah as his own manifesto. He announces a God who is very different from the one the authorities claim as their own: " . . . He has sent me to bring the good news to the poor, to proclaim liberty to captives . . . to proclaim the Lord's year of favour" (Lk. 4:18-19). His listeners understood very well the content of this discourse for the re-establishment of social justice. It resulted in his first confrontation with the chief priests who were also large landowners and exploited the impoverished peasants through the heavy taxes that they set. They made a first attempt at assassination and never ceased to hound him until the end. At the very beginning, Jesus showed his "identification card" to the disciples sent by John to learn if he was the one "who is to come" or if they should "wait for someone else." As a sign, he again spoke the words of Isaiah, but conscious of the clash that would certainly result from such a scandalous gesture, he added " . . . happy are those who do not lose faith in me" (Mt. 11:2-6).

He never ceased defending the rights of simple people against the Laws, those concerning the Sabbath, for example, or others such as the pure and impure. He challenged the interpretation of faith that made the poor, the blind, the crippled and other sick persons the outcasts of God. We can almost hear him in our day, replying to the decision-makers who try to convince us that the sick and the "losers" are unproductive, non-competitive and useless (in the eyes of the religion of the market), that they cost too much and that we should drop them? Instead, Jesus calls them "blessed". "Feeling sorry" (Mk. 1:41) for these least among his brothers and sisters, Jesus sided with them, cured them and reinstated them socially.

The New Testament is woven through with expressions of God's project to re-establish solidarity among the people, starting from the fringes of society. The attitude of the Samaritan is given as a sign and a standard for the Kingdom. In Zacchaeus, who wanted to share his possessions after his conversion, Jesus recognized "a son of Abraham"; in other words, someone who has rejoined the people of God through his solidarity (Lk. 19:9). The meaning of Jesus' anger against the merchants in the temple is no different: God and religious piety were being used to abuse the pilgrims who were obliged to buy doves to offer ritual sacrifice. Is it not society today that is the "temple of God"? People are not goods or business opportunities but "images of God." The theologian Douglas Meeds was right when he spoke about the "Economist" [37] God, in other words, who jealously cares for his "house" which is humanity, and where God's spirit, "that renews the face of the earth" to make it fraternal, is always at work. At the end, sensing the failure of his appeals, Jesus wept over Jerusalem: "How often have I longed to gather your children, as a hen gathers her chicks under her wings . . . and you refused" (Mt. 23:27) and predicted catastrophes (Lk. 19:41-44).

The apostles subscribed to the same movement. Paul admonished the Corinthians who claimed to communicate in the Eucharistic body of the Lord while they broke his social "body" (1 Co. 11:17-22). As for John, he warned, "Those who do not love their brother whom they see, cannot love God, whom they do not see" (1 Jn. 4:20).

Contrary to the word of the preachers, the Gospel is not socially neutral. Unlike the gods of the neighbouring peoples whom the strongest call to their support, the movement of the biblical revelation presents a God who always sides with the victims. God takes the part of the assassinated Abel; of Joseph, sold by his brothers; of David, ignored in the choice of a future king; of the rejected prophets; of the weak despoiled by the powerful. This closeness to those who do not count reaches the point where Jesus, like them, becomes a victim. Crucified outside the walls, he suffers the ultimate exclusion. In Matthew 25, Jesus identifies for all time with those who were first destined to receive his good news. This God had nothing in common with the title of a homily posted one day in front of a church on Sherbrooke Street in Montreal, *"Our God doesn't take sides!"*

After the Resurrection in which God sided with the One who had shown solidarity even unto death, the time of the Spirit began. This was the Paraclete, the Advocate who would appeal Jesus' condemnation (Jn. 16:7-11). This revision of the trial, carried on throughout history, calls new witnesses to the bar. Is it not practising solidarity with those who today are "sacrificed" to economic or other idols that alone is worthy of faith, or that can attest in a convincing way that, like Jesus, the "losers" are the victims and not the guilty?

In a very significant manner for our subject, the Bible ends with the promise of the victory of the Lamb and the Christians who are resisting the empire. The domination of the empire is so total that one can no longer speak of prophecy here, a term that applies to an order that can be rectified, but rather of *apocalypse*, because in this case, even hope must be reconstructed. The author announces the fall of imperial Rome whose "traders were the princes of the earth" and claims that "all the nations were under your spell." And why will the empire fall? Because "In her you will find the blood of prophets and saints, and all the blood that was ever shed upon the earth" (Rv. 18:23-24). Neoliberalism will not survive because it too has gone too far. In its frenzy, it has touched what is vital to us and is in the process of rousing the populations against it.

The testimony of the first Christians

The practice of acting in solidarity with the outcasts of the empire always constituted a touchstone of the faith in the first centuries of the Church, beside the intellectual defence of the faith against the heresies. This attitude went hand in hand with the refusal to recognize Caesar as "God". Regarding Caesar as sacred was well understood to be the keystone of a vast system of social and fiscal injustice. This tradition of solidarity culminated in the fourth century, in the doctrine of the universal destiny of goods. Often trained in the law, that they did not confuse with charity, the Church Fathers affirmed that "if God is God, all human beings have, as such, the right to what they need to live." Furthermore, they affirmed that this principle prevailed over any other, even that of private property. To summarize, we can use the words of Saint Irenaeus, "the glory of God is the living person." It was the last flash of a prophetic tradition that would almost die out over several centuries and that we have barely begun to revive.

2. "What I want is love, not sacrifice" (Hosea 6:6)

I have already emphasized, at least indirectly, that God's project of reestablishing solidarity by favouring an alliance with the marginalized did not include their sacrifice. Let us be more precise. [38]

The biblical tradition shows that idolatry bears the mark of sacrifice and always leads to human sacrifice. The God of Israel was never shielded from manipulation in this direction. An old concept of the Jewish tradition defined the relationship to God in terms of debt or an observance of faith that was always in default, thus inducing guilt and requiring compensation through sacrifice. Another interpretation of the faith, based on Abrahamic freedom, breaks with this concept and relativizes the Law in favour of the concrete life. Jesus brings this last interpretation to its culmination. In the Lord's Prayer, for example, the relationship with God is always presented in terms of debt, but God "forgives" and does not demand repayment. God merely asks that we forgive others their debts to us (Mt. 6:12), as confirmed in the parables of the ruthless debtor (Mt. 18:23-35), the workers who arrived during the last hour (Mt. 20:1-16), and the prodigal son (Lk. 15:11-32). The God of Jesus did not calculate; therefore, there could be no sacrifice. Any institutional order, always based on the recovery of the debt rather than on its forgiveness, is thus relativized. This position was at the heart of Jesus' confrontation with Jewish power that eventually caused him to be executed precisely in the name of the God-Law: "We have a Law and according to this Law, he ought to die" (Jn. 19:7). The sacrificial reason could then freely resurface: "It is better for one man to die for the people" (Jn. 18:14).

Saint Paul also discovered the deadly power of a Law that, cut off from the freedom of faith, could overturn its own meaning and kill. He was mindful of structural sin that came not from transgressing the law but from its observance. This is why he was the harbinger of the freedom that Christ gained for us with regard to all "the Sovereignties and the Powers" of yesterday and today, by "cancelling every record of debt that we had to pay" (Col. 2:14-15). This same dominant characteristic was retained during the ten centuries that followed.

In the eleventh century, Saint Anselm tragically reversed the Pauline interpretation of the law. The relationship to God was separated from the relationship to others and the law of absolute repayment of debt was installed at the heart of the Trinity, thus legitimizing the inflexibility of usurers. God must be paid what is due despite humanity's insolvency. Accounts would be settled at the only price that could match the extent of outraged honour: the blood of His Son. The law now regulated the action of a God who was nothing more than the deification of worldly powers, while concealing their historical responsibility. Heaven remained closed to debtors until they had done as Christ did by paying with their blood. This sacrificial interpretation of the faith prevailed until the twentieth century. It could only predispose Christians to submit themselves to its secularized version: capitalism with the contract and the absolutization of the law of the market as the basis of all human relations, including the corresponding sacrificial consequences. It is not surprising to hear Michael Novak declare, "If God had thus wished that his beloved Son should suffer, why would he spare us?" and to derive from it an argument in support of resigning ourselves to capitalism, an attitude associated to Christian "realism." [39] And how many politicians today call on our "sacrifices" to justify budget cuts, alleging that "we don't have any choice" and that we have to reimburse our deficits and our debts . . . ? Will our faith be able to rediscover its fibre of solidarity in time to stop the neoliberal planetary holocaust that is eclipsing the paternal and maternal face of the God of Jesus?

Amazingly, the current signs of the times are leading us to rediscover the identity of this God that we have so traditionally learned to name "Trinity," in other words: community, society.

"Solidarity" is, therefore, both the proper name and the invention of our God. He came to reveal them to us on the very terrain of anti-solidarity, to the extent of being crushed by it. If grace is "the life of God within us" and "among us," is it not this solidarity that the "images of God" need for their survival, so submerged are they in a society organized structurally in an anti-solidarity manner that they are disintegrating as persons? As a result, the logic of the simple market is exposed as "atheistic," not because of an open declaration, but through the mediation of socio-economic structures that are falsely viewed as sacred. This is because in tearing the social fabric to the innermost layers and producing outcasts through its "normal" operations, it underhandedly denies God's project. The irruption of this God is "bad news" for those who make the wheels turn, but "good news" for the "stones rejected by the builders" of the social order, as long as there are hands willing to transform it into "good reality."

IV

WHAT DOES "FOLLOWING JESUS" AND "LIVING COMMUNITY" MEAN IN A WORLD THAT IS "DE-COMMUNITIZING," OR OUR "ZEAL" FOR THE "HOUSE" OF THE LORD (PS. 69)?

Before embarking on the paths to an alternative suggested by our journey up to this point, it is important first of all to extract from it a new light on the meaning of the Church and our mission as carriers of the "good news."

After the period of numbness caused by the death of Jesus, the Apostles rallied or were rallied by the Holy Spirit to pursue the movement of God's involvement in history. They intervened publicly. Do we not talk about the *Acts* of the Apostles? As already recalled, the first Christians understood their faith or "sequel to Jesus" as their entry into the "social" involvement of God, who determined that solidarity was not a simple means of salvation but was related to the very fibre of this faith and this salvation.

Here, we are at the heart of the prophetic model that presupposes that the Church mission constitutively takes the societal dynamics into account. However, an examination of the latter with its components of social de-communitization and the sacrificing of the losers who have no possible recourse, indicates at the outset that the "sequel to Jesus" is counter-current, according to the very expressive title of a recent book by Carlos Mesters. [40] It is in such a tradition that a growing number of Christians are registering, as evidenced by the participation of 450 people at the most recent *Journées sociales* in Rimouski on the theme, *Intervenir à contre-courant. De nouvelles pratiques de solidarité* (Counter-current Intervention: New practices in solidarity). We took pleasure at that meeting in relating the traditional representation of Christ, "ICTHUS" in Greek, to a fish, the image of the courageous salmon, whose fertility can only be expressed after it swims upstream.

Neoliberalism collides with us in a number of ways. Something within us is indignant first of all at the social ruin that it is provoking. Even the Church, which is expected to be essentially a process of doing "community," stands out in new relief in our time. In the image of God, who is in His very heart "community," humanity has a vocation to solidarity. God is haunted by this dream, "May they all be one." "Father, may they be one in us as you are in me and I in you . . . " (Jn. 17:21), Jesus said in his last hours, as if he were revealing his ultimate secret. As a result, the Church "community" can no longer be a mere refuge in a hostile world; it has meaning only when it turns outward, as a "laboratory" for another form of society. The Eucharist with its social implications can serve as a paradigm for this perspective. If God takes bread and wine, "fruit of the work of human hands" or of the economy, as the basis of Divine presence, is He not in this way calling us to make the economy the basis, the sign or the "sacrament" of God's paternal and maternal presence within a society that is organizing itself as a fraternal household so that each one may live?

If the Church's involvement is necessarily "political," in other words, linked to the places where human togetherness is being negotiated, it cannot exactly make up the numbers of those who represent political parties and civilian associations. Its manner or its specific criterion to be "political" is disclosed at the point where the manifestation of a God who scandalously goes to the defence of victims is refuted head-on by a neoliberalism that systematically rejects the weakest. This is the meaning and the proper place of the mission of the Church in its relation to today's world: the breach where the least among us see their dignity and their living conditions threatened. This is where the Church will rediscover its Lord. This involvement is more important than ever before. At the time of Keynesian prosperity, the modernity model, although insufficient, had fewer negative consequences, because society institutionally supported the most destitute. The adoption of this same model today would have tragic consequences under a neoliberalism that abandons people to the violence of the strongest. Would the Church be lost in this option? On the contrary, as Bishop Romero testified shortly before his death:

> This coming closer to the world of the poor is what we understand both as incarnation and as conversion. The changes that were needed within the Church and in its apostolate, in education, in religious and priestly life, in lay movements, which we had not brought about simply by looking inward upon the Church, we are now carrying them out by turning ourselves outward toward the world of the poor.[41]

It is, in fact, when the losers rediscover their transcendental (founded in God) and absolute right to avoid being sacrificed and when believers take their side, that the God of Abraham and of Jesus, sensitive to the "Isaacs" of history, is again becoming *visible*; the deification of the market then appears as *theologically* impossible, and we receive the assurance that the "house of the Lord" no longer owes anything to anyone nor to any fate whatsoever, other than its own. Nietzsche was right to thus rage at Christians who had created the option for the losers:

> The individual was made so important and so absolute, by means of Christian values, that he could no longer be *sacrificed*, despite the fact that the species can only be maintained by human sacrifices. . . . Genuine love of mankind exacts sacrifice for the good of the species—it is hard, full of self-control, because it needs human sacrifices. *And this pseudo-humanity which is called Christianity would fain establish the rule that nobody should be sacrificed.*[42]

V

"PREPARING THE WAY OF THE LORD" FROM THE "STONES REJECTED BY THE BUILDERS" OF THE SOCIAL ORDER

It is obvious that neoliberalism causes a society to sink. Instead of continuing this relentless pursuit, would it not be better to backtrack and start over in another direction? Just as neoliberalism has corrupted reality at several levels, it is also from several angles that we must examine the contours of a potential alternative.

The alternative as horizon of meaning and as mysticism

The analysis of societal dynamics has shown us that neoliberalism had raised its society project, the rules of the market and its sacrificial implications for the losers to a transcendental level. Our detour through the founding references of Judaeo-Christianity has relativized these pretensions and presented other bases to the alternative.

In the human context, everything begins with a dream, a utopia, (*u-topos*: a possibility that as yet has no place), without which historic projects could not be carried out nor measure their own relativity nor thus avoid retreat into totalitarian madness. Inversely, current capitalism has decreed the end of utopias, a decree moreover, that is itself utopian! It has thus tried to block the imaginary and to destroy the hope of any other. Yet, our own belief in history actually began with the hope of the *yes* of the promised land or a return to Jerusalem, without which the Hebrew people could not have said *no* to Egypt or to exile. We can indeed dream, even in the neoliberal exile, on condition that we have *another* point of view. Our societies urgently need some profession of hope in order to counter the fascination with death and collective suicide that plagues them.

The rediscovery of the freedom of Abraham and Jesus vis-à-vis any law also enables us to refuse to regard the rules of the market as sacred and to consider that obedience to God, after Jesus, implies disobeying the laws of neoliberalism when they become totalitarian. Is this not the case when the obligation to repay debts contracted by corrupt leaders in the Third World leads to the sacrifice of children's lives, or even here, when deficit reduction is carried out in large part at the expense of the most destitute. No, the market is not divine and no person's life and dignity are negotiable. This mysticism of the incompressible dignity of the "images of God" and of "zeal" for the social "house" of the Lord make it possible, not necessarily to win, but to refuse to bow our heads before the neoliberalism that would like to break our spirit. The logic of the "remnant," of the wisdom that is "folly in the eyes of men" and of the "stone rejected by the builders" but which "became the cornerstone," is sufficient to make us "prepare the way of the Lord," for it is a "theo-logic," capable of bringing the humble to their feet and of "pulling down the princes from their thrones" (Lk. 1:52).

The alternative as ethics of solidarity and as ideology of the "socially correct"

From an ethical point of view, as a concretization of the horizon of the meaning outlined above, the alternative implies challenging the reduction of ethics to the mere rules of competition. Woven for a number of centuries already with the thread of individual interest and anti-solidarity, we must reweave ourselves with another thread, the thread of solidarity, particularly with the weakest, with all the probabilities of a collision with the ethics of the market.

If we inscribe this proposition on the horizon of history, we must return to the programmatic slogan of modernity, "liberty, equality, fraternity." Tragically, these three ideals have been isolated from each other, thus provoking their denaturation and decline, for they have meaning only within the dialectic unity that they form together. The West has favoured liberty, but by cutting it off from the egalitarian objective and from their mutual "soul"—fraternity or solidarity. The result is a caricature of liberty, reduced to the absolutization of individual initiative. As for the East, it has wagered everything on equality. The curb imposed on the liberty of the abusive privileges ended quite simply in dissolving liberty itself. Equality, without the project of fraternity, could only impose itself superficially, by force. These two totalitarianisms have proved that the projects of liberty and equality become completely disoriented, contradict each other and deny themselves when they cease to be propelled by the solidarity that cannot be decreed, but without which, Solzhenitsyn reminds us "no village can stand. Nor any city. Nor our whole land."[43]

We are well aware that Third World populations have not benefited from the liberty and equality that has been monopolized by the North. They have survived only because of something that the North did not even want, a solidarity that is today severely tested through the penetration of neoliberalism. At a time when darkness is spreading through our world, should we not, in all urgency, stand the modernity project upright once more by putting fraternity back into the central perspective? More precisely, this would mean rediscovering the flame of hope on the side of the losers, on the side of all those who are sacrificed by neoliberalism in the North as in the South. Is it not significant that the *International network against neoliberalism and for humanity* was launched by the marginalized, the Chiapas Indians?

At the ideological level, I will merely propose this idea of setting against the "economically correct" a public opinion that is itself defining what will be "socially correct." [44] The limits of rectitude are known, but how can we give some ideological strength to the ethical criteria of an alternative instead of remaining at the mercy of the sole standard of blind "tolerance" that flings us bound hand and foot before the throne of the totalitarian ideology of the market? The "socially correct" must of course be marked out, but was it not something of this kind that roused American opinion against companies gaining prestige from thousands of layoffs and compensating their top executives proportionately as a function of the layoffs?

Does the "socially correct" not mean naming the "very visible hands" that set the rules of the game, whether for example, by vigilance concerning decisions of the high international economic authorities or through public information on the manoeuvring of business lobbies; in short, by forcing the true actors on the economic stage to come forward from the wings and urging them to collectively adopt (since they cannot do it individually) rules compatible with social cohesion?

The alternative as reconstitution of the social subject

The following level calls for a reversal of the movement in which the economy swallows up the political and the social, or the process of the marketization of the world. Translated into terms that are of interest here, the three values of the slogan of modernity would be equivalent to the market, the State and civilian society. Like fraternity, the third actor, society, has also been pushed aside and dissolved, with the result that the other two have been led astray as evidenced in the neoliberalism of the present day.

The broad perspective emerging here, that has taken on the scope of a global movement and will eventually counterbalance neoliberalism, is a reestablishment of social solidarity, a reconstitution of the social subject, the only player eventually capable of bringing us out of the sterile oscillation between State and market, and capable of controlling them and setting the agenda without destroying them. This is the enormous task of reconstruction that humanity is called to perform on itself rather than remaining at the mercy of the market. Society must be its own salvation instead of counting on the welfare-state or the welfare-market as it does at present, even if it means delegating a part of this responsibility to them. In very simple terms, the task is to reconstitute ourselves as "we." *Social citizenship* is the indispensable mould for political citizenship and economic citizenship that constitute its relays or mediations.

This perspective can give unity, coherence and hope to millions of the most diverse initiatives and from as many points in every setting. This common conscience could compensate for the extreme decentralization of the social movement, that like a thread woven in so many stitches, might one day contain the "monster." And the corresponding process lends itself to infinite participation by people, from mutual help in the neighbourhood to the transformation of structural relations at the level of nations. It unites solidarity and responsibility. It is on this both moral and very concrete criterion of the re-establishment of solidarity that the state of society should be judged. Counting on contagion or the ripple effect throughout the social fabric to be rewoven, this process makes solidarity not only the meaning, the ethics and the ideology of the alternative, but also its culture and its society project.

The new civil society is not obsessed by the immediate takeover of power, but tries to create the conditions of a different kind of politics, by promoting what the State and the market have always neglected: man-woman complementarity, community organization, [45] the rich diversity of cultures and ethnic groups, ecological and territorial as well as religious and spiritual dimensions. Finally the reconstitution of the social subject would have no meaning if it did not, as a priority, take into account those whom neoliberalism leaves by the roadside, or, described in terms of the society project, in the way of the Zapatista movement in Mexico, *una sociedad donde quepan todos* (a society where there is room for all).

The alternative as politics

We are now back at the most tangible level, that of economic and political orientations and practices. It is the level at which the civil society is not content to be *one of the poles* of the trio already mentioned, by developing solid labour and community movements, for example, but where it seeks to *hem in economic and political fields* in order to provoke structural changes. It is in this way, that guided by the perspectives outlined above, it will make its presence felt in political parties or create new ones, it will make representations vis-à-vis governmental authorities, participate in public consultations on various subjects, present alternative budgets as is the case at present and support the most destitute as they organize themselves in a search for just reforms.

It is in this way, moreover, that the civil society will take the initiative to reconstitute a social and political regulation of economic activity at the regional, national and global levels, and create favourable conditions for the coexistence of a plurality of types of economy (private, community, public, cooperative . . .). With regard to the problem of employment for example, only a profound social movement can force businesses and governments into a reorganization which will enable a resolution of the equation of socially necessary working time, taking account of the current productive capacities of the economy and employment income as a condition of access to necessary goods. We could multiply the examples of the spread of the new perspective. Let us summarize here by defining solidarity at the present level as an effective and vigilant exercise of citizenship and as politics in the plenary sense of the term, starting with its first step that is essential for empowerment: joining a group, and then a network, of citizens.

This is a potential framework in which we could register our personal and collective initiatives, for the alternative is also a daily practice and a way of life. I have tried to insist, negatively and positively, on the societal process underlying concrete arrangements. A clearer vision of both the current dynamics and another possible trajectory can liberate a population's creativity and help it to stay on course beyond short-term success or failure and to gain an understanding of its route rather than leaving it to experts and pseudo-messiahs. Perhaps the following three criteria could be useful in discerning the way to an alternative that always presents itself, concretely, in the form of propositions or projects: (1) Does this initiative promote the re-establishment of solidarity among peoples? (2) Does it re-establish solidarity with the losers or the marginalized? (3) Finally, does it aim for structural change, at least in the long term, so that over and above emergencies we can go beyond the perspective of a "Christmas fund-raising" Church or society?

Moreover, nothing will be given automatically, nothing can substitute for the passion to live differently and the mindful will to form a "we." We are returned to our reasons to live and hope, hence the journey upstream, like the salmon, to the sources of our faith to rediscover the Spirit capable of transporting beyond themselves our fragmented, hesitant interventions.

At the end of this reflection, I would like to return to a nineteenth-century prophet, the novelist Dostoyevsky. In *The Brothers Karamazov*, he describes with an exceptional lucidity, the individualism, rivalries and competition that lead to social disintegration. And that will last, he explains, until we understand that "the true security is to be found in social solidarity rather than in isolated individual effort," and until all realize:

> how unnaturally they are separated from one another. . . . And then the sign of the Son of Man will be seen in the heavens. . . . But until then, we must keep the banner flying. Sometimes even if he has to do it alone, and his conduct seems to be crazy, a man must set an example, and so draw men's souls out of their solitude, and

spur them on to some act of brotherly love, that the great idea may not die.[46]

Are these words written in 1879 not the words of tomorrow? They are merely the echo of a Word that comes to us from a yet more distant tradition. Neoliberalism is again presenting the old problem that confronted the people of Israel. In opposition to the hypocritical ritualism and the fundamentalist reliance on the law combined with the oppression of workers and the poor, Isaiah proposed the "fast that is pleasing to Yahweh," the liberating justice with regard to "your own kin," and from whom "you cannot turn" (Is. 58:7). To the one who undertakes such practices, Yahweh promises "your wound will be quickly healed"; he promises to "give you relief in desert places" and to make you like "a spring of water whose waters never run dry" (vv. 8-11). And in the context of neoliberalism, let us take good measure of these words from verse 12, "You will be called Restorer of ruined houses," or perhaps we might translate it as, "one who re-establishes solidarity in dismantled 'social houses'!" Here it is perhaps, the "door" that God "has opened" before us through the signs of the present times, the door that "nobody can close" (Rv. 3:8).

NOTES

1. *Le Devoir,* 24 February 1997, A1 and A12.

2. *Shakedown: How the economy is changing our lives* (Doubleday, 1996).

3. *Shakedown,* p. 307, quoted by Michel Venne, *loc. cit.*, A12.

4. *Ibid.*

5. *Ibid*., p. 248.

6. M. Venne, *loc. cit.*, p. A12.

7. This term designates the new economic and political model that now governs societies and that will be analysed in greater detail in a subsequent section.

8. *Justitia in mundo*, No. 38.

9. My summer job at the factory where my father was a labourer made me realize time and time again how much the meagre salaries cost the employees in physical exhaustion and the abnegation of their best faculties in order to ensure their families' survival; and they still had to exhaust

themselves in English to be heard, if not hired, in a province that was nevertheless ninety per cent Francophone!

10. *Justitia in mundo*, No. 7.

11. Quoted in Pierre Haubmann, *P.-J. Proudhon, Genèse d'un antithéiste*, Tours, Mame, 1969, p. 186.

12. Readers will recall, for example, the reaction of the Canadian political authorities, in 1983, when the Catholic bishops expressed criticism of the Federal government's economic policies; they were accused of meddling in something that did not concern them! As for the faithful, as the theologian Gregory Baum shrewdly observed, they begin "coughing" to express their uneasiness when their pastors evoke the Church's teaching on social justice!

13. We could mention the encyclical *Quadragesimo anno* (1931), as well as various initiatives that transmitted this "new social doctrine of the Church," including l'*École sociale populaire* and the *Semaines sociales du Canada* (1926-1958).

14. *La Presse*, 6 June 1992; *Le Devoir*, 4 March 1994.

15. *Rerum novarum*, No. 2.

16. *Quadragesimo anno*, No. 117.

17. Marc Blondel, *La Lettre A*, 15 February 1996, quoted by I. Ramonet, "Davos," in *Le Monde diplomatique*, March, 1996, p. 1.

18. Quoted by I. Ramonet, *loc. cit.*, p. 1.

19. Statistics Canada, 1991.

20. N. Delisle, "Un emploi ne met plus à l'abri de la pauvreté," *La Presse*, 24 April 1997.

21. S.H. "Leçon d'économie moderne," *Le Monde diplomatique*, February, 1996.

22. *La Presse*, 9 April 1996.

23. On this subject, see the Message of the First of May of the Quebec bishops: *J'étais là, m'as-tu fait de la place?*, Montreal, 1997, 8 p.

24. Quoted by I. Ramonet, *loc. cit.*, p. 1.

25. *Essai sur le marché*, Paris, Syros, 1995, pp. 188-190.

26. Quoted in Associated Press, "Les compagnies américaines ne se vantent plus de faire du dégraissage," *La Presse*, 4 June 1996. The italics are mine.

27. Adam Smith, *The Theory of Moral Sentiments*, ed. D.D. Raphael and A.L. Macfie (Oxford: Clarendon Press, 1976), p. 86.

28. "From P.C. to E.C.," *The New York Times*, 12 January 1993.

29. R. Petrella, "La fiction de la mondialisation," *Forum* (University of Montreal), 21 April 1997, p. 4.

30. *Le Devoir*, 24 April 1997.

31. *Une éthique économique. Les valeurs de l'économie de marché*, Paris, Cerf/La Boétie, 1982, p. 412.

32. "Marché et Royaume, la double appartenance," *Documents Épiscopat,* 12 (July-August 1992).

33. Adam Smith, *An Inquiry into the Nature and Causes of the Wealth of Nations* (Edinburgh: Adam and Charles Black, 1863), p. 319.

34. Interview in the Chilean newspaper, *El Mercurio*, 19 April 1981.

35. See V. Labrie, "Histoire de décroissance et de carottes," *Relations*, January-February 1996, p. 4-5. In this article, the author outlines the convergent opinions of three top managers on the way to manage the decline in the Quebec health sector.

36. G. Fraser, "Hors du marché du travail, point de salut," *Le Devoir,* 26 September 1995. The italics are mine.

37. *God the Economist* (Minneapolis: Fortress Press, 1989).

38. For the following, I am referring to my own article "Sotériologie capitaliste et salut chrétien," in J.-C. Petit, J.-C. Breton (dir.), *Seul ou avec les autres? Le salut chrétien à l'épreuve de la solidarité*, coll. "Héritage et projet" 48, Montreal, Fides, 1992, p. 260.

39. M. Novak, *op. cit.*, p. 411.

40. C. Mesters, *Suivre Jésus à contre-courant,* coll. "Déclic", Montreal, Paulines/CPMO, 1997, p. 110.

41. *Voice of the Voiceless: The Four Pastoral Letters and Others Statements* (Maryknoll, New York: Orbis Books, 1985), p. 180.

42. Nietzsche, *The Will to Power*, Book 1 (London and Edinburgh: I.N. Foulis, 1914), pp. 202-203. The italics are mine.

43. A. Soljenitsyne, "Matryona's House," in *We Never Make Mistakes* (Columbia: University of South Carolina Press, 1963), p. 100.

44. A sort of equivalent to what the historian E.P. Thompson called the moral economy.

45. Quebec, for example, has four to five thousand community groups, the highest proportion in the Western countries of the North.

46. F. Dostoïevski, *The Brothers Karamazov*, Modern Library (New York: Random House Inc.), pp. 326-327.

CHART 1:
The Evolution of Economics, Labour and Policy within Twentieth-Century Capitalism

ERA	ECONOMIC	ECONOMIC POLICY	SOCIAL POLICY	SOLIDARITY	IDEOLOGY
Prior to 1935 CLASSIC LIBERALISM	Capital vs. Labour Max. exploitation 1929: S>D Employment precarious	None except via military spending	None or virtually none State complements Private assistance	"Charity" + Mutual aid - Local - Family - Informal	Self-regulating free market (19th Century) "Laissez-faire"
1935 to 1968 FORDIST-KEINESIANISM	• Growth based on equilibrium S=D (spiral) • Mainly national • "Normal" Unemployment: 3% = Fordism	Support for S via support for D (taxes, interest %, etc.) Govt. intervention = Keynesianism	Support for S via support for D through social programes and availability of work Public "social" security Welfare State	Institutionalized at Provincial and National levels	Capitalism with a human face (Political control for redistribution)
1968 to Now NEOLIBERALISM	Restructuring supply Transnationalization of production, (S) mergers, acquisitions, technology Market conquest (D) D=Demand (world, national) Employment: "normal" Unemployment: 10%; more precarious =Neoliberalism (or supply economy)	Reorientation of economic role of state: direct support for S: subsidies, tax measures, international development assistance, privatization, deregulation, trade liberalization "Corporate Providence" Neoliberal state "Neoliberalism" = 20th Century liberalism + Direct state support "Make it work"	Reorientation of social policy: – Support for S via employment measures – Progressive dismantling of social programes From "social" security to "income" security Indifferent or "Workfare State"	Dismantling of institutionalized solidarity Social dislocation Responsibility for dis-advantaged given to society without appropriate funding Return to private, informal, non-organized "charity" in fragmented society: - Telethons - Philanthropy - Church works, etc.	• Competition, "Excellence" "Winners" • Society subject to free market • Position of state / "Traditional Solidarities" (volunteer, works...) • Markets and corporations as new "Providence"

S = Supply   D = Demand

Michel Beaudin, Faculty of Theology, University of Montreal

CHART 2: Three Models of the Relationship between the Church and Society and their Implications

Model Scheme	Representative	Type of Christians or in disorder	Society in order	"Justice"	Era(s)	Status of the social reality
"Christendom"	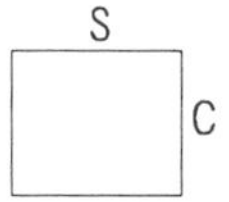 S C	"Assimilators"	Order	Status quo and "works" Micro-ethical perspective	From the 4th to the 18th Centuries (1960 in Quebec)	Passive and controlled by a faith formed beforehand
"Modernity"	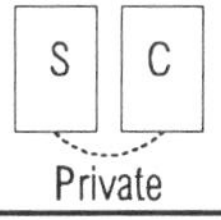 S C Private	"Accommodators"	Order (faith not involved)	Status quo and "works" Micro-ethical perspective	From the 18th Century (varying according to the regions)	Social reality and Gospel mutually reduced to silence
"Prophetic"	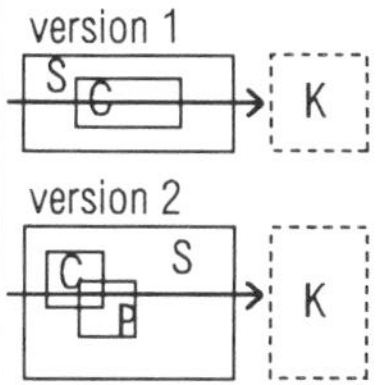 version 1 S C K version 2 C S P K	"Socially committed"	Disorder to be put in Order	Structural transformation of society Macro-ethical perspective	- Biblical and patristical tradition until the 4th Century - From the end of the 19th Century	- Constitutive of faith development - Church and society converse without mutual reduction

C = Church   S = Society   K = Kingdom   P = Poor or Marginalized

Michel Beaudin, Faculty of Theology, University of Montreal

2

"tomatoes"

Adding a bit of spice

SPIRIT AND SINEW:
AN ABORIGINAL PERSPECTIVE

PRISCILLA SOLOMON, CSJ

Priscilla Solomon, an Ojibway, a Sister of St. Joseph of Sault Ste. Marie, and a Companion of Kateri, lives in Sudbury, Ontario. Trained as an elementary school teacher, a spiritual director, a retreat director, and a pastoral counsellor, she has spent the last two years living the Ojibway tradition of caring for her elders. She has been the primary care-giver for her ageing and ill parents, both of whom died since she began her contribution. She dedicates it with love and gratitude to them: Eva and Art Solomon.

*Some of the stepping stones on my faith journey that have developed my consciousness of justice issues are described in my writing (*Spirit and Sinew: An Aboriginal Perspective*). Besides the powerful influences of my parents and my family-of-origin, especially my sister Eva, I also recognize the transforming power of the deep soul-searching and visioning that my religious congregation has done during the years since Vatican II. Every four years we have communally challenged ourselves to examine how we are living the Gospel message and our own specific charism of Unity and Reconciliation. Over the years, we have made deliberate choices to develop a social consciousness and to respond to the needs of people who are disadvantaged and oppressed.*

One specific living experience which influenced me radically was a nine month stay in Guatemala in 1975-1976. I look upon it as a pregnancy for consciousness! I lived and worked among the people of Gualan and Guatemala City. I also visited La Union. In the midst of incredible poverty and oppression, I saw hope. I met people whose faith enabled them to laugh, to play, to cry out to God and to confront systemic injustice against what seemed like impossible odds, doing so with the confidence that change would come. When I returned home, it was as though scales had fallen away from my eyes and I could see the injustices to which my own people were subjected. My eyes and ears were opened. I could now hear the bottom line: "Justice with compassion."

To provide a faith reflection on the socio-economic realities of our times invites one to ask such searching questions as: Does my faith really touch my life experience? Does it influence my behaviour? What relationship does my faith, my behaviour and my life have to that of others? What does my faith have to say to socio-economic realities? Is my understanding of the socio-economic situation adequate? Can and will my response make a difference? What are the gifts I have to offer in such a reflection? Without pretending to answer all these questions directly, I have decided to share with you some of my response in faith.

Other authors in this book have already given excellent and enriching responses to these and similar questions. What I would like to do is give you some sense of how I see our socio-economic realities, as well as what I see are some of the faith resources I have found. It is my hope that what I have to say will touch the mind, the heart, the spirit and the body of those who read it.

I suppose I have a fairly simplistic understanding of the socio-economic realities of our present times. I will state it this way. I can see that not only in this land but globally human beings are more and more clearly becoming part of one of two groups. One group has, to a greater or lesser extent, privileges, advantages, money, wealth, unrestricted access to land and resources, even the power to manipulate and control economies, governments and societies, as well as oppress other people. The other has penalties, disadvantages, a lack of finances, restricted or non-existent access to land and resources, a lack of external power, and frequently little awareness of the inner personal power they have that seems so overwhelmed by the manipulations and control of the other group. The boundaries between these groups are less and less geographic, although some of the geographic boundaries still exist very clearly. Among the former, there are some who perceive themselves to be underprivileged and disadvantaged, often because they see clearly what they want but do not have, rather than what they have. In fact, as political and economic power and finances get more concentrated in the hands of fewer and fewer people, many others do have less. Many more people are squeezed into situations of bankruptcy, economic and social disarray and even poverty and despair.

There are also many whose faith influences their life and does not allow them to live comfortably with the inequities and injustices of these socio-economic realities. In all honesty, I count myself among the privileged, though not among the wealthy, because I have, or have access to, so much. And I believe I can count myself among those who are not willing to live comfortably with the inequities.

From my perspective, the free market, the huge trading blocs for free trade, the lending policies of the World Bank and other big multinationals and transnationals are all contributing to the widening of the gap. Capitalism itself seems to have taken on a life of its own like that of a huge monster. As capitalism grows more powerful, it becomes easier for capital to move where its masters please, even when that means trampling to death anyone and everyone who does not and cannot hold its reins. To put it in another image, capitalism, as it has grown today, is like a huge river that flows unrestrictedly. However, this river waters fewer and fewer gardens while more and more land becomes the desert of peoples' pain, desperation, death and destruction.

In my simple analysis, I also see that some in both groups resort to violence, both militarily and economically: one to maintain or improve their advantages, the other to change their position and gain some advantage. Arms trade today may not seem as threatening as the build-up of nuclear weapons and nuclear arsenals that we feared in the late sixties, the seventies and the eighties, but we cannot deceive ourselves into thinking all is well. We still live with an incredible world weapons market!

Of the other group, what can I say? Daily television reveals their faces, or their ravaged bodies. Systemic injustice ensures their continued existence. But I find I cannot absorb this reality easily. Instead, I need to put an individual face to it. I think of a young woman, Mary, whose husband left her with three small children. She has no money to pay a sitter, very little support from her family, and cannot find work although she tries each day. I think of Jose, a Guatemalan refugee friend I worked with a few years ago, who said: "Will you help us study the Gospel so we can understand why this oppression continues and what we can do about it?" I think of a homeless man, Irwin Anderson, who died in the cold of a winter night on a street in Toronto.

I realize that there are many nuances to our socio-economic reality that I have not identified. I acknowledge that although I identify two major groups for the sake of simplifying my description, the reality is much more complex. I could also have said there are three major groups, some of whom are very wealthy, others of whom are very poor and some who are managing comfortably enough. However I describe it, the basic fact remains that in this land and around the globe some people suffer and die because the basic resources they need are not available to them, even though the resources do exist. Both my faith and my culture tell me that this reality is not acceptable.

I believe very strongly that faith cannot be separate from life. My life, my choices, my vision, my experiences are all influenced and coloured by my faith. As an Aboriginal woman, I realize that my faith can and does touch and influence me physically, mentally, emotionally and spiritually. Daily I am challenged to recognize in my brothers and sisters in the human family the very God who created them and is revealed in them. Daily my response is called forth mentally in the way I perceive them and think about them: emotionally, in the way I respond to them; physically, in what I actually do concretely to express the love I profess to have in Christ; and spiritually, in the way I allow my spirit to be moved in intercession, or gratitude, or blessing for them, or in communion with them.

One of the gifts I think I have to offer in this analysis is a belief that however bleak and distressing our socio-economic realities are, there is still room for hope. My faith tells me there is a God who is compassionate and caring—a God who eventually will say, "In so far as you did this to one of the least of these . . . , you did it to me." (Mt. 25:40). I believe there are people with faith and values who see that our situation can be different. I believe there are people who are willing to live and die to make a difference.

Another gift, that gives me the courage to respond, is the gift of a perspective that comes from another faith tradition and another culture. By birth I am cross-cultural. I was born of parents who are Anishnabe (identified also as Ojibway) and French Canadian. I would like to share with you some of the richness of my Aboriginal spirituality and world view. It is my hope that what I share will facilitate your own faith reflections and responses to our socio-economic realities.

When I was a child, I was fascinated with the mystery of how a kaleidoscope worked. I remember twisting it and turning it, amazed at how each slight move created such a different picture. More recently, I have seen a different little instrument—a teleidoscope. It looks much like a kaleidoscope but it does not reflect light refracted from little bits within it. Instead, it takes light reflected off the surrounding objects and transforms it into an amazing array of colour and design.

Each of these is for me an image, however inadequate, of the cultural dimension of faith and life. Culture takes the bits and pieces, the fragments of our faith and life, our beliefs and our experiences, and puts them together in comprehensible patterns. I suppose one might also say that faith gives meaning to culture, and that experience tests faith. Culture is also the container, like the tube of the kaleidoscope or the teleidoscope. It houses the communal aspect of one's faith and experiences. At the same time it can be, and often is, the expression or concretization of one's faith and one's personal life experiences.

Similarly, culture can take the light of eternal wisdom and reflect it off all the bits and pieces of life, both within and outside of one's culture, for the benefit of the people of that culture. For one who believes in Christ, the light that transforms and gives meaning to those bits and pieces is none other than Christ, the Light.

For years, I identified myself as French Canadian, although that is by far the smaller part of my heritage. In my world I was ashamed to identify myself as Aboriginal, because what I heard of the Native peoples from others was that Natives were "dirty," that we were "drunken Indians," that we were "lazy."

My reality was that emotionally and psychologically I could not claim the kaleidoscope of my own culture, even though the patterns in the kaleidoscope of another culture often did not make sense to me. They did not give adequate meaning to my life and experiences. Yet for more than thirty years I tried to fit in, to measure up to expectations, values and interpretations of my experience that were not really able to touch the core of my being.

When I was a young religious in the Congregation of the Sisters of St. Joseph, my parents, Eva and Art, began seriously to look at this issue of faith and culture for themselves. My father especially began to make personal choices that frightened me. His concern and outrage for the injustices done to our people by both governments and churches terrified me. I was too naive then to realize one can criticize and yet value, even love, what one criticized. I identified with the Catholic Church, and every criticism or condemnation I heard, I took as personal. I felt judged. I felt condemned. I felt rejected.

Not only did I feel threatened by him and some of the many Aboriginal visitors who frequently visited my parents, but also I anguished over what seemed to me to be my parents' loss of the faith. They no longer went to Church. They could no longer be identified as "practising Catholics." That is to say, they no longer were regular Church-goers; they no longer volunteered their services in the Church; they no longer financially supported the Church.

If I had been able to stay with that understanding of Catholic, I suppose it would have been easier to find relief in my own turmoil. But much of this took place during and after Vatican II. As a consequence, I struggled to put together my experience with the new teachings and new emphases of the post-Vatican II Church.

Among the changes brought about by Vatican II was the refocusing of our personal relationship with God. There was a recognition that a solely vertical relationship was not enough. We were being taught that our personal relationship with God must find expression in the horizontal or communal dimensions of life. The social doctrine of the Church was given more attention. The Church began to see itself as finding holiness not by withdrawing from the world, but rather finding holiness in engaging with the world and being light in the world.

At the same time, we as Catholics were being encouraged to read and pray over Scripture. In doing this, I was meeting with Jesus who fed the hungry; who reached out and touched the unclean, the lepers, the outcasts and the little ones. I met the Jesus who dared to challenge the leaders and teachers whose call was to serve Yahweh and the people of Yahweh. I met the Jesus who dared to eat with sinners; who talked with a Samaritan woman; and who raised people from the dead. He is the one who said that in the end I, and every follower of Jesus, would be judged by whether or not we fed the hungry and clothed the naked. He said we would be blessed if we visited those in prison and those who are sick.

These were the things I found my parents doing. I would go home for a visit and find strangers welcomed at their table. The little they had would be shared with whoever was there. I saw them, especially my father, going into prisons; bringing with him hope, healing, the sacred medicines and the sacred pipe, as well as powerful challenges to the penal, justice and religious systems of this country.

On a few occasions I went with them into a prison or to other gatherings. I watched women, and sometimes men, come and just sit by my mother to find strength and comfort. Sometimes they would talk to her and pour out their hearts. I knew they found comfort, peace and love because when it was time to leave, they hugged her and held her like she was their own mother. I watched and listened as men and women, young and old listened to the words of my father and found hope, courage and new meaning for their lives. For many, it was the first time they had heard anything of a spiritual nature that truly touched their hearts and their lives.

Again and again I found myself asking: "How could they be wrong? Are they not doing what Jesus said his followers must do? Are they not carrying out the works that Jesus said would be the very things that would be the core of our final judgement? Aren't they really being 'practising Catholics' in a much deeper and truer sense?" I leave the final answer to my questions to God's wisdom, mercy and compassion. But that witness and those questions have had an irrevocable impact on me and my practice of my faith.

During that time my sister Eva, who is also a Sister of St. Joseph, was beginning her own journey of inculturation of her faith. At the time I did not know such a word. I just knew that as she found new meaning and richness and shared that with me, she began inviting me to look at what was missing in my life. I was afraid. I did not want to risk walking into the unknown. It was the unknown, because we had grown up as strong Catholics who had accepted and believed the pre-Vatican II teaching that the ways of our ancestors were pagan. I believed that all those teachings had to be rejected if I were to be Christian. Anything of my culture was suspect. Only much later did I realize how much of my culture, values and teachings my parents, especially my mother, had passed on to us.

At the urging of my sister, I attended with her the Beatification of Blessed Kateri Tekakwitha, the Mohawk and Algonquin Christian who, to some extent at least, lived her Christian faith in the context of her Mohawk culture. Together we attended the Tekakwitha Conference in the United States where annually thousands of Native Catholics and their non-Native brothers and sisters, the religious and clergy who worked with them, met to begin the process of inculturation of the Christian faith. My understanding grew and my fear lessened. Eva's faith, her courage and indomitable commitment to understand and live the process of inculturation of her Christian faith both challenged and encouraged me to do the same. This too had a tremendous, irrevocable impact on me. I began to burn the sacred medicines in prayer. I began to attend pipe ceremonies, sacred circles and sweat lodges. Each time I did, I felt a deep and powerful sense of coming home. I felt the rightness of what I was doing. It took a while for me to break through the feelings of guilt and fear that I was making a mistake, but the sense of rightness was stronger. It was as though I had picked up the kaleidoscope of my own culture, and with the light of Christ shining into it, I saw patterns that had much more meaning and more connectedness for me than any I had previously found. I felt more whole.

Gradually I began to understand that the process of inculturation of my Christian faith was essential. I could only be who I was called to be if I began by recognizing who I already am—an Aboriginal woman who is called to follow Jesus Christ. I began to understand that, as Pope John Paul II has said in his encyclical letter, *Redemptoris Missio*: "Inculturation means the intimate transformation of authentic cultural values through their integration in Christianity and the insertion of Christianity in the various human cultures." [1]

As in any culture, a process of discernment is required to determine what are the authentic cultural values and which rituals and ceremonies facilitate and/or express Christian faith. To which of these values, teachings, practices, ceremonies and rituals does the light of Christ bring a new dimension? Are these not the same questions we believers need to ask ourselves of the contemporary society in which we live? We can, I believe must, ask those questions in the material, the economic, the spiritual, the religious, the political, the social and the personal spheres.

In a society that values individualism, we need to examine the relationship between the individuals we affirm, support, honour—or criticize, ostracize and reject—and the extent of their material wealth. Is it the individual or the material wealth that we value? If we err, the Gospel would have us err on the side of persons, that is, of affirming and supporting those who have less.

Deliberate choices to respect the disadvantaged and dispossessed in our land call forth from us a radical faith that reveals itself in practical actions and responses. I think of it as radical because it includes and goes beyond intellectual assent. It includes emotional involvement; something many of us find uncomfortable and often distressing. It requires a deep spiritual awareness of our shared humanity, our own capacity for brokenness and failure, and an irrepressible hope and confidence in the resilience and goodness of other human beings. It requires a physical response, whether that be as basic as holding open a door for an elderly or physically challenged person, or perhaps pouring out our energies and creativity on transforming our immediate social, political and economic milieu into a truly loving, compassionate, life-giving reality. It challenges us to look more deliberately and critically at the cost-cutting actions of our governments and to question which of these actions reflect a genuine concern for the well-being of all our citizens; to question which actions reflect the values of love, care, community, and personal worth by virtue of one's humanity rather than one's possessions; to ask which reflect true peace-making and justice?

Inculturation is an essential contemporary process that involves a continual discernment of the operative values in our daily lives as much as the ceremonial rituals and communal religious services in which we participate. Pope John Paul speaks of intimate transformation. Intimacy involves knowing and being known. I think an active personal engagement in the on-going process of the transformation of one's cultural values is intimate in as much as one actually knows what the true values are in the culture and how those values are lived out in one's own daily life. It is a process of consciously actualizing, or incarnating, what one believes. The transformation cannot be superficial. It touches every aspect of one's life. It is intimate also in the sense that it is not a solo performance, but rather a process lived and reflected upon in the presence of one's God.

To continue my story: for me, ritual and ceremonial expression was followed by a much closer look at, and greater awareness of, some of the teachings and values of my Aboriginal culture. It is some of these teachings that I believe are essential, not only for me as an Aboriginal Catholic and for the rest of my people, but also for the enrichment of other cultures and for survival on this earth. They are not values and beliefs to be imposed. Rather, I think that unless many more people come to similar values and beliefs, particularly, although not solely, people with power to influence the economics and politics of our global reality, we humans will continue to make the entire planet non-sustainable. We will destroy ourselves and every form of created life that has been given to us by our Creator. We are doing that already. As the free markets expand, and new ones are created, environmental and social issues and concerns are being pushed further and further aside.

Among the teachings of my people, and also in the Christian faith, is the teaching that not only does each one of us have a purpose for being here, but also each one has gifts given by the Creator. We believe that each people is given gifts as well. In the great circle of the human family, we see yellow-skinned people, red-skinned people, black-skinned people and white-skinned people. Each of those symbolic races, from our Aboriginal perspective, has gifts to be shared with all the rest of creation. One of the gifts of the white-skinned people, though not exclusively, is the capacity to develop technology. But this gift, like all gifts, can be misused. As technology advances, the sheer power it gives, as well as the lure of possibilities it offers, seems to blind its creators and users to morality and conscience.

Advances in technology are both improving life and destroying life. Human suffering is being alleviated. Lives are being saved. At the same time, through technology, rain forests are being wiped out. Rivers, lakes and oceans are being polluted. More and more toxins are spewing into the air around us. This living, breathing presence we know as Mother Earth is being raped, ravaged and choked continuously. In one of his poems titled *They've Gone Too Far* my father says:

> And it seems like there have always been
> Those who were obsessed with
> "Progress and Development."
> But I have rarely found anyone who asked:
> "Is this progress forward or backwards?"
> ". . . And this development,
> Is it for people or is it for money?" [2]

Of the Aboriginal or First Nations people, my father often says, "We are the final teachers in this sacred land." [3] He does not say it with arrogance but with deep sadness and anger for the way in which a materialistic culture uses and abuses our Mother, the earth, and all her gifts and resources. He says it with the pain of knowing that, despite all the violence that has been done to her, we who believe we were placed on this land by our Creator were given the responsibility to care for our Mother. We still have that responsibility. In our efforts to carry out that responsibility, we realize we must share with our brothers and sisters of other cultures our sense of the sacredness of all creation. He and I recognize that not every person of our own culture is prepared to live these values. Even those who are willing also fail at times. Is that failure to put belief into practice not also true of other believers? Other humans? Is such failure cause to abdicate our responsibilities? I think that despite failure we must continue to try to close the tremendous gap between our faith and our living. We must continue to try to harmonize our body, our mind, our emotions and our spirit in every choice we make. We must do everything in our power to carry out the responsibility given us to be caretakers of this land.

The teachings and values we have within our culture that help us to understand how intimately we are connected to our Mother come from thousands of years of lived experience and reflection upon that experience. They arise out of thousands of years of a sense of accountability to the Creator for the life that throbbed in and around and under the people of this land. They include a belief that we do not own the land. It belongs to the Creator. Instead we were put here with the responsibility to care for the land, the plants, the animals, the air, the very rocks and earth that we know to be our life-sustaining Mother.

Our aboriginal cultures have taught us to recognize the presence of the Creator in all of creation. We see ourselves as spirit beings who have been sent into this physical world with a purpose given us by our creator. We are called to fulfil that purpose and return to the spirit world. For us the spirit world is a constant presence as real as the physical world around us. It can and does reveal to us the Creator. The web of life around us is permeated by the Spirit. Our response is one of respect. That is what we are taught. We are taught to respect all life around us. We respect the creator, the source of life, and we respect the spirit life within the created being. We understand that even the most simple or least significant in the winged world, the animal world, any part of the physical world can reveal to us the sacred. The sacred is in all of it. All of it is responsive to the Creator. Any part of it can call us to honour the Creator, the Spirit.

Let me share with you a story. Story-telling is one of the most powerful ways of communicating in our culture. The story respects and honours the faith and experience of the story-teller. At the same time, it honours the experience and faith of the listener. It says to the listener: "This is my reality. I offer it to you so that, if you choose, you can reflect on your reality and perhaps come to some new insight or understanding." Here is my story.

A few years ago my sister, Eva, organized an eight day retreat. It was open to religious, other laity and clergy, Native and non-Native. If non-Catholics had applied they too would have been accepted. It was a retreat in which we as Aboriginal Christian women shared our faith, our teachings, our ceremonies and rituals. There were ten or eleven participants. On one of the mornings, I had agreed to lead morning prayer. It was to be a ceremony with the sacred pipe. Our retreat was being held in St. Joseph's Motherhouse, a building that faces Lake Nipissing in Northern Ontario. Much of the adjacent shoreline is huge boulders and rocks but there is one smooth granite rock that slopes down to the lake. I had sat many times on this rock. I liked it. There was a picnic table nearby on the north side. To the east was a small cove with trees, low bushes and grasses at its edge. To the south was the lake. And to the west were huge boulders. I thought it would be a good place to pray. I set everything up as the others gathered in the pre-dawn darkness. Some sat on the bench of the picnic table. Some sat beside me. It was only after I began the prayer that I realized that we were unable to complete the circle because the rock sloped too steeply.

Traditionally, we sit in a circle for ceremonies. It is a powerful visual and experiential symbol of inclusion, equality and the mystery of the entire web of relationships that are a basic part of life. This time no one was sitting in the east and no one was sitting in the south.

While I was preparing, I had noticed a pair of ducks swimming about in the cove. When I faced east and held up the pipe to pray, I watched in amazement and awe as the ducks swam toward us in the circle. When they were quite close they stopped and stayed quietly facing into the circle. When I turned to face the south with the pipe, I was once again overcome with awe. The ducks slowly swam from the east side of the circle to the south side. Once again, they stopped when they reached the centre of the south side of the circle. Then they faced inward and stayed there until I finished and turned to face the west. I was sitting in the west side of the circle along with another member of the group. When I faced west, the ducks turned and flew off in that direction. Later as we completed the prayer the same two ducks flew back from the west, along the north side of our circle, and returned to their nesting site in the cove.

I always allow time for participants to talk after we have prayed with the pipe. I also share. I decided to say nothing about the ducks until the others had been given an opportunity. After the invitation to share everyone sat in silence for a few moments. Then with a sense of awe and what seemed like a little bit of fear that perhaps she had imagined it, one of the retreatants asked: "Did you see those ducks?" Everyone had witnessed what I had witnessed. Everyone had been amazed. Among us there was a tremendous sense of the sacred, and of the mystery of our connectedness with all life. One might say it was an accident. Another might say we had piqued the curiosity of the ducks. None in that circle said such things. I say that for a brief period of time, we witnessed and experienced the radical oneness of the circle of life. For a brief moment, we experienced a transparency of the spirit world when our spirits and the spirits of those ducks shared in praise and gratitude to our Creator. Could we as privileged First World people continue to ravage the web of life if we had such an awareness of the presence of the sacred in our world? If we were more aware and had a greater respect for the spirit within other forms of life, could we be so violent toward it?

Another of the teachings of our culture is that there is always a lesson for us in what happens. There is some teaching hidden in every mistake we make, if we are prepared to look for it and learn from it. I learned to always make sure that physically the circle can be completed by those who are participating. I have no right to impose upon the spirit world around me. For me the most powerful teaching, however, was the depth of the spiritual as well as physical interrelatedness of all life on our Mother Earth. Everyone and every form of life belongs in the circle of life. I consider this inclusion of all creation an authentic value of my culture. My faith as a Christian affirms that belief and challenges me to recognize that I am called not to judge or exclude others from that circle—even those whose values, beliefs and actions are radically different from mine. I don't have that right. However, I am called to judge and work to change or transform behaviours, systems and structures that exclude, dehumanize or prevent others from taking their rightful place in the circle.

From early childhood I had a strong sense of connectedness with life around me: my family, my community, the plants, the animals, the lakes, rivers and streams, the night sky, the moon, the sun and the rain. This sense of connectedness was fostered by my parents. I was given an appreciation of the beauty, the mystery and the presence of the sacred in all of the visible world. I was also given a strong sense of the reality of the spirit world that was as real and as close as the visible world and could be revealed through it. I was taught to respect the natural world and to understand my place in it. As an adult Catholic engaged in the process of inculturation, I heard articulated clearly what I already knew from experience, namely, the strong value my culture places on the sacredness of all that comes from the hand of the Creator. I realized that for us as Aboriginal peoples, each person is but a small part of a web of life, a web of relationships that connects us with our Creator, with each other, with our very self and with the natural world around us. We are significant because we have been given life and purpose by our Creator, not because we are superior to plants, animals, rocks and water. They can all exist without us. Rather, we are dependent upon them for our very survival. Spontaneously we think of physical survival. Aboriginal peoples around the world are very aware of how intimately linked our spiritual survival is to the web of life. Each and every part of the web can be for us a revelation of the Creator present in it and a point of contact with the Creator.

Like thousands of my ancestors before me, I have learned that I can go out into the bush or sit by a lake and find peace, healing or communion with my Creator, or even find myself again. More and more people in our society today are realizing technology and wealth cannot give what is given in the song of a bird, in the beauty and grandeur of old growth forest or in the mystery, complexity and simplicity of life anywhere and everywhere on this planet.

One of the philosophical differences between the Aboriginal world view and that of peoples who came to this land from countries with Judaeo-Christian and European world views is that while we Aboriginals consider humans the most dependent upon all other forms of life, and the most responsible for caring for all other life, Judaeo-Christians have been taught that humans are the apex of life and have a responsibility to dominate and subdue the earth. These are two very different kaleidoscopes, two very different ways to understand our place and our responsibilities in this life. Each can claim illumination from the same source of life. Each has something to offer. It seems to me though that unless the latter is tempered by the former, or by the tenets within itself that approximate the former, our Mother the Earth cannot much longer sustain the abuse. Neither can our brothers and sisters in Third and Fourth World situations sustain the ravages of the untrammeled freedom of the so-called "free market."

Both as a human being and as a Christian I am called to reach out, to speak out, to challenge the forces that violate my Mother and my brothers and sisters. I cannot ignore the situations of the Lubicon Cree, the Innu of Nitassinan, the Tema-Augama Anishnabe, the Mohawks of Kanehsatake, the Nuu-chah-nulth Nation in internationally known Clayoquot Sound and the Anishnabe at Stoney Point. These are but a few of the many situations in which Aboriginal inherent and treaty rights are being denied. In other lands our brothers and sisters are sustaining similar abuse. Mother Earth is ravaged in South and Central America, the Middle East, India, Africa; wherever money and control take precedence over her natural beauty and bounty.

I recognize that I do not have a plan to create a new economic and political reality in this land. I don't know what the specific materials or dimensions are, but I know that my faith as a Native Christian tells me that the foundation requires respect for all life and the inclusion of all in the circle.

From the teachings of my ancestors, I have been impressed with the understanding that we humans have been entrusted with the awesome responsibility of caring for every form of life, every resource, every gift that has been given us by the Creator. Two of the criteria for that caring are that it be out of respect for the spirit life in the created being and out of concern for the life of the community, not out of personal gain or profit. Quite possibly the very concrete reliance upon both the natural world and the community in which previous generations lived, as well as some fear of the power in the natural world, played a part in their beliefs. So also did their intimate knowledge of the strengths of community and the world around them play a significant role.

Frequently, I have been told that our spiritual way is not a religion but a way of life. It is concrete. It is practical. It values respect, honesty, kindness, caring, strength, courage, balance and integrity. It is, in the words of my father, "the natural way." For many of my people these values facilitate a life of honour, respect and integrity. For me, an intimate transformation of these values inherent in the natural way comes about through the process of inculturation of my faith. As a Christian, I know personally the very source that empowers me to live these values is Jesus Christ through the indwelling of the Holy Spirit. I know the Great Spirit to be the source of both my faith and my practice. My faith then is more than an intellectual assent. It is also the practical way in which I live out my responsibility to care for and foster all life around me. It is made real in my efforts to care for my parents, my brothers and sisters, my neighbour, the condition of the atmosphere, the rain forests, the people who are being politically and economically oppressed.

It seems to me that balance is absolutely essential. When I fail to acknowledge and rely on the very source of life, God, it becomes much more difficult to live in a balanced, peaceful, just, caring and compassionate way. It becomes easy to slip into the kind of separation of belief and the practice of virtue or goodness that make it possible for neoliberalism to flourish. In other words, it becomes very easy for some of the best values of a culture to be co-opted and corrupted.

One of my personal struggles for balance is the struggle to articulate both my own personal reality and the reality of my people. It is easier for me to try to share my story, my perceptions, my experiences and my personal struggles for justice. It is a tremendous challenge for me to try to articulate the same for Aboriginal peoples across this land.

The First Peoples of this land have thousands of years of co-existence, some shared and some distinct spiritualities, many similarities of lifestyle, and over five hundred years of shared experiences of colonization and its effects. We also have uniqueness and differences among ourselves. Consider the uniqueness and differences among the peoples of Europe, a much smaller land mass. No one expects them to speak as one. Even now as they attempt to establish a common economic arrangement, there are great differences. Why then do Canadians expect that the different Aboriginal Nations should speak with one voice? Or act in concert?

Recently I was asked by a colleague, "What are the effects of neoliberalism (also described as neo-conservatism) on the Aboriginal Peoples?" Just what are they? They are generally destructive, demoralizing and devastating. That's a pretty strong statement. But I don't think it is inaccurate. Once again let me interrupt myself with a story.

You were out exploring one day. You came upon a beautiful old home with immense and magnificent gardens. As you walked up to the home you saw that the front door was open. No one seemed to be around. You walked in. It was filled with treasures. You decided to gather up these treasures and claim them as your own. While you were doing this, someone else walked in. It was not the owner but the gardener. The gardener called in the police. The police came but when they attempted to arrest you, you convinced them that there was something there for them too. All they had to do was delay the arrival of the homeowner, tie things up with paperwork, and give you time. And they'd get their share. Then you worked on the gardener, again buying time. You removed treasure after treasure, inside and outside. You took possession of the home as though it were yours. You even carved out a little corner of the land for the gardener and his family to live on as long as they liked. When one of the policemen made it clear that he could not be bought, you took care of him. When the gardener showed signs of resistance to your plan, you worked on his family and convinced them they would profit immensely.

Finally, one day, the homeowner returned from another of the places he frequented. In shock, he turned to the police and the legal system. And yes, you're right! They ruled that you had no right of possession. You had stolen and destroyed what belonged to another. You were a criminal. The law was on his side. And justice was served. You were imprisoned.

Except for one significant detail and its implications, this story parallels the stories of the first peoples of this land. And that detail is this: the same law that protects ownership of home and property in this land upholds the concept of *terra nullius*, the concept that this land was empty of human life when the European explorers laid claim to it! Yet, for thousands of years, Aboriginal peoples had cared for this land and ensured that it would be here and would provide for the generations yet to come.

No one would be fool enough to say that you, in my little adventure story, could truthfully and justly claim the house and gardens you found. Yet how many Canadians accept unquestioningly the decisions of Canadian governments to deny, even extinguish, inherent Aboriginal rights or prosecute Aboriginal peoples for exercising them? How many Canadians perceive as justifiable the actions of federal and provincial governments that delay settlement of land claims at the same time as they authorize mining companies and logging companies to proceed?

The recent ruling by Newfoundland's Supreme Court Justice Ray Halley is a case in point. I was angered and distressed that Justice Halley ruled against the Innu Nation and the Labrador Inuit Association in their bid to have the Newfoundland environment minister reject the Voisey's Bay Nickel Company's application to construct a new road and airstrip into Voisey's Bay.

What's a road, you say? But it's not just a road. It's a road, and eventually mines, being constructed on land that is part of an unsettled land claim. It is being constructed before an environmental assessment has taken place. The company would have us believe no environmental damage takes place during exploration! And, in my view, the road and airstrip will undoubtedly facilitate the explorations to the point that Inco, the Newfoundland government, and other major transnational investors will soon find themselves saying (if they haven't already done so), "We've invested too much now to stop. We can't let land claims issues and the social and cultural issues of the Innu stop us now. Let the land claims wait until we've got what we want." They may even be thinking of the Innu, "All we have to do is buy them off."

This is not the first visitation of destruction and disaster upon the Innu. Some of these same people, the Innu, have lived thirty years of hellish existence in Davis Inlet. Years of social and cultural breakdown. Years of broken dreams and broken promises. Years of despair, drunkenness and family violence. And years of judgement and condemnation by those who think, perhaps unconsciously, "It's their own fault. If they would only be like us (not so lazy) they would have had a better life with running water, flush toilets, good roads." Or, "If we can only get enough social workers in there . . . "

In baseball the rule is: "Three strikes and you're out!" It's a good thing the Innu aren't engaged in playing baseball! Their third strike follows the Davis Inlet disaster and more than a decade of Federal government contracting of low-level flying by NATO planes that have disturbed both the lives of the people and the caribou herds which are so significant to them. But the Innu are not out! They're not giving up! And I think they won't. This is the essential message captured in the following statement from the Royal Commission on Aboriginal Peoples in *People to People, Nation to Nation*. It reads: "Assimilation policies failed because Aboriginal people have the secret of cultural survival. They have an enduring sense of themselves as people with a unique heritage and the right to cultural continuity." [4]

Another situation that concerns me is that of the Lubicon Cree of Northern Alberta. They have been fighting the transnational pulp and paper giant, Daishowa, for about ten years. Once again, the situation exists in which a provincial government has given unilateral authorization to a company to access traditional lands that are part of an unsettled land claim for close to thirty years. Lands have been clear-cut. Profits have been made. The company has fought not only the Lubicon Cree, but has even legally fought the Cree nation's non-Aboriginal supporters, the Friends of the Lubicon.

How many Canadians would continue to negotiate after years (centuries) of abuse, oppression, broken promises and broken treaties? Aboriginal peoples have known for a long time that our very existence and survival as nations and peoples is in jeopardy. It would appear to me that overall government policy toward Aboriginal peoples is still assimilation. It's still: "Be patient. Do as we say, not as we do." How different from Jesus's approach. He said, "I give you an example . . . "

As you know, in 1991, the Canadian Government established The Royal Commission on Aboriginal Peoples. In the ensuing five years the commission met with Aboriginal and non-Aboriginal groups, visited Aboriginal communities and carried out a host of other activities in the effort to discharge its responsibilities. It met with hope, suspicion, acceptance and opposition from both Aboriginal and non-Aboriginal groups. Its final five-volume report has since been published, along with a smaller book entitled *People to People, Nation to Nation* subtitled, "Highlights From the Report of the Royal Commission on Aboriginal Peoples." Who has seen it? Who has heard of it? More distressing still: Who cares? Does anyone?

I remember watching the news on television the night the report was published and the commission was finished. What struck me was that the overriding message presented was how much it financially cost Canadian taxpayers. And it seemed to me that fears were raised about how much it will cost if implemented. While I realize that is an important issue, I have to say I was deeply disappointed that there was no acknowledgment of how costly, not only financially but also morally, culturally, ethically and spiritually the policy of assimilation has been for both the Aboriginal and the non-Aboriginal peoples in this land. More depressing still is the realization that so many Canadians don't even perceive this as costly. I am aware of how little public awareness, even interest, there is in this matter or in the report.

I offer one final response to the question: "What effect does neoliberalism have on Aboriginal peoples?" Aboriginal peoples are not just nations and communities but also individuals. As individuals we too get caught in confusion, greed, wrong-doing, failure to act in the common good, to serve the needs of the people in a good way. There are Aboriginal people, leaders and others, who have been compromised by the glitter and promise of money, wealth, control, and power over people. There are Aboriginal people who have been successfully co-opted. There are also Aboriginal people who have believed they were acting in the best interests of their people, only to find out otherwise, just as there are non-Aboriginal peoples in such situations.

The essential issue for me is not Aboriginal versus non-Aboriginal. It's a systemic issue. It's a war. It's a war between a system that values material wealth, accumulation of property and accumulation of power over peoples and nations; that disregards its destructive impact on Mother Earth, the atmosphere, the oceans and waters of Mother Earth, and the peoples of the earth; a war between that essentially evil system and systems that value human life, justice, the sacredness and vitality of the earth and the very existence of future generations. In this war, the capitalist neoliberal system uses divide and conquer tactics, double-talk, coercion and enticement. In my understanding its tell-tale statement is: "The bottom line is profit." For the sake of profit, and to the god of profit, are sacrificed human lives—the lives of individuals, families, communities, and nations, economically, physically, emotionally and psychologically as well as spiritually. It's fruits? Look around you. Also sacrificed: old growth forests, fragile eco-systems, personal integrity, national political and governing power, the integrity required to honour commitments and treaties, the will of individuals and peoples to be their truest and best selves.

Facing this monolith is a variety of systems, or perhaps better identified as individuals and groups, who have a different vision. Their bottom line is "justice" or better still, "justice with compassion." Not just justice because frequently the justice system stands hand in glove with the monolith, serving "Just Us," as my Dad would say. For those for whom justice with compassion is the bottom line, the significant elements are persons and their lives: the well-being of their families and their communities; their rights and freedom; the environment; the earth itself and its future; future generations; conscious living and conscientious choices about life; true peace and harmony among nations and peoples; respect; integrity and other such values. There are many of these groups and individuals throughout the world but their bottom line is never as readily heard, nor as readily accepted, as that of the neoliberals. Instead it is questioned and challenged. Its proponents are confronted with every conceivable argument to prove that their bottom line is invalid, indefensible and impossible to achieve. It's much more difficult for them to speak with one voice.

What is amazing though is that wherever and whenever anyone truly hears that voice and listens to it with not only their ears but also their heart, and their hopes for a more human life, they hear an invitation to accept and live by the same bottom line: justice with compassion that leads to truth, life, wholeness, and godliness, better described as true humanness. This happens even if the listeners have truly heard the voice of even one individual who is committed to that same bottom line. Also amazing is the fact that sometimes the speaker has lost the capacity to act as well as speak, but the message itself has transformative power.

In today's world, it will take massive attitudinal and cultural changes to develop the level of awareness that will ensure the existence of rain forests, old growth forests, and clear lakes and rivers. Even though it may seem impossible, my faith assures me that in Jesus the forces of life have overcome the forces of death. For this reason and with this hope, I speak, I write letters, and I sign petitions to try to bring about the changes that will give life rather than death and destruction, empowerment rather than powerlessness, humanization rather than profit.

I realize that an individual response is not enough to challenge the tremendous powers that are at work today; systemic change is necessary. I also realize that a few scattered rain showers did not create the devastating floods in Quebec a year ago, and more recently in Manitoba and Europe. Neither did a few snowfalls create the six and seven foot snow banks that surrounded my home in mid-winter. In the same way—like the accumulation of individual raindrops or snowflakes resulting in transformations of significant proportions—essential personal conversion effects transformation. A personal commitment to the Gospel virtues of faith, hope, love, justice and compassion is absolutely necessary, not optional, for us as believers in our contemporary society. Such a commitment to living justly is vital to being a truly free and whole person, I think. At the same time, the accumulation of individual conversions and efforts is not enough unless it results in the collaborative efforts that effect systemic change.

In the society in which we live, it has become very easy to separate our spiritual self from our physical, mental and emotional self, to compartmentalize one's self as well as one's life. In fact, to acknowledge either one's spiritual self or one's emotional self is frequently unacceptable in the "business of living." How sad! It is only when we have the courage to engage our total self that we will also find the courage to examine society and its values.

One of my greatest challenges, as I have said, is to try to live in balance: to bring together as a whole my faith, my practice, my thoughts and my emotions. I am often aware of how easily my life can get out of balance. I realize that all too easily I can neglect one or more aspects of my whole self. When I over-emphasize one aspect and neglect the others, I become less free, less whole, and less capable of living fully all my other relationships. The balance I speak of is not only internal balance. It is also the balance of my relationship with God, with other humans and with the natural world around me. Intimacy and communion with God are the source of the fire within that propels me to be socially conscious and to do justice. When I neglect that relationship, even if it is through over-emphasizing my other relationships, I discover that the other relationships are diminished as well. I need to ask myself: How do I bring into balance my use of the conveniences technology provides with my respect for the earth and my concern to protect my Mother Earth from pollution? How do I honour my own personal call to fulfilment and at the same time ensure that I am not simply being egocentric? In Christian terms: How do I genuinely love my neighbour and at the same time genuinely love myself? How do I live in a balanced way the invitation "to act justly, to love tenderly and to walk humbly with your God?" (Micah 6:8).

One of my favourite prayers that serves as a reminder to me of what it means to be a faith-filled and faithful person in today's world is a simple little prayer that is frequently used in funeral services. The prayer goes something like this: "May every gesture, every mark of affection you give, be for you a sign of God's peace." I am sure that prayer is intended to be a source of comfort, and it is. But for me it is also a reminder of the intimate connection between faith and life as well as the incarnational connectedness between divinity and humanity. It is also a challenge and an invitation. In these current times do I dare accept? Do we believers dare accept?

Notes

1. *The Mission of Christ the Redeemer* (Montreal: Éditions Paulines), p. 77.

2. *Songs for the People: Teachings on the Natural Way: Poems and Essays of Arthur Solomon*, Michael Posluns (ed.) (Toronto: N.C. Press Ltd., 1990), p. 184 (Available from ARC).

3. *Eating Bitterness: A Vision Beyond the Prison Walls: Poems and Essays of Arthur Solomon,* Kathleen Knee and Michael Posluns (eds.) (Toronto: N.C. Press Ltd., 1994), p. 70 (Available from ARC).

4. *People to People, Nation to Nation: Highlights from the Report of the Royal Commission on Aboriginal Peoples* (Ministry of Supply and Services Canada, 1976), p. X. This information was provided by the Privy Council Office and reproduced with the permission of the Minister of Public Works and Government Services Canada, 1997.

Resources

Besides the books quoted, and a wealth of others and personal contact with First Nations and Aboriginal organizations; the following groups are excellent resources for anyone who wishes to learn more, or become involved. The purpose and vision of each group is unique. Neither the author of this chapter, nor the collaborators and editors of this book, necessarily agree with each group, but we recognize that each has something to offer in the dialogue of justice with compassion in our current reality.

• Aboriginal Rights Coalition (ARC) (Project North)/
La Coalition pour les droits des Autochtones (Projet nordique)
153 Laurier Ave. E, Ottawa, ON K1N 6N8
Tel: (613) 235-9956 Fax: (613) 235-1302 e-mail:arc@istar.ca

• Assambly of First Nations (AFN)
1 Nicholas St., Suite 1002
Ottawa, ON K1N 7B7
Tel: (613) 241-6789 Fax: (613) 241-5808
Web site: http://www.afn.ca

• Canadian Alliance in Solidarity with the Native Peoples/
Alliance Canadienne en Solidarité avec les Autochtones
427 Bloor St. W, Room 261
Toronto, ON M5S 1X7
Mailing Address: P.O. Box 574, Stn P, Toronto, ON M5S 2T1
Tel: (416) 972-1573 Fax: (416) 972-6232 e-mail:casnp@pathcom.com
Web site: http://www.pathcom.com/~casnp

• Friends of the Innu c/o Canadian Environmental Defence Fund
347 College St., #302 Toronto, ON M5T 2V8
Tel: (416) 323-9521 Fax: (416) 323-9301
Web site: http://www.web.net/~cedf

• Friends of the Lubicon
485 Ridelle Ave., Toronto, ON M6B 1K6
Tel: (416) 763-7500; e-mail: fol@tao.ca
Web site:http://www.kafka.uvic.ca/~vipirg/SISIS/Lubicon/main.html

THE PERMANENT WAR ECONOMY

LEONARD DESROCHES

Leonard Desroches is a writer and drywaller who lives in Toronto where he is a resource person for the exploration of the spirituality and practice of nonviolence. He has a B.A. degree from Wilfrid Laurier University, Waterloo, ON. He recently published Allow the Water: Anger, Fear, Power, Work, Sexuality, Community and the Spirituality and Practice of Nonviolence, *1996.*

Since my youth I have searched for a deeper sense of power. The predominant form of power (organized violence) was obvious to me. I hungered for another form of power which I could not name. Martin Luther King's capacity to love in the face of hatred began to name this soul force I'd been searching for—especially his mystical understanding of Christ's challenge and invitation to love our enemies. And just in time! I was beginning to question whether the church was not deeply irrelevant to a world hacking away at itself and the earth. Then I began to realize that within the stifling corporate church which marched to the rhythm of the Empire, there was a more radical, fully alive church community which was living out gospel nonviolence—much as in the first three centuries of the church's life. Since then I have searched for and tried to live out this soul force in my relationships, in my work and in my resistance to injustice and violence. I have also spent many years exploring nonviolence as a resource person for retreats, workshops and training for specific nonviolent responses to injustice. Today, I would sum up gospel nonviolence as the life-long apprenticeship in the love of enemy and love of earth.

From Three-piece Suits to Bloodied Army Fatigues, Back to Three-piece Suits: Militari$m as a Way of Life

"The sinews of war are infinite money." These words were spoken by Cicero in his *Orationes Philippicae, V.* All the way back in the Roman Empire, this man already understood the very heart of warfare. (As with "agribu$ine$$" and "mega-$port$," the spelling of "militari$m" is important.) The following dangerously familiar information is to be read slowly—very slowly: every minute about 15 children die of hunger and inadequate health care while the world continues to spend $1.6 billion on war. Militari$m. [1]

War is the profound moral laziness and cowardice of sending the young to die and to kill for us. Militari$m is the day-to-day maintenance of a permanent war economy.

Militari$m is made up of the everyday activities which are necessary for the perpetuation of war—as, for example, taxation. Not long ago, while on a train, I overheard this extremely dangerous, irresponsible and unfortunately, very common comment: "All you can do is pay your taxes and shut up." Very few things could be more conducive to war-making. That attitude is exactly what guarantees "infinite money," as Cicero put it, for the "sinews of war." As long as we provide the money, the military-industrial complex will be there to lead the politicians into war. Each year, every Canadian man, woman and child gives more than $344 to the military—one of the world's most expensive, where the cost per member is $127,000, compared to Belgium's $74,000. The average pay of a General/Lieutenent-General in 1996-1997 was $117,000. [2]

Here are just a few basic facts. The Canadian government's 1997-1998 military budget is $10,306 billion. Have we not become dangerously blasé about such enormous amounts of money—which represent so much energy and time on our part? Canada is among the highest military spenders in the world and among the top 10 per cent of arms exporters. The ratio of the military budget to the environment budget in 1997-1998 is 25/1. There may be bigger armies in the world, but 118,251 people are a lot of people paid with our taxes to do ultimately one thing: fight wars. There are 64,996 active forces, 30,000 reservists and 23,255 civilian defence employees. Imagine just a fraction of that—say, 50,000 people—paid to develop and maintain civilian-based defence (CBD). CBD is the serious organization of active nonviolent defence of the country. (More on CBD later.)

While the USA poured $150 billion into General Thieu's repressive police state during the Vietnam War, Canada quietly profited. Most of the nickel used in US planes, missiles or vehicles came from Canada. "Explosives for US Up Sharply in Canada," reported the *Globe and Mail* newspaper on April 7, 1966. In May of 1967, *Maclean's* magazine announced: "We're making millions out of Vietnam." "Defence Sharing is Truly Big Business," stated the *Financial Post* on February 4, 1967. In his important book, *Quiet Complicity,* Victor Levant lists seventy-seven different Canadian-made products used in Vietnam. He states that "On the basis of an official Pentagon survey of contracts worth $200,000 or more for the years 1968-74, it appears that at least 37.5 per cent of all Canadian defence sales ($447,023,000) consisted of materials destined for the Southeast Asia theatre." Litton Systems in Toronto produced parts for two US bombers during the Vietnam war. For the F-4 Phantom fighter-bomber, Litton produced the INS (inertial navigation system) and weapons release computer sets. Litton also had a contract to build the INS for the F-11 fighter-bomber.[3] Now Litton is making new profits from selling radar systems to the Indonesian army which has been involved in the illegal occupation and the massacre of the people of East Timor. Militari$m.

What about nuclear weapons? As Bill Robinson of Project Ploughshares put it recently in a letter to me:

> More than fifty years after the advent of the nuclear age, Canada still maintains a fundamentally ambiguous policy toward nuclear

weapons. The Canadian government rules out acquiring its own nuclear weapons, opposes nuclear proliferation and supports, at least in principle, the abolition of all nuclear weapons. But it also supports the continued possession for nuclear weapons by its allies, participates in a nuclear-armed alliance, and [does] not foresee any future need to change any aspect of NATO's nuclear posture or policy. The Canadian government continues to believe that the defence of Canada relies on the nuclear umbrella that the United States and other NATO allies have unfurled above this country, and it continues to provide both physical and political support for those weapons in a variety of ways. In short, while the Canadian government condemns any reliance on nuclear weapons by non-allied countries, it continues to treat those same weapons as a useful—even necessary—element of Canada's defence and those of its allies.

After the horrors of the Persian Gulf war, even Prime Minister Brian Mulroney had to admit that the pushing of arms all over the globe was at the root of the violence and starvation in the human community. Yet, as Ken Epps of Project Ploughshares noted,

> In the same September week that the Parliamentary Sub-Committee on Arms Export issued a report calling for tighter Canadian military export controls, New Brunswick's Saint John Shipbuilding announced it had received Ottawa's approval to pursue a $1.5 billion sale of three patrol frigates to Saudi Arabia. After the end of the Gulf War, five Canadian ministers toured the region in an effort to help boost Canadian arms sales, especially in Kuwait. [4]

Canada is involved more and more in international peacekeeping efforts. Yet, as eminent Canadian military researcher, Ernie Regehr, pointed out, "The failure of states to control collectively the shipment of arms to regions of conflict renders peacekeeping impossible." [5] Of the 38 third-world countries Canada has sold arms to in recent years, 29 were cited by Amnesty International as human rights violators, and 11 were at war. Almost 80 per cent of these countries use repression in extreme form against their citizens (torture, disappearances, political killings). Still, in these times of the globalization of greed, we continue to profit from pushing arms. Militari$m.

History of War, History of Lies

We continue to perpetuate wars partly because we have been lied to about the real history of war. Imagine a history book that had the courage to present war from the perspective of the victims. We are finally beginning to see this happening. We are just beginning to hear about the sex slaves of the Japanese armies; about the rapes in the US army; about the ravages of wartime racist policies such as led to the internment of the Canadian citizens of Japanese origin. We are just beginning to hear of how in 1898, when the UK seized the Philippines as their colony and foothold in Asia, more than 250,000 Filipinos were killed; of how Stalin confiscated the bountiful harvests of the Ukraine and caused the starvation of 10 million Ukrainians.

To be read slowly: between 1962 and 1982, there were at least 10,700,000 people killed in 65 wars in 49 countries—that's an average of 1,465 people killed every day! There were more wars fought in the 1980s than in any other decade in recorded history. The historic shift in the 1990s is from state-versus-state wars to civil wars: Peru, Guatemala, Somalia, former Yugoslavia, Rwanda.... We are being confronted with a critical lesson: with or without nuclear weapons we are capable of mass murder and massive destruction of the animals and the earth.

Nonviolence questions the myths inherent in war and in the "history" of war: What does "victory" mean? Is the military-industrial complex really "good for business?" Whose business? Who defines our enemies for us? Why? Why are we so afraid of telling the amazing history of nonviolent resistance to war and violence—e.g. how 5,000 farmers in Le Cambon, a small village in Nazi-occupied France, saved 5,000 Jews? What are the real reasons we don't explore seriously civilian-based defence (CBD)?

The final question in an honest history of war is: what does it mean that a war "ends" neatly on such and such a date? What does it mean to say the Vietnam war "ended" when almost as many US soldiers committed suicide as were killed in action—approximately 50,000? What about the soil still poisoned by "Agent Orange" and still poisoning the people's food? What about the mines left behind by the US military—which they were bound by the Paris Peace

Accords to remove but didn't? Land free from mines is still in very short supply. There are about 100 million "anti-personnel" land mines scattered in 62 countries. Worldwide, at least 500 children, women and men are killed or maimed each month. Why? Over 95 manufacturers in 48 countries profit from the production of 5-10 million antipersonnel mines each year. Militari$m.

When we say a war ended, what about the direct environmental effects?

What about the social effects of war? What about the cultural effects of war? What about the psychological effects of war? What about the deadly spiritual numbness that has poisoned our soul?

Who pays for all this? Who pays for all the deep healing and rebuilding required by all this mass killing and destruction?

Choosing a Career, Living an Adventure—the Degradation of Good Work by the Permanent War

Echoing Cicero's insight that "infinite" (i.e. tax) money is essential for war, General Electric's president, Charles Wilson, noted in 1944:

> The revulsion against war not too long hence will be an almost insuperable obstacle for us to overcome. For that reason, I am convinced that we must begin now to set the machinery in motion for a *permanent war economy* (my emphasis). [6]

Yes, as in 1944 there is still a "revulsion" against war. Unfortunately revulsion is by far not enough. Revulsion is not conversion. Revulsion is not revolution of values—for example, the research, teaching, building, and maintenance of civilian-based defence. There has never been a cultural conversion or a revolution of values when it comes to war.

A "permanent war economy" has poisoned every aspect of work in North America—and elsewhere. To quote from Joseph Goebbels, Hitler's chief propagandist: "Even if we lose, we will win, because our ideals will have penetrated the hearts of our enemies." The ideal of the permanent war needs the ideal of the "permanent war economy." Both ideals have penetrated our hearts! There is no way that the Nazis lost the moral war: the festering, pus-filled sores of day-to-day militari$m cover this sweet earth like cancer from some massive, pathetic addiction. Between the former USSR and the USA, Somalia was turned into an arms bazaar, leaving first one, then many war lords to starve and kill and maim thousands of their own people. Militari$m.

About 75 per cent of Canada's military industrial production is exported to about 60 countries—mostly in the developing world. Not long after ARMX 87 (Canada's arms bazaar), at the time of the government's "White Paper" (pushing for the greatest possible share of the profits to be made from arms spending), the magazine *Aerospace Canada International* eagerly changed its name to *Aerospace and Defence Technology.* Militari$m. Permanent war economy.

Working Directly for the War Machine: Choosing a Career, Living the Adventure

In Canada, as many as 100,000 people work in the arms industry. A local neighbourhood newspaper recently dedicated two full pages presenting a "career" in the military. It was headlined by the Canadian military's own current, clever logo: "Choose a Career, Live the Adventure." I wrote to the paper:

> I was disappointed that you presented the military purely in terms of a career. The bottom line of the military is the ability and willingness to kill other people when ordered to do so. We are being dishonest not to present that, when we present the military as an option for young people. I am very aware that most Canadians are under the impression that there are no serious alternatives to the military. This is a profound misunderstanding. After decades of work, civilian-based defence (CBD) is finally acknowledged as a very urgent alternative to war in resolving our international conflicts. I hope that young people will be given all the options when presented with career opportunities. The possibilities for the development of civilian-based defence are very exciting. [7]

I was somewhat surprised when the paper not only printed the whole of my letter (the above is just an excerpt), but headlined it with: "Kill when ordered bottom line of military career." This demonstrated how normalized a "career" the military has become—and how sometimes, by grace, publications actually welcome being reminded of the real implications of presenting the military to young people as simply another job.

Working Indirectly for the War Machine: "I Just Put Wires Together"

"I'm not really that much for war." These lukewarm words from a young Canadian bank worker just out of university says much about being passive fodder for the permanent war economy. If I'm "not really that much for war," I'm certainly not that much against it.

Over the many years of leafleting the workers at Litton Systems, many of those who sincerely did not approve of the weapons being built there told us: "We just put wires together." Unfortunately, in a permanent war economy every cog in the war machine is indispensable. We can no longer say, "I just do the research at the university," or "I just make the laws," or "I just test the weapons."

When Albert Einstein realized how his work was used to bomb Hiroshima, he boldly declared: "If I had known they were going to do this, I would have become a shoemaker." To make his intention clear, Einstein declared: "Non-cooperation in military matters should be an essential moral principle for all true scientists"—and researchers, designers, factory workers, lawyers, judges, bishops, welders, security guards, suppliers . . .

In the case of Litton Industries of California, the parent company to Litton Systems Canada, a 1971 US congressional investigation charged that Litton created "an image of technological and organizational superiority by developing flamboyant sham into an art and [it] had made overstatement a way of life. It is adept at concealment, misdirection and incomplete statement."

Litton and the US Navy ended a nine-year court battle in June 1978 over construction costs for American assault ships and destroyers. Litton ended up building fewer ships (five instead of the original nine) and received more money! At least six times during 1971-1981, Litton refused to bargain with unions which had been certified by the Labour Relations Board. In 1971, Litton president

Roy Ash stated the company global goals: true internationalization of both management and capital. [8]

In 1987, Auditor General Kenneth Dye exposed that the Department of National Defence (DND) paid a Canadian supplier $8,613.23 each for 10 butterfly valves that sell for $912 each in the US. The *Ploughshares Monitor* reports that in 1991-1992 Canada spent $26 million on military bands—more than five times the budget ($5 million) of the Canadian Institute for International Peace and Security, which has since been closed as a cost-cutting measure. Imagine $26 million for research related to Civilian-Based Defence (CBD).

Selling

As I sat in a courtroom waiting through the proceedings related to our arrests for blockading the entrances to ARMX '89, I decided to read some of the arms merchants' glossy literature which I had picked up. "Every individual or group that kills has to think of the cost: even the serial murderer has to consider if he can afford the weapon needed." I was struck by the honesty—as grotesque as it was. It then went on to talk about the "lowest cost per kill"—referring to the All Weather Smart Projectile (ASP) for the NATO 155mm Autonomous Precision Guided Munition (APGM). This goes on all the time secretly. Armx and all the other arms bazaars are simply self-confident times of public orgy.

Wars Serving the Right and the Left: The Need for a More Thorough Liberation

I rarely use the language of disagreement: it's seldom what's needed. This is one of those rare times when I do need to speak this language: I strongly disagree with those who see war as an issue that's remote from the more immediate forms of violence such as wife battering, sexual abuse, or racism, unemployment, homelessness. I am utterly convinced that as long as we do not practically and publicly renounce war we can never free up our full spiritual energy to resist what seem to be the more immediate forms of violence. (Immediate and remote forms of violence are more intimately connected than might be apparent.) For both the right and the left, war is knowing that someone (young), somewhere, somehow will kill (and die) for me if push comes to shove. Therefore they don't need to be involved in a life-long apprenticeship of nonviolent resolution of conflict—they are "too busy" with pressing, local problems. For as long as war is an option—a final solution for both right and left—*all the injustices leading to war* will continue. To accept war and its *necessary* daily militari$m is to have our imaginations enslaved. Renouncing militari$m frees up our collective imagination. Ours is a kept imagination. This is dramatically demonstrated by the way we have organized society: virtually everyone has agreed that *all* their plans (family, holidays, work, friendships) are contingent on the demands of war. We will set all aside for months or even years if the state calls a war. (Recall the Gulf War.) I now know that within this normalized, sick war culture, I need to live in a community with others where everything is also contingent on war—*but rather on its renunciation, non-cooperation and active nonviolent resistance.* Put most simply: I need to live! To be in denial about the very foundation of our culture—the Gun—is not living. It may be normal, but it is not spiritually sane. An impeccably logical economic discourse—right or left—which perpetuates militari$m may sound impressive, but it is totally false. It becomes sane only when it takes into account how much we live off the Gun. Our usual, polite economic discourse is only logical if we accept the *premise* that mass killing and destruction is the state's right.

Hopelessness Defied: Lucas Workers Spark a Revolution of Values

In the hard struggle of dismantling the genocidal war machine, the word Lucas defies hopelessness. Lucas Aerospace is one of Europe's largest designers and manufacturers of aircraft systems and equipment. In 1974 a committee of Lucas workers got together and drew up a plan to stop the massive layoffs and convert military production into useful and needed products, such as road-rail vehicles.

This is what the workers learned as they involved themselves in creating practical alternatives to war production: "We've demonstrated beyond any doubt the ability of so-called ordinary workers to decide what products they should make, how they should make them and in whose interests they should be made. And so much so, that they've seen through the whole *myth of hierarchical management.*"

The myth of hierarchical management is at the heart of the permanent war economy, as it is at the heart of armies. We have been lied to for so long we barely believe we're capable of radical cooperation and intelligent decisions. To continue to allow the military corporations' insatiable appetites to determine how we define and structure work in our culture is slowly sapping all spiritual life from us. We are loosing the will, let alone the capacity, to be active, cooperative participants. The myth of hierarchical management in both the economy and the military denies our capacity to respond as a community to the Spirit's graces and clues, as we try to resolve our conflicts without hatred or mass killing.

Capitali$m and Militari$m are Inseparable

Too much of our wealth goes to too few people. As of 1993, major Canadian corporations owed in excess of $40 billion in deferred taxes. Statistics Canada reveals that 50 per cent of the deficit is due to tax breaks for upper income earners and corporations and only two per cent can be attributed to government spending on social programmes. Capitalism is the most logical way to make a tiny percentage of the community wealthy (though not necessarily happy by any means) while too many are either deprived or seriously suffering. Capitalism is the most highly developed system of greed. Its facade of efficiency is a laughable, vicious sham built on the blood and backs of the poor. Dorothy Day was a US journalist who saw through the sham. She helped found the *Catholic Worker* movement during the Great Depression. She gave her life both to solidarity with the victims of capitali$m/militari$m and to active nonviolent resistance. This North American prophet and saint once declared: "Our problems stem from our acceptance of this filthy, rotten system."

Capitalist economists refer to human beings as "factors of production." Under the North American Free Trade Agreement (NAFTA) we—as factors of production—are becoming part of a huge free trade zone without standards, where transnationals can move production to suit themselves. As a global community, we need to find different ways of managing international trade. We need to *translate* cooperation into even the global level of practical economics. A nonviolent economy is one built on a radical respect for the common wealth of God and one built on love of enemy—not on the Gun as final authority. A violent economy—one built on power over people and the earth, one built on the mass killing of state-designated enemies—will always eventually unravel.

An Alternative to War—Civilian-Based Defence (CBD)

"The world is round! Really!"

Imagine the shock that must have been felt when this was first uttered—likely in the 12th century, while the fearful keepers of the status quo proclaimed: "That's ridiculous! We'd fall off!"

Now there is even more shocking news: a world without war—without armies—is possible! "Really!!!" "Ridiculous!" say the politicians and church leaders—to the great relief of the arms makers and arms pushers. "We'd all fall!" "High tech warfare is the only thing that can protect you. Trust us!"

When the global community finally accepted that the world was round, it made the necessary adjustments. We named the force that kept us from falling off "gravity." It is now time for another historic readjustment. The force that could keep us together this time is not physical as much as spiritual. It is already at our disposal. Some have done and some are doing marvellous explorations with it. It is called community. Not dependent on high tech machines, its power resides in truthfulness, trust, generosity, respect, intelligence, imagination, courage and the powerful tools of "nonviolence," "satyagraha," "agape," "people power," "relentless persistence."

In the past, when we wondered if the world was indeed square or round, we investigated. Recently the Second World Congress on Violence and Human Co-existence explored whether or not people were naturally violent. It concluded that there's no scientific basis for the belief that violence among humans is ingrained or inevitable.

From global community comes a global "common security," exposing the illusion, the lie, the dangerous myth of "national security." Community takes us beyond the dangerously brittle notion of "patriotism." Patriotism—and its consequent "national security"—depends entirely on the physical power of the "armed forces." Jean Goss, a one-time prisoner of war, who became one of France's greatest exponents of nonviolence, used to say simply that nonviolence is life—life is community. Community ("We are a great people among other equally great peoples")—and its consequent "common security"—is dependent on what the great Canadian prophet in politics, J.S. Woodsworth, called "spiritual forces." Challenging the new country of Canada to rely on the soul force of nonviolence, Woodsworth stated clearly:

> For me the teachings and the spirit of Jesus are absolutely irreconcilable with the advocacy of war. . . . According to my understanding of economics and sociology, war is the inevitable outcome of the existing social organization with its undemocratic form of government and competitive system of industry. . . . There is little dependency on spiritual forces. . . . It seems to be taken for granted that we must follow the example of European nations and proceed to arm. . . . Now I would like to challenge the implication that in order that we may become a self-sufficient nation it is necessary for us to maintain a militia force. Now is the time when we should decide whether or not an armed force means or makes for peace. . . . I recognize that the policy which I have advocated would involve risks, but the present policy involves not only risk but almost certain failure. Why not take those risks which are incident to the development of the *new means of protecting our nations?* (my emphasis). [9]

In the "new means of protecting our nation" Woodsworth was prophetically pointing to civilian-based defence. In the Philippines, Benigno Aquino bluntly asked: "Can the killers of today be the leaders of tomorrow? Must we destroy in order to build? I refuse to believe that it is necessary for a nation to build its foundations on the bones of its young." Woodsworth and Aquino, as politicians, were challenging the very foundation of the state: that the final authority resides in the Gun. Aquino was assassinated. Woodsworth's challenge was shamefully abandoned—and has never been taken up by either the church or the NDP (New Democratic Party), the successor to the *Canadian Commonwealth Confederation* (CCF), which Woodsworth helped to found. It remains an aborted Canadian dream. The divine right of the Gun remains the final authority. It is on that foundation that we continue our pitiful attempts to end wars—when we could literally be in a process of ending war itself.

Politicians know the real consequences of such a fundamental rearrangement of the very structure of the state. They know it every bit as much as the kings and queens whose shrieks of protest we can still hear echoing through the centuries in reaction to the challenge to abandon their "divine right." The consequences for a king or queen were indeed great: to forgo living apart and above the rest and to take the same risks as everyone else in the helping to build true common security. This implies egalitarianism, cooperation, conflict resolution. Indeed this does require a whole fundamental rearranging of society—a revolution of values, as Martin Luther King put it.

The risks of J.S. Woodsworth's challenge to the Canadian state are even greater than those presented to those frightened monarchs of old. Even when we got rid of the divine right of monarchies, we did not, as a society, face the even more fundamental divine right of the Gun. The implications of getting rid of that divine right are very real: rather than being the *last ones* to risk physically in times of aggression or invasion, the elected political leaders would necessarily be the *first ones* to face the risks involved in organized Civilian-Based Defence. I believe that is the final, silent fear which we have to be much more honest about: the fear of risking *our own lives* (not just those of the young) as adults and as community/political leader/servants. Imagine how much less romantic, macho or careless our politicians would necessarily be if they knew that dealing with war automatically meant dealing with the risk of their own lives first.

In state warfare the question is not, "Will someone get killed?" The question is, "Who will get killed?" It is never the wealthy and politically powerful. The politicians and religious leaders do not rot in the trenches. Martin Luther King started to go beyond resistance to racism alone when he realized that in capitalism both white and black poor people were being used as fodder in the Vietnam war.

This is why I see war as profoundly cowardly and lazy: what could be easier than to order someone else—the young—to kill and die for you (patriotism) and to have their terror and torture and death bring you both political points and quick-fix economic benefits? What could be more realistic, courageous and fair than to risk your own life as the "prime minister"—the first servant—in putting in motion a country-wide response of nonviolent resistance and non-cooperation in case of invasion or aggression? This is just what the Danish people did in their resistance to the powerful Nazi war machine. As Thomas Merton put it so well: "Denmark was not the only European nation that disagreed with Hitler. . . . But it was one of the only nations which offered *explicit, formal and successful resistance to Nazi power*" (my emphasis). [10] The King of Denmark declared that he'd be *the first* to wear the yellow badge that the Nazis wanted to use to identify Danish Jews. This decisive and organized non-cooperation at the state level rendered the invaders impotent.

This critique of war applies to the official leaders of the various religions. In fact, they might have the greatest power of all to advance genuine civilian-based defence as an alternative to war. What if religion no longer hid behind the protection of the state (which in turn hides behind the lives of the young)? Would we not be forced to deal with this system which perpetuates so much endless suffering? When the North American prophet Dorothy Day cried out: "Our problems stem from our acceptance of this filthy, rotten system," she explicitly focused *on the system.* It's one thing to accept the luxury of choosing which war you will eloquently denounce. It's a whole other reality to daily pay the price of the long loneliness of denouncing the very system of war itself as being the cornerstone of the state. If I as a male refuse to renounce rape itself and merely make pronouncements on individual rapes, I have no solid foundation with which to face male violence. If the church refuses to renounce war itself and chooses to simply address individual wars, it has no real foundation with which to face war-making and its necessary daily economic brutality. Without this foundation, the day-to-day building of a culture of gospel nonviolence barely survives: conflict resolution, resistance to injustice and the building of alternatives to violence—including war itself.

"It's a matter of living our lives in drastically different ways," warned Dorothy Day. The more thorough our "pilgrimage" into all this—going to the very edge, to see for ourselves—the more we begin to see the day-to-day implications. They are costly—personally and collectively; as a church community, as a culture. But, as the great French exponent of nonviolent defence (a former decorated army general), Jacques De Bollardière put it:

> This strategy is accessible to the masses . . . at its worst, this struggle without arms and without hatred would not provoke the same massacres as violence, would not accumulate the same ruins, would not lower the level of civilization. . . . As an officer, I have constantly asked young men to accept to be killed. And they accepted, *often without understanding,* simply out of obedience to a discipline, because they were trained for that. Why would not young people today accept to sacrifice themselves for something that they understand and believe in? [11]

As for the Christians, maybe it is time to take a collective pilgrimage to the "end of the earth" to see for ourselves if it is round or square. Maybe this pilgrimage needs to take place inside our collective selves. Joseph Beaulieu, a former captain in the Canadian Armed Forces, took such a scary pilgrimage. He wrote, standing at the edge:

> My military career, which was supposed to last twenty years, began in the autumn of 1962. I was at that time at the University of Montreal. I thought it was a good idea to enrol in the Canadian Air Force, for after all, I needed money to pay for my studies and the general opinion was that the Armed Forces were a place where a young person could work for peace, even giving his life if necessary to defend his country! I was thus not very aware of military policy and programmes.
>
> I had the opportunity, during my career, to visit nearly all the military bases in Canada. I worked at six of them, including two with nuclear arms. I had to come to grips with the fact that the *raison d'être* of the Armed Forces is to train people for war and eventually to enter into combat and kill human beings. This understanding was confirmed one day at the Cold Lake Base, when a superior officer gave us a disciplinary reminder in these terms. "Don't kid yourself, fellows, you are part of a violent organization and its purpose is violence!" I was also told that as an officer, if I carried a revolver during exercises while my men carried guns, it was because I was supposed to shoot them if they refused to shoot

> the enemy. The training that we gave to the young men included a lot of pressure and frustrations, in order that they would come to the point where they would obey without question. It seems that is a necessity for combat!
>
> All these violent events created in me an internal conflict which lasted many years with many sleepless nights. *I thus undertook a long pilgrimage which led me to the discovery of an alternative to the army, that of non-violent civil defence.* This alternative has been more effective than violence in many historical conflicts, even when there has been no previous training. . . . This non-violent method also made me see clearly the madness of military thinking in which we kill a man, our brother, in order to destroy the evil which is in him! We are struggling against a false enemy! (See Ep. 6:12) The non-violent alternative will surely lead us to go beyond the concept of the "just war," in order to dare to move towards the biblical solutions of forgiveness of sins, love of the enemy, and resolution of conflicts in truth and total respect for the human person. I place my hope now on the fact that love is stronger than hate and life is stronger than death. This is the basis of the Hope which gives me life.[12]

Once we have come out of our collective pilgrimage and clarified the spiritual questions, we can begin to focus on the practical tactics involved in civilian-based defence. In Quebec, a good place to begin is the book *Pour un pays sans armée,* edited by Serge Mongeau and printed by Ecosociété, Montreal. For a brief but excellent study of how CBD could apply to Canada, there is George Crowell's *The Case for Nonviolent Civilian Defence Against External Aggression* in the Ploughshares Working Paper number 90-4. There are also the books of others from around the globe: Jean-Marie Mueller, Gonzalo Arias and Gene Sharp among others. [13] We will soon need to invest at least the same amount of resources and taxpayers' money in the serious exploration and implementation of CBD. In keeping with the spirit of nonviolence, bold imagination is utterly urgent in all of this.

Stephen Dale, writer on Canadian military matters, noted not too long ago:

> In the early eighties, Laval University political scientist Alver Legault calculated that, between 1949 and 1980, Canada's

> peacekeeping costs not reimbursed by the UN amounted to a cumulative $266 million—less than one half of one per cent of the total military budget during that period . . . [Meanwhile] the activities that led to the carnage of January 1991 are still going on. Canada and its multi-national weapons-producing partners continue to develop more sophisticated generations of weapons for the next war. While the peacekeepers occupy the front page, nobody notices the armies of anonymous bureaucrats and scientists—ordinary civilians with high-paying jobs and respectable lives—who spend their days refining the technology of death. [14]

The Canadian peacekeeping tab for 1992 was approximately $120 million—less than 1 per cent of Canada's military budget of over $13 billion for 1991-92. Militari$m.

If it had been prepared for genuine nonviolent intervention in Bosnia, Somalia, Rwanda, Zaire . . . the UN would have put in place mechanisms whereby thousands of nonviolent, international peacemakers could be deployed. We have indeed advanced greatly in the use of sophisticated, expensive, high-tech military equipment. Now much of the military work is much easier—often as easy as pushing buttons. The sad irony is that genuine nonviolent conflict resolution has probably become correspondingly harder. The minds and hearts of the people have been captured, lulled, and numbed by the military myth, the myth of the quick-fix "redemptive violence," as scripture scholar Walter Wink describes it. I found it quite symbolic that the attempted parachuting of food to those besieged in the former Yugoslavia was such a failure: we have practised pin-point accuracy when it comes to the Cruise missiles' mass murder capacity, and yet we don't know what we're doing when it comes to the strategies and tactics of practical nonviolent intervention. This we have not practised with the same dedication and financial resources.

We need to dare to imagine, on the government level, the turning of Canadian Legion halls into exciting centres of study and practice of CBD—for the young and the elders all across the country. Along with the work of CBD, these centres could be used for the on-going development of local neighbourhood conflict resolution programmes (such as have just begun to blossom here and there). Could we imagine, on the Church's part, the use of its halls as exciting centres where the spirituality and practice of gospel nonviolence is explored and developed with relentless persistence? Imagine, for example, if the Roman Catholic Church took advantage of our recently more honest understanding of the history of violence done to the First Nations peoples of the Americas by both Columbus and his "knights" *(conquistadores)*. Imagine the Knights of Columbus transforming into an exciting movement for gospel nonviolence and renaming itself after Bartolome de las Casas, the Dominican monk who denounced his fellow Spanish Christians' violence against the First Nations peoples. Imagine young people being introduced to a rich, on-going apprenticeship in the love of enemy! I am convinced that young people would be open to being challenged to explore the love of enemy in their day-to-day lives. Young people haven't yet gone into denial about the horrors of war. They would say in amazement, "I didn't know this kind of vibrant alternative community is what 'church' meant!" They can't say that yet: shamefully, "church" does not stand for that.

We sometimes talk of "historic decisions." At this volatile time in history, all our major decisions related to global conflicts are by definition historic. If we choose (it is a choice) to continue to prepare for war (as we are actively doing) we will have made a historic choice in one direction. If we choose (and we can) to develop nonviolent civilian-based defence, we will have made a historic choice that will necessarily alter the very course of history for our children's children.

We simply will not survive unless we change. Civilian-based defence is as "unthinkable" as Solidarity was in Communist Poland, or glasnost in the USSR, or the fall of the Berlin Wall. As French nonviolence historian, Jean-Marie Mueller, observed, *"Il est plus difficile d'inventer la paix que de se résigner à la guerre"*—It is more difficult to invent peace than to resign ourselves to war. [15] When 100,000 people took to the streets of Sarajevo in March 1992, and when students mobilized in Belgrade, they asked Europe for support—e.g., for European ambassadors to be posted in Belgrade. There was no such support given to the initial nonviolent resistance. As a global community our imagination is so seriously stunted that we can only imagine a military reaction to international conflicts. Thus all our resources are swallowed up by militari$m and its permanent war economy. Just as it is more difficult to invent peace than to resign ourselves to war, so it is more difficult to invent a genuine peace economy than to resign ourselves passively to a permanent war economy.

Origen, an early church theologian, noted: The greatest warfare is not with human enemies, but with those forces which make people into enemies. In the third century after Christ, the young war resister, Maximilian, declared to the Roman proconsul Dion, in North Africa: I will not be a soldier. . . . I am a Christian. Given the death penalty, as required by law, Maximilian cried out: "God lives!" Cicero referred to money as the infinite sinews of war. Such a permanent war economy demands an obedient generation of youth to kill and die for the empire's permanent war economy—the sinews of war. Maximilian's refusal—our refusal—is not an act of bravado or even defiance; nor is it a competition against the state. It is a prophetic invitation and challenge to live community with each other and with every creature on this small, wondrous earth and with the Creator.

God lives! Community is possible. A world without war—without a permanent war economy—is indeed possible.

NOTES

1. The position sustained in this chapter can be substantiated by Project Ploughshares whose research has provided the principal source for the data presented here. Project Ploughshares is a Canada-wide church and citizens coalition dedicated to monitoring Canada's military involvements. For further information about the issues raised in this chapter, contact Project Ploughshares at Conrad Grebel College, Waterloo, ON, N2L 3G6; Tel: (519) 888-6541.

2. *Ibid.*

3. Victor Levant, *Quiet Complicity* (Toronto: Between the Lines, 1986).

4. *The Ploughshares Monitor*, Dec. 1992—c/o Project Ploughshares.

5. *Kitchener-Waterloo Record,* 20 Jan. 1993.

6. G.E. internal publication, 19 July 1972—as quoted in *National Boycott News,* Winter, 1992-1993.

7. *St. Jamestown T.O.*, 16 Nov. 1992.

8. Len Desroches, Tom Joyce and Murray MacAdam, *Arms Maker, Union Buster—Litton Industries: A Corporate Profile.* Published independently by the Cruise Missile Conversion Project, with financial assistance from Project Ploughshares. In one of our leaflets to the Litton workers (on the outskirts of Toronto), we quoted Russ Messino, an engineer at a US G.E. war plant. He had quit his job because he could no longer justify the "middle class welfare" which paid him "handsomely for work that does not make a positive contribution to society. . . . Why is the defence business allowed to divert our resources and talents from areas that could make a positive contribution to the world?"

9. Kenneth McNaught, *A Prophet in Politics* (Toronto: University of Toronto Press).

10. Thomas Merton, *The Nonviolent Alternative* (Farrar, Straus and Giroux), p. 165.

11. Jean Toulat, *Combattants de la non-violence* (Paris: Cerf, 1983).

12. Joseph Beaulieu, in *Notre défense et nous* (Comité œcuménique sur la défense nationale au Québec).

13. There is an ongoing source of news and analysis of CBD in the newsletter *Civilian-Based Defence* (P.O. Box 92, Omaha, NE, 68101, USA). A recent issue reports on how Professor Albert J.F. Lin, a Taiwanese-Canadian has been instrumental in beginning an exploration of CBD in Taiwan.

14. *THIS Magazine,* March/April 1993.

15. J.-M. Mueller, "Non-violence," in *Actualité*, Feb. 1993.

3

"corn"

Serving the soup

OBSTACLE IN THE COURSE OF THE MISSION, THE IMPASSE OF RELIGION

André Myre

André Myre, biblical scholar, PhD in Intertestamental literature at Hebrew Union College-Jewish Institute of Religion (Cincinnati), was a professor at the Faculty of Theology at the University of Montreal from 1970-1997. He is the author of Un souffle subversif. L'Esprit dans les lettres pauliniennes *(Montreal, Bellarmin/Paris, Cerf, 1987) and* Scandale! Jésus et les pauvres *(Montreal, Paulines/CPMO, 1993).*

How do we arrive at an awareness of social justice? Do we ever come to this awareness? Reflecting on my life, I recognize a number of influences: the Bible, read time and time again; cherished Biblicists who opened my eyes to the meaning of texts that had never appealed to me until then; sisters and brothers especially, passionately loved in the faith; brother Jesuits here at home, the prophet Arrupe from over there, heroically faithful social activists, admirably human religious; and so many others, drawing me forward by their friendship, teaching me to reread the Bible with new eyes and to discover myself, despite appalling limits, as their brother and friend and therefore as the brother and friend of Jesus.

I have never forgotten the content of this sentence. A few years ago, the Canadian Catholic bishops published a text on the economy that aroused the indignation of some God-fearing people. After reproaching the bishops for discussing the economy although they were not economists, the chief editor of *Le Devoir*, who was neither an economist nor a theologian, reminded them quite curtly of their responsibilities: “Tell us instead about the eternal truths.”

The whole problem facing the Christian mission is contained in this last sentence: “Tell us about the eternal truths.” When Christian revelation passed from a people to a community of faith, it inevitably faced the temptation to transform the world mission into a religious mission. As long as God is considered to be the God of a people, He is necessarily involved in their affairs. In the life of a people, however, religion is not a domain apart, separate from the others. Rather it is a dimension that influences the totality of their existence, even disappearing, it might be said, into the reality of their lives. When a people, as an entity, has a common God to which it refers, its culture, lifestyle, foreign relations, politics and gatherings are coloured by this common God. In that reality, nothing is purely religious, but nothing is separate from religion.

The synagogue in Jesus’ time is a good example of this reality. The word quite simply means “assembly.” When Jesus goes to the assembly, most of the time he does not enter a building. He participates in a village meeting that deals with the business of the community: legal disputes, safety, human relations, commerce, etc. There are moments of prayer, of course, because prayer is a part of life. But strictly speaking, the assembly is not a religious reality; it is the meeting of a human community that deals with all the questions concerning the community. God is present there because He is interested in human affairs.

In passing from a people to a community situated within several cultures, Christian faith inevitably had to ask itself what distinguished it from the surrounding societies. Naturally, it did not find these distinct realities in political organization, economic development, financial realities or strictly cultural activities but in the domain of religious symbolism. There is no harm in that. Religion is a fundamental dimension of human life and pervades it through and through. But there is a very real temptation to transform faith into religion, to carve out a sacred zone in reality, to make God's revelation an invitation to perform a series of activities independent of the normal course of life and, thus, to trivialize human existence in the interests of an ideal great beyond or a supernatural for which it is worth sacrificing everything else. Is there any need nowadays to demonstrate that Christianity has yielded and continues to yield to this temptation?

Each time that human reality is diminished in the interests of religion, the Christian mission suffers because of it. And at the present time, it suffers greatly, particularly here at home. Where are the Christian communities that are serious about the demands of justice, the necessity to disassociate themselves from the politics of the current global economic Empire, the cries of the poor, the enormous disparities between continents and peoples, the enslavement of human beings to the demands of commerce? Admittedly, initiatives are taken, relevant documents written, donations made, solidarity is demonstrated. But the task is not really taken seriously because it appears to be of secondary importance in comparison to religion. International solidarity is a good thing, we say or are told very often, but it is only a sign of universal salvation. Giving bread is commendable, but the real bread is that of the Eucharist. Human communion is desirable but it is only truly accomplished in the communion of the Church. Mutual pardon is praiseworthy but it is inferior to the pardon dispensed by the priest. Regaining one's health deserves thanksgiving but in the hope of the absolute health of the Resurrection. Everything is a function of the religious and the sacred. It is not surprising, therefore, that the proponents of liberation theology are accused of horizontalism or of neglecting the supernatural; that those who work in the direction of a Church serving mankind are reproached for neglecting the task of drawing people into the Church; that Christians concerned by the monster of neoliberalism are told that they ought to be involving themselves, above all else, in the traditional battle against sin.

How do we escape from the impasse, break open the log-jam? How do we rediscover the meaning of the mission in a world that God loves so passionately? We must begin humbly perhaps, by offering a contribution aimed first of all at releasing the religious ideal. Let us return therefore to the life of the Man from Nazareth, situating him as concretely as possible among his people in order to gain a better understanding of his approach to human life. Then we shall examine how the Gospel deals with these same realities. In conclusion, we shall look at where this exercise has brought us.

Galilee

It is S. Freyne who deserves the credit for having shown in 1988, the importance of Galilee in understanding the Man from Nazareth. As he himself wrote:

> If historians of Jesus have made little serious effort to explore the Galilean roots of his career, christologians have also paid little attention to this dimension, even in their quest for the historical Jesus. [1]

Since that time, studies have multiplied and, recently, a major book by R. A. Horsley, *Galilee: History, Politics, People* was published. The pages in this section rely on Horsley's book for the data that will help us to formulate a more discerning question on the meaning of Jesus' deeds. [2]

Controlled militarily from Jerusalem under David, subjected to taxation and forced labour under Solomon, the people of Galilee quickly became disillusioned by the Davidic royalty and, after the death of the second king, were quick to reject the power of the monarchy and of the Jerusalem Temple. The cycles of the prophets Elijah and Elisha allow us to gauge the vigour of the Galilean resistance to oppression and foreign cultural influences. From the fall of Samaria at the hands of the Assyrians, Galilee lost its elite and its history was distinct from that of Judaea. It was administered separately and the small Galilean villages followed their own habits and customs. The situation was repeated under the Persian and Hellenistic regimes. Between the death of Solomon in 931 B.C.E. and the Hasmonean conquest in 104 B.C.E., there were barely twenty years of direct influence on Galilee from Jerusalem under Josiah. It was not long enough, however, to create loyalty toward Jerusalem as a cultural centre and place of worship. Life continued, expressed in the oral traditions of the people, independently of Jerusalem, without a central city of culture that was strictly Galilean, without a Temple or sacred literature.

In 104 B.C.E., the Hasmoneans seized Galilee which Judaean officers controlled from fortresses such as Sepphoris. For the first time since Solomon, Galilee was subjected to the Jerusalem high priests, to the Temple and to priestly taxes. The Roman conquest of 63 B.C.E. confirmed the Hasmonean domination of Galilee, except that Roman taxation was now added to the first. Troubles broke out, in Magdala particularly, reflecting the Galileans' alienation with regard to Jerusalem as much as to Rome. With the Romans' blessing, Herod the Great seized Galilee in 40 B.C.E. and governed it from Jerusalem, via Sepphoris, until his death in 4 B.C.E. Although they continued to retain their local traditions, the Galileans were now subjected to a third level of taxation, that of Herod. Thus, sporadic revolts erupted, aimed at establishing a native king who would shake off the foreign yoke and free them from the crushing burden of taxes.

On Herod's death, insurrection broke out under the direction of the native king Judas, son of Hezekiah. Sepphoris was captured and burned. Roman repression was very severe in the surrounding villages.[3] The Romans subsequently entrusted Galilee to Herod Antipas who governed it from 4 B.C.E. to 39. During nearly the entire first century of our era, Galilee had an administration separate from that of Jerusalem. In 4 B.C.E., Antipas rebuilt Sepphoris, to the great resentment of the Galileans, and, approximately fifteen years later, founded Tiberias from which he governed Galilee. Flavius Josephus would say of the Galileans that "they have the same hatred for the inhabitants of Tiberias as they have for those of Sepphoris."[4] It was from there, in fact, that they were taxed by non-Galileans who had no interest in promoting the establishment of links with Jerusalem since tax collection was a highly competitive business. As Horsley declares, "Sepphoris and Tiberias were in but not of Galilee."[5] The construction of these cities, as well as their cultural, economic and political development depended on taxes that were basically drawn from agriculture. And it was in the time of Jesus that the impact of the construction of Tiberias was most keenly felt. In fact, the Galileans had no contact with these cities except when their representatives came to collect the taxes. Their resentment is understandable; they received nothing in return. It is not surprising that from 47 B.C.E., Galilee was the scene of a great deal of banditry, since large numbers of those who had lost everything turned to violence, or that it witnessed the rise of a certain number of native kings in whom the peasants concentrated their hopes for liberation.

At the time of Jesus, Galilee was much less Judaean in spirit than is commonly believed. As in the case of the leaders named by the Romans, the lower classes, to all intents and purposes, had no contact with the representatives of the authorities in Jerusalem except when taxes were collected. It was not the ideal way to establish good relations. And contrary to what is also believed, Galileans did not go to Jerusalem much more than once during their lifetime.

> For a very rough sense of such Galilean pilgrimage [to Jerusalem]: if by a high estimate, 1,000 Galileans made a pilgrimage each year and, by conservative estimate, there were 100,000 inhabitants in Galilee (with life-expectancy of between twenty-five and fifty years), then well under half would have made a pilgrimage to the Jerusalem Temple once in their lifetime. [6]

The Galileans' degree of devotion to the Jerusalem Temple should therefore not be overestimated. Since there was no indigenous priestly aristocracy in Galilee at the time, identity was maintained much more through local traditions than through external institutions.

> . . . [I]n the early first century B.C.E. Galileans may well have seen the Temple and the high-priestly regime in Jerusalem as remote and the "laws of the Judaeans" as odd versions of Israelite traditions, imposed from the Jerusalem that their ancestors had rejected, according to their own Israelite traditions. [7]

Against this backdrop, it is not surprising that "Jesus . . . (apparently) stands opposed to specifically Jerusalem institutions such as the Temple and high priests on the basis of an alternative understanding of Israel."[8]

Finally, it must be recognized that Galilee was a frontier area with a long tradition of resistance to oppression from the outside. It separated from Judaea at the time when the latter established the Temple and the Torah as its central institutions. In Galilee, there was neither indigenous ruling class, nor priestly aristocracy nor central institution. Apart from taxation, Judaean customs had not been imposed. But the weight of the taxes demanded by the various levels in question had provoked several revolts under the direction of a native king. As might be imagined, all of this is not without importance in understanding the man from Nazareth.

The Galilean

Jesus lived for his people of Galilee. It is remarkable, when studying the Synoptic Gospels, to see that all his activity, except his key encounter with John the Baptist and his stay in Jerusalem at the end, took place in Galilee. It is equally noteworthy that the texts never mention Jesus at Sepphoris, Tiberias or even in the city itself of Caesarea Philippi. It would perhaps not be inferring too much from this silence to refer to the problems around Sepphoris that followed the death of Herod the Great, and the horrors that Jesus had witnessed as a child or about which he had heard. He knew from experience the violence of Roman oppression and the unbearable weight of Roman, Herodian and high-priestly taxes. The meaning of his life did not direct him toward the oppressors but toward their victims, namely, his own people. As Horsley writes,

> [. . .] Jesus was not teaching some sort of new lifestyle to individuals, but addressing local communities about their disintegrating social-economic relations. [. . .] Jesus also pronounces God's condemnation, not of Israel (let alone "Judaism"), but of the Temple, the Jerusalem rulers and their representatives, the scribes and the Pharisees, who "come down from Jerusalem." [. . .] The impact of Roman and Herodian rule [. . .] is felt in the disintegration of households and local village communities.[9]

Faced with a power whose decisions contributed to the breakup of the social fabric, Jesus strove for the reintegration into community life of those who had been excluded and gave hope for a new way of life for the whole people in the kingdom of God. He therefore appointed twelve disciples, a sign of a new society conforming to the original intuitions. Jerusalem would no longer hold central power, exploiting the people with taxes and forced labour, but the people would find themselves again as twelve tribes, negotiating as equal to equal, each tribe led by one of its own, under the guidance of God. And he was and would be their servant, and not their king. Consistent with his experience of God, it was important for him to establish the programme of the kingdom without holding the power. [10]

To wait for the kingdom of God means to prepare it. Naturally, the priority goes to those who are currently on the fringe, marginalized by the system in place. For those who were excluded because of illness or social function, Jesus expected nothing less than reintegration into their milieu. He announced the remission of debts in the kingdom of God, a remission that would begin immediately."Forgive us our debts, as we have forgiven those who are in debt to us" (Mt. 6:12). Besides, the Roman taxes were illegitimate: since we owe everything to God, we owe nothing to Caesar (Mk. 12:13-17). This is the same attitude he displayed in condemning the Temple, the priesthood [11] and priestly taxes. Even knowing the danger, he showed no hesitation in going up to Jerusalem a short time before the end of his life and making a frontal attack on the Temple, the heart of the system of collaboration with Rome. He announced its complete destruction: there would be no need for it in the kingdom of God.

The characteristics of Jesus' activity allow him to be situated in the line of Israel's social prophets. The one who had been given the responsibility of bringing, on a human scale, the good news of the kingdom *of God* obviously did not perceive himself as a king, except in this precise meaning, to show by word and gesture, what kings should do and not do, and therefore what He, God, would do.

A reading of Ps. 146 provides an essential element for explaining Jesus' hope in the kingdom of God. Even if the man from Nazareth, like the vast majority of his contemporaries, especially in the Galilean villages, was probably illiterate and had perhaps never heard proclaimed the psalm, the instrument of work of the Temple priests (notice the liturgical framework of vv. 1-2 and 10b), the similarity between the psalm and Jesus' activity is remarkable. This text very likely reflects a similar spiritual sensitivity and experience of life.

> [1] Alleluia! Praise Yahweh, my soul!
> [2] I will praise Yahweh all my life,
> I will make music to my God as long as I live.
> [3] Do not put your trust in princes,
> in any child of Adam, who has no power to save.
> [4] When his spirit goes forth he returns to the earth,
> on that very day all his plans come to nothing.
> [5] How blessed is he who has Jacob's God to help him,
> his hope is in Yahweh his God,
> [6] who made heaven and earth,
> the sea and all that is in them.
> He keeps faith forever,
> [7] gives justice to the oppressed,
> gives food to the hungry;
> Yahweh sets prisoners free.
> [8] Yahweh gives sight to the blind,
> lifts up those who are bowed down.
> [9] Yahweh protects the stranger,
> he sustains the orphan and the widow.
> Yahweh loves the upright, but he frustrates the wicked.
> [10] Yahweh reigns for ever,
> your God, Zion, from age to age.

The experience that prompted the writing of the psalm is presented in vv. 3-4: *earthly kings can no longer be trusted.* Now there is hope only in Yahweh (vv. 5-6). Then follows a list of Yahweh's priorities (vv. 7-9), with the conclusion providing the key for interpreting the psalm: Yahweh will reign forever (10a).

Nothing closer to Jesus of Nazareth can be found. This psalm shows that radical criticism of and opposition to human political power are the *sine qua non* of commitment in preparing the kingdom. He who renounced placing his trust in human power in order to aspire to and to announce the kingdom of God could not consider himself as a messiah. The spirituality of the psalmist was the spirituality of the man from Nazareth. This psalm is therefore most enlightening in understanding the Jesus of history. This attitude which represents fundamental opposition to the king is eminently the attitude of a prophet. [12] The gesture directed against the Temple is perhaps the most beautiful example of a traditionally prophetic action. It supports both Jesus' non-messianic vision of his role (it is the prophet who is opposing the government) and the Galilean perspective of this gesture, which focuses on the symbolical and actual origin of the oppression suffered by the people of Galilee.

A human being, however, cannot control the opinion that others have of him. It was impossible for Jesus to prevent the lower classes, who witnessed his actions and were impressed by the vigour of his social, economic and political criticism, from dreaming of him as a native king in his Galilean tradition. [13] What a good king he would make, this person who understood them so well and in whom they could not but recognize their hope for freedom! The Messianic interpretations of the life of Jesus can be traced back to this groundswell that roused a people. It explains both the movements of the crowds who glimpsed the end of their oppression and the reluctance of Jesus whose actions were only announcing the coming of the kingdom of God. It also explains the apathy of the Romans who, before the gesture against the Temple, were unconcerned about the symbolic revolution of a man who was virtually alone, without a structured organization, troops or weapons. Jesus did not view himself as anyone's king, but simply as a servant of the servants of the Great King.

There comes a time, however, when liberty disturbs, when the symbol roars. Jesus' liberty and the symbolic power of his gestures came together in his anger against the Temple. It was too much for the Romans and the proof is in the sign they wrote for the Cross, a sign that was an expression of their spite. [14] This is what they would do to the one whom the Galileans would like to crown as their king: they would crucify him. Let there be no doubt in anyone's mind. Jesus died because of his actions, of course, but perhaps more so because of an interpretation of his gestures that did not come from him. In an irony of history he died and rightly so, but for the wrong reason. In addition, the sign proclaimed that Jesus was the so-called king of the "Judaeans." It was the name the Romans used for the inhabitants of the conquered country, and this is the second irony of history. In addition to dying for the wrong reason, Jesus found himself endowed with a title that was repugnant to a Galilean.

The wording of the sign was a result, and this must be repeated, of the desire of numerous Galileans to anoint Jesus as a native king who would liberate them from the Romans and the onerous burden of the taxes collected from Judaea, and it undoubtedly contributed to the messianic reinterpretation of the life of Jesus. This same wording, just like the first Christian sermons in Jerusalem as well as in Judaea, must have played an important role in the Davidic expression of the Galileans' dream of a native king. The mechanism of enculturation was rapidly put in place. But in a strict sense, faith in Jesus as the messiah could not depend solely on his crucifixion as king of the Judaeans. It is therefore necessary to refer to the fundamental experiences that prompted an awareness of the exaltation of Christ. Christian faith in Jesus the Messiah was born. The history of the birth of this faith is therefore understandable even if Jesus of Nazareth, strictly speaking, undoubtedly never considered himself as the messiah.

The Messiah and Son of God in Mark

The evangelist Mark tells us at the outset (1:1) that he does not intend to talk merely about the Galilean, but that he will deal, in a larger sense, both with Jesus and the person that he became after His death, namely, Messiah and Son of God. It is very interesting to see how Mark, who is writing in Rome, at the heart of the Empire, presents the one who is at the origin of the new faith. The angle of the approach used in the following pages is that of the relationship between Jesus and God. [15]

At the beginning, in the middle, and at the end of his text, Mark offers his readers God's viewpoint on Jesus. In 1:1-15, he shows Jesus invested by the Spirit hearing, through a voice from heaven that is God's own voice, that he is God's beloved Son. Mark concludes his presentation by saying that in Galilee, Jesus proclaimed the Gospel of God, namely that the kingdom of God was near. From these very first lines, the readers know who will be talked about in the text, which is not the case for the characters in the story. Further along, in the middle of the account, Mark once more presents God's view of Jesus, always for the readers, but this time, directing it at the three principal disciples; Jesus is indeed God's beloved Son and they are invited to listen to him (9:2-8). Finally, in conclusion, using the code of the man in white to express the heavenly origin of the faith, Mark tells us that Jesus has risen (16:1-8).

In the entire Gospel, *God will not do anything more than this.* All that Mark says about the action of God is that the latter raised Jesus from the dead and presents him as His Son. Yet, the Resurrection took place in the magnitude and the mystery of God. In the story, God merely creates solidarity with Jesus in the minds of certain people, nothing more. Human beings, including Jesus, will have to struggle in the ambiguity of life. Let us look at how Mark presents this struggle and the place he gives to the religious dimension of existence.

In the first part of the Gospel (1:16-8:21), the word "God" is mentioned fourteen times: four times by persons possessed (1:24; 3:11; 5:7 [x2]); once by the scribes (2:7); once by the witnesses (2:12) ; eight times by Jesus (2:26; 3:35; 4:11,26,30; 7:8,9,13).

In these chapters, Jesus is very active. He appoints his disciples and gives them their mission. He cures the sick and demoniacs (the demoniac in Capernaum, Simon's mother-in-law, lepers, a paralytic, a man with a withered hand, the Gerasene demoniac, the woman with a haemorrhage, the daughter of a Syro-Phoenician woman, the deaf man with a speech impediment). He raises a young girl from the dead. He eats with tax-collectors, argues with scribes and Pharisees, calms a storm, visits Nazareth, multiplies loaves, walks on water. It is a great deal, and typical of him. Only on two occasions is he in a gathering where all sorts of topics, including religious issues, are discussed. On both occasions, he performs a cure when he has no right to do so; the second time, a death threat hovers over his head. The remainder of the time, his work is oriented toward life; he focuses on the physical and psychological health of the people; he demonstrates his solidarity with social outcasts; he wants the people to feel secure; he foretells a world where the poor will have enough to eat. In his activities he has manifestly little interest in official religion. This does not mean that God does not interest him—on the contrary. But he has his own way of being interested in God.

When he cures the demoniacs, it is they, not he, who speak about God. When he cures the paralytic, it is the scribes and the witnesses, not he, who talk of God. When therefore does Jesus talk about God? He talks about God in response to the Pharisees who denigrate his disciples (2:26; 7:8,9,13), and to his family, including his own mother, who want to divert him from his mission (3:35). And then, when he takes his disciples aside, he clarifies for them the sense of the kingdom of God that inspires him (4:11,26,30). That is all, and it is very telling. But let us see what the rest of the Gospel has to offer on the subject.

In the second part of the Gospel (8:22-15:47), the word "God" is used thirty times, [16] once by the Pharisees (12:14), once by a centurion representing Mark's Roman community (15:39) and once by an anonymous narrator (15:43). The remainder of the usage is by Jesus himself. Unlike the first part of the Gospel, here Jesus speaks much more frequently than he acts. His actions include curing two blind persons and an epileptic. He goes up to and enters triumphantly into Jerusalem. He drives the merchants from the Temple after withering a fig tree. Finally, chapters fourteen and fifteen deal with the last days of Jesus.

The words, more numerous than is often thought, are focused a great deal on the inevitable suffering awaiting those who agree to struggle in the way of Jesus, on that which makes the grandeur of a human being, on scandal, the right or not to divorce one's wife, the conditions for access to true life, the attitude to wealth, the conditions for access to power and its exercise, the human condition in the afterlife, the greatest commandment, the alienation caused by the teachings of the great, the future of humanity, etc. In all these questions that all generations and societies ask themselves, Jesus puts the human being, liberty, justice, inner honesty before all else. Most of the time, this bias lands him in difficulty with his questioners who force him, so to speak, to put the issue of God on the carpet, although it had not been his primary intention. Because Peter refuses suffering, the inevitable consequence of following in Jesus' footsteps, his thoughts are not of God (8:33); he will understand one day perhaps, if he is there to see the kingdom of God coming in power (9:1); no stone must be left unturned, however, in avoiding the scandal of this refusal of suffering (9:47). As for the disciples, they are far from God if they do not welcome these disenfranchised, the children (10:14,15); similarly, they understand nothing about God if they think that the rich will be favoured in His kingdom (10: 23,24,25,27). On the question of divorce, (10: [6],9) or paying taxes to Caesar (12:17 [x2]), the Pharisees know nothing of God; the ideal in human life is not divorce, and since we owe everything to God, we owe nothing to Caesar. To the rich man who says he is good, he replies that only God is good (10:18). In Jerusalem, he simulates the end of the Temple, this cavern of thieves oppressing his people (11:17), by withering a fig tree in the name of God (11:22) and overturning the tables of the money changers. To the Sadducees who have a very physical view of the Resurrection, he replies that they misjudge God (12:24,26 [x4],27). To the scribe who questions him about the greatest commandment, he replies that he is not far from the kingdom of God (12:29,30,34). In all these cases, it is not Jesus who takes the initiative to talk about God. He does it because he is challenged or questioned.[17] Jesus speaks about God of his own accord on three occasions only: at the end of the Last Supper when he announces to his disciples that he will drink the new wine with them in the kingdom of God (14:25) and on the cross when he asks God why He has abandoned him (15:34 [x2]). He had besought this Father who had twice presented him as His Son (1:11; 9:7) to save him from death (14:36), but without success. God's response was not to be pronounced in history but in the hereafter. How then, from this side of death, could he not feel horrifyingly abandoned? Death seemed to contradict everything that he had said about God under the pressure of objections, and to justify the traditional image that others gave of Him. He died after giving a great cry.

At the end of the journey

At the end of this journey, what do we keep in mind to allow ourselves to heed the call, forever renewed, to the mission?

First, the importance of Galilee in understanding the Man from Nazareth: several elements are striking—for example, the tradition of resistance in the face of foreign oppression, the absence of centralized institutions and indigenous governing elites for the entire territory and, especially, the preservation of local traditions independently of Jerusalem institutions. In the time of Jesus, rabbinism did not yet exist, and the image that we often have of a Galilee controlled by an army of scribes, responsible for educating the people about how to do things in the Jerusalem way, is not exact. It seems that the Temple authorities had their work cut out collecting taxes in Galilee. As for the customs of Judaea, they had no opportunity to be imposed for the simple reason that to all intents and purposes, since the very beginnings of the monarchy, Galilee had existed as a region independent from Judaea, with different ways of following the ancestral traditions. A basic fraternity could exist of course, but Jerusalem was always "the other"—threatening. They remembered the harshness of Solomon and their ancestors' decision to rebel against the power of Jerusalem. They were still strangling on the priestly taxes imposed by the Hasmonean power. For the Galilean peasants, nothing good could come out of Jerusalem.

Secondly, it is worthwhile to remember Jesus' very human existence. During his entire life, the Galilean had been a man of his people. [18] He suffered to see them subjected to a foreign power. He liked the Romans well enough, but in Rome. For his own people, he wanted the end of oppression through taxes, the return to the land of their fathers, the remission of debts, bread on the table, an end to the anxiety that causes disease of body and soul, reintegration into the community, the re-establishment of full human dignity, liberty in relation to the various levels of government as well as to the public servants who were the instruments of their domination. Too realistic to try himself to undo the noose that had a fatal stranglehold on his people, he looked to the kingdom of God. He could only give the principal directions through his activities, but these directions were clear. They were a reflection of God's boundless interest in seeing that humans are happy *here below.*

There, where God reigns, empires are defeated and their subjects increase in stature, to the great displeasure of all those who would claim for themselves the right to oppress others and leave "the eternal truths" to God. They made no mistake when they cut him down in his prime. And since then, from one generation to the next, they continue to put him to death by misrepresenting the meaning of his life, transforming it into a defence of religion and the sacred at the expense of the appeal to struggle against the Empire.

Thirdly, even a summary consideration of Mark's Gospel shows that Jesus' actions are much more secular than is often thought. He is concerned about realities as close to life as health, human dignity, work, integration into the human community, bread on the table, wine at the feast and friendship, a government that is decentralized and close to the people, the freedom to be faithful to oneself. These realities are valuable in themselves and deserve, in love, that we give our lives for them. They are not a spring-board to something else, nor do they exist solely in relation to greater realities. Human life is oriented, quite simply, to happiness here on earth. It is within this call to struggle for the least among his people that Jesus meets his God whom he names the God of the kingdom. It is to this God that he prays, it is in this God's dynamism that he renews his soul. When he cures the sick, he implicitly witnesses the importance of human health for God, quite simply because, in his culture, all reality is impregnated with the dynamism of God. He does not feel the need to discourse on, to hold forth about God. For the Jesus of the Gospel, God is expressed in a free, healthy people, at liberty to make their own decisions, in relation to their local community within a work environment that allows them to make a living. The remainder is a counter-argument. As for Jesus, his God is not sending him out to preach about the Godhead or to participate in one religious celebration after another. There are matters of much greater urgency. It is the others who confront him with their religion and their sense of God and challenge him to clarify his own vision of God. In doing so, he says exceedingly beautiful things that reflect the strength of his inner life. But when he speaks of God in this way, he is not evangelizing. He explains, defends himself, attacks. When he evangelizes, he is healing, consoling, liberating, reintegrating. He speaks about God *after* evangelizing, and not to the poor, but to his and to their adversaries, who normally are not interested in the Gospel and the God of the kingdom.

Finally, it is important that Jesus' disciples not fall into the trap of words. To evangelize, in the Gospel sense, is not to hold forth about God. It is to bring to the people and to the poor, the good news that inevitably clashes head on with the powers of this world and religions more interested in the "eternal truths." That is why it is quite in line with the Galilean and the Jesus of the Gospel to struggle against the Empire of neoliberalism, even if in doing so, we do not talk about God or contribute to increasing the ranks of the Church. Today, the role of the Romans, of Herod and the high priests in the time of Jesus, is played by this Empire of neoliberalism. It smothers the people and the least among us who are waiting for the good news of liberation. And this Empire always invents for itself a God that justifies its atrocities. The only way to counter this false God is to do our share so that the actions heralding the good news of liberation for the poor will be made to happen immediately, even if only on a small scale. Once these actions have been taken, the time for discussing God will surely come, as in the case of Jesus, with the problems foretold by the Gospel. Each thing in its own time.

Notes

1. S. Freyne, *Galilee, Jesus and the Gospels: Literary Approaches and Historical Investigations* (Philadelphia: Fortress, 1988).

2. R. A. Horsley, *Galilee: History, Politics, People* (Valley Forge, Pa: Trinity Press International, 1995); by the same author, also see *Jesus and the Spiral of Violence: Popular Jewish Resistance in Roman Palestine* (Minneapolis: Fortress, 1993); *History and Society in Galilee: The Social Context of Jesus and the Rabbis* (Valley Forge: Trinity Press International, 1996).

3. No doubt including Nazareth, situated a little over five kilometres from Sepphoris. Jesus would have been three years old at the time. Old enough to remember . . .

4. Flavius Josephus, *Life*, 384.

5. Horsley, p. 174.

6. *Ibid., p.* 316, No. 30. According to Flavius Josephus, besides the cities of Sepphoris and Tiberias, there were 204 villages in Galilee. Most of these villages had less than 300 inhabitants. At the time of Jesus, Nazareth had approximately 500 people and Capernaum had 1,000 (pp. 190-195).

7. *Ibid.*, p. 156.

8. *Ibid.*, p. 252.

9. *Ibid.*, pp. 280-281.

10. When the crowds were hungry in the desert, it was not Jesus, but the Twelve, in keeping with their symbolic role as chiefs of the people, who distributed the loaves and fishes to the people. Significantly, when the food had been distributed, there was still some left over, a sign that they should continue their task of pastor. The famous "Do this in memory of me" of the Last Supper only makes the meaning of these leftovers more explicit. As far as Jesus was concerned, he had shown the road ahead, it was now up to his disciples to embark upon it. In passing, it is important to note that the Last Supper refers to the multiplication of the loaves as the rite to reality and *not the reverse*. For Jesus, the essential was that his people had pastors so that the loaves would be available to them. He would have been horrified to learn that one day those venerating him would turn the call to sharing into a mere advertisement for the Eucharist, a terrible overgrowth of religion at the expense of human life.

11. According to J. P. Meier, "Reflections on Jesus-of-History Research Today," in J. H. Charlesworth (ed.), *Jesus' Jewishness: Exploring the Place of Jesus within Early Judaism* (New York: The American Interfaith Institute-Crossroad, 1991), p. 89, the parable of the Good Samaritan is an anticlerical joke, told by a layman to other Galileans who detested the priestly aristocracy.

12. It is understandable that from a distance, Gospel commentators interpret Jesus' activity as that of a prophet. The texts lend themselves well to such a verdict, much more so than one that would make Jesus a messiah, a title to which he had always shown the greatest reluctance. But it would be difficult to prove that he saw himself as a prophet. As a rule, it is the witnesses who bestow such a title on an individual. The person in question devotes all his energies to responding to the inner vision that compels him, and to suffering the consequences. In his opinion, the cause he defends is more important than his own person. In the case of Jesus, his life is only the advertisement, on the human scale, for what the kingdom of God will bring; as Meier puts it, "For Jesus, however, the revolution is the one that will be accomplished not by humans but by God Himself" *(Ibid.*, p. 92).

13. For example, see Jn. 6:15, for Galilee; Mk. 11:1-11, for a Jewish retranslation. On this popular vision of Jesus, read Horsley's conclusion in *Jesus and the Spiral of Violence*, pp. 318-326.

14. No doubt there is irony in the way Mark understood the sign; see T.E. Schmidt, "Mark 15:16-32, The Crucifixion Narrative and the

Roman Triumphal Procession," *NTS* 341\1 (1995). But at the historical level, because the Christians certainly did not invent this sign, the Roman spite for these indomitable Jews or Galileans is evident. See R.E. Brown, *The Death of the Messiah: From Gethsemane to the Grave: A Commentary on the Passion Narratives in the Four Gospels,* Vol. II (New York: Doubleday, 1993), pp. 962-968.

15. The theme is a large one. The concentration here is on the passages where the word "God" is used, mostly omitting synonyms and related concepts.

16. 8:33; 9:1,47; 10:9,14,15,18,23,24,25,27; 11:22; 12:14,17(x2),24, 26(x4),27,29,30,34; 13:19; 14:25; 15:34(x2),39,43. The use of the concepts of "Heaven" (11:30,31), "Father" (8:38; 11:25; 13:32; 14:36) or "Power" (14:62) to mean God, most often in a context of controversy or dispute, should be noted as well.

17. In 13:19, Jesus also speaks about God in reply to a question from the disciples about the time when the end would come and the sign that it was about to happen.

18. That the Risen Christ and Lord, in the dimension of God, had made the decision to found a Church to begin his mission of liberty and solidarity with the poor throughout the world is a matter of faith that does not have to be measured against the historical life of the man from Nazareth. This statement, far from separating Jesus from the Christ, affirms the opening of the initial project, which had been restricted to the limits of one people, to the whole of humanity.

NEW FEUDALISM, NEW SERFS

Mary Boyd

Mary Boyd is an adult educator and researcher. She worked for over twenty-one years as Director of Social Action, Diocese of Charlottetown, P.E.I. At present, she is Director of the Meckillop Centre for Social Justice. Her publications include From the Grass Roots *and* From Resistance to Transformation: Coalition Struggles in Canada, South Africa, the Philippines, Mexico *(Ottawa: Bonanza Press, 1996).*

My awareness of social justice is a life-long process which began when our grade six class was shown a movie on the life of St. Frances Cabrini, entitled "Too Small A World." Something in this woman's story triggered my interest that God calls us to social causes and awakened my consciousness to the wider world. Growing up in Antigonish, Nova Scotia and making friends with students from southern countries who came to study Father Moses Coady's philosophy; writing my B.A. thesis on the Black people of Nova Scotia; becoming active in the International Grail Movement and spending a year at a community college in Loveland, Ohio where I was exposed to the Civil Rights Movement; and participating in Martin Luther King's march from Selma to Montgomery, Alabama, all constituted one block of a process of awareness up to my early twenties.

The second block began with a six-and-a-half year stint in Nigeria and Ghana where I became aware that the distressing poverty experienced by people in impoverished countries is largely caused by economic, political and social structures orchestrated in the Western world. This was also the time of refreshing breakthroughs in Catholic social teaching, the theology of liberation and conscientization. Studies in Paris at the International Ecumenical Institute for the Development of Peoples (INODEP), based on Paulo Freire's "conscientization" methodology, gave me a more focused methodological approach, as did an M. A. in Sociology on applying Freire to Atlantic Canada. More than twenty-one years of service in the Diocese of Charlottetown as Director of Social Action enabled me to deepen my understanding of church social teaching, to research the root causes of poverty, develop education and action programmes and cooperate with initiatives of the Social Affairs Commission of the Canadian Conference of Catholic Bishops.

In 1989, a group of Third World theologians declared that "we are faced with a *kairos* moment." For them *kairos* is a moment of crisis that challenges, a moment of truth, a time for decision, a time for grace, a God-given opportunity for conversion and hope. Some of the theologians were from South Africa, which has indeed experienced a time of grace with the end of Apartheid. But for those who came from several other countries, the *kairos* moment was about much more than the sinful system of Apartheid. It was about the powers that rule our world, dividing Christians into those who uphold the present economic and political system and those who are victimized, even executed by it. They deliver their message in strong language:

> We wished to make it quite clear that those Christians who side with the imperialists, the oppressors and exploiters of people, are siding with the idolaters who worship money, power, privilege and pleasure. To misuse Christianity to defend oppression is heretical. And to persecute Christians who are oppressed or who side with the oppressed is apostasy—the abandonment of the Gospel of Jesus Christ.[1]

This anguished cry comes from people who see too much suffering and death. They lay bare the causes and extent of misery. But they also hold out hope for the world. They know that change can come if Christians and their institutions choose to practise the real meaning of the Gospels, that it is the poor—and not the powerful who oppress them—who are blessed. Their declaration wants the worship of "no Gods except the God who was in Jesus. I am Yahweh your God who brought you out of the land of Egypt, out of the house of slavery. You shall not have Gods except me" (Ex. 20:1-3).

Creeping Globalization

For the most part, we Christians in industrialized countries still live in a dream world. While we sleep through our daily routines of work, television and entertainment, we fail to recognize that the whole world is now ruled by the laws of the marketplace, nor have we analysed the powerful forces at work in our globalized world. All but a small minority are blind or indifferent to the way that globalization has crept up on us. While our sisters and brothers are increasingly overcome by neoliberal policies, we turn our heads, offer little solidarity and ignore the larger societal questions.

As we approach the new millennium, five million Canadians are trapped in poverty. The federal government, true to its neoliberal ideology, introduced fiscal restraints that cost close to a half-million jobs in two years. Women bear the brunt of those slash-and-burn measures. Policies built on this ideology keep the unemployment rate close to 10 per cent nationally and as high as 26 per cent in Cape Breton, Nova Scotia. Some other areas of the country, especially in Atlantic Canada, are not far behind. But this is apparently not enough punishment for the victims. Cuts to Unemployment Insurance reduced the number of people eligible to draw benefits from 87 per cent in 1990 to less than 40 per cent in 1997. At the same time as this was happening, the federal government handed Canadians the Canada Health and Social Transfer (CHST) which eliminated the Canada Assistance Plan (CAP) and robbed welfare recipients of rights such as protection against having to work for welfare. It also cut transfer payments to the provinces and changed the format of payment to block grants. These reduced revenues, which are not designated to any particular programme, guarantee increases in student tuition fees, cuts to sparse welfare payments, and erosion of health services as social programmes are played off, one against the other, at the provincial level. As neoliberal policies continue, the results are record bankruptcies with huge numbers of people losing their homes. As the rich get richer, the rest of us march towards feudalism and serfdom.

Instead of a huge public outcry against this trend, we often hear that everyone could have a job if not for laziness. These myths are planted by the powerful who benefit most from the system of corporate capitalism and its "profits-before-people" ideology—the direct opposite of Catholic social teaching, which places people first.

The recession of the early 1980s, contrived by Ronald Reagan and his corporate friends to break the power of labour unions, set the stage for an increase in poverty and powerlessness reminiscent of the "dirty thirties." The first Church response to this monetarism as it crept into Canada came in January, 1983. The Social Affairs Commission of the Canadian Conference of Catholic Bishops and the Commission's co-directors, Tony Clarke and Bernard Dufresne, critiqued the neoliberal belief that the "free market" is the engine of growth in the economy. No Church document to that date had laid bare the system so succinctly. The Church, through its bishops, took a stand against the corporate agenda and, by doing so, filled a leadership vacuum that existed throughout the country. In a ten-point programme, they took aim at the deepening moral crisis in our country and the loss of human dignity that befalls its victims.

Then came the Canada/US Free Trade Agreement which restricts Canada's power to act in the interests of it own citizens. Social programmes were attacked and downsized. As the globalization agenda advanced throughout the world, the gap between rich and poor kept increasing.

As corporatism accelerates its pace into the twenty-first century, islands of prosperity are becoming more identifiable, but so are the seas of misery that surround them. People are attacked, defeated and shut out of the economy. We don't even need imagination to visualize the wealthy living in their royal palaces reminiscent of the days of Pharaoh and Solomon.

Royal Households

On the eve of the twenty-first century, our world looks more and more feudal with its royal households of transnational empires. The lifestyles of their wealthy owners and Chief Executive Officers (CEOs) dwarf even Solomon's splendour. As they control more and more of the world's wealth, they can afford to plan a long-term future while the vast majority of people are left in poverty and powerlessness.

The royal household of corporatism assures its power through control over the media, technology and its ability to move around the world forcing people to "race to the bottom." Slave wages, the lowest possible taxes, the lowest possible environmental standards, and the worst possible working conditions for employees are but a few of the corporate demands.

Our elected politicians have opted to support this imperialism by trading their obligation to safeguard the common good for membership in the royal corporate households. They forget what they were mandated to do, and allow themselves instead to be simpletons for the corporations who reduce them to the state of rich and privileged hangers-on. The fallout for the people is enormous. Few are fighting back.

Canada and the South

The most poignant examples of the impact of globalization come from the poorer countries of the southern hemisphere where transnational corporations eye huge profits. They unscrupulously extract the livelihood of future generations for profit which they share less and less with people, including those in their home countries. For example, in Southeast Asian countries like the Philippines, restraints and burdens imposed by large-scale mining operations on inhabitants of mining communities are extensive, according to Vitoria Tauli Corpuz, Director of Tebtebba Foundation (Indigenous Peoples International Centre for Policy Research and Education).

Women bear the greatest burden because of their role and lower status in society. The feminine face of poverty is evident as they are robbed of their traditional lands and their economic role as producers of food. There is even a decrease of productivity in non-confiscated fields as wild foods are poisoned along with marine life and animals. As traditional lands disappear so do traditional values and customs, the key to sustaining community, tribal, clan, family solidarity and unity. Subsistence economies are forced to give way to cash or market-based economies controlled by forces beyond the grasp of the people. Women are robbed of social and economic power needed to protect themselves from further victimization. Erosion of traditional values is manifested through increased prostitution, incest, wife-swapping, infidelity, alcoholism, drug addiction and gambling.

The disappearance of traditional roles subjects women to increased tension, stress and even mental illness as they are pushed into the informal economy in order to survive. As their traditional role diminishes, they suffer serious consequences, which include an increase in domestic violence and even commodification of their persons.

Women are not the only ones affected. Once land is appropriated for mining purposes, there is massive displacement of people and destruction of agricultural lands. Environmental destruction is enormous as mountains are levelled and forests are stripped, causing erosion, siltation and desertification. Production of natural food is affected as soils and rivers are saturated with toxic chemicals used in the extraction and processing of mineral ores and the toxic mineral by-products of the mining process. Mining accidents (i.e., through acid mine drainage) are frequent due to the collapse of underground tunnels and bursting or overflowing of mine tailing dams, causing further pollution of lands, rivers and oceans. The result is decreased marine bio-diversity and the killing of plants, animals and even humans.

Mine workers experience serious health problems including skin diseases, respiratory diseases, like tuberculosis, silicosis, asbestosis, gastro-intestinal disease and cancer. Their families, communities and any people on the receiving end of mine toxins face similar health problems. Reproduction is affected through frequent miscarriages and malformed babies. Mental illness is on the increase, as are AIDS and other sexually transmitted diseases; all this can be traced back to the disruption of traditional community life.

Miners are subject to poor and high risk working conditions full of occupational hazards that cause accidents and life-long disabilities. Increased mechanization and automation results in high unemployment, under-employment and the accompanying undermining of unions. The original inhabitants of the land are the last to be hired and only for the most easily replaceable jobs. Child labour is a growing phenomenon.

At this point in time, there are thirty-five Canadian mining companies either in the Philippines or waiting for permits to take advantage of the Ramos government's new policy. This policy allows foreign companies 100 per cent ownership of their operations under the Medium-Term Philippine Development Plan, known as "Philippines 2000." This five-year development programme attempts to make the Philippines a major player in the globalization race in the hope that the country will achieve a dragon economy status by the year 2000.

Philippines 2000 opens the door to increased large-scale mining by transnational mining corporations from the United States, Canada, the United Kingdom and Australia. Loans to Asian governments from the World Bank (WB) and the International Monetary Fund (IMF) assist those corporations in a major way to build infrastructure for their mining operations (roads, energy sources, etc.). The IMF and the WB even give direct loans to the mining companies to help them to draw up their economic blueprints.

These are the same institutions that imposed Structural Adjustment Programmes (SAPs) on the Philippines and other countries in the name of debt reduction. The people of the Philippines, especially the impoverished, are still reeling from the effects of SAPs which led to tightening of government budgets with accompanying cuts to social programmes, especially health and education; reform of tax codes; the liberalization of agriculture to emphasize exports; easier entry of imported agricultural products; removal of subsidies; devaluation of currency; and privatization of state-owned corporations, including mining. All this was done to allow entry of foreign mining corporations that demand liberalization of investment codes, mining codes, and agrarian reform codes. Corpuz states that:

> The history of mining is a history of land appropriation, displacement of peoples from their lands, a history of environmental devastation, and further marginalization and oppression of people belonging to the lower economic sectors of society and of women. It is a perfect example of how nations and countries who are endowed with rich natural resources are still wallowing in poverty and oppression. [2]

To their credit, people are increasingly resistant to this corporate carnage. But the companies fight back through their bureaucratic and political allies by using increasing militarization and violations of human rights. Once the mineral deposits are depleted and the lands are devastated, often beyond rehabilitation, these corporations move on in search of new privileges and prey. The impact of their action on impoverished countries is horrendous and immoral.

The policies of the IMF and the WB are no longer confined to debt-ridden countries of the South. Canadian representatives to these institutions, like Marcel Masse, fed into the ideology behind SAPs, especially the neoliberal budget cutting that characterized the Mulroney years and the Chrétien years to date. They advocated that similar measures be taken in Canada and other Western countries. While the countries of the South are still much poorer than we are, there is a qualitative change in Canada as the same policies, driven by the same ideological forces, are applied by federal and provincial governments. Impoverishment is on the increase. More situations in this country bear striking similarities to the Third World. Another means used by the corporations and their political allies to promote corporate interests is the Asia Pacific Economic Co-operation Forum (APEC) which is composed of eighteen countries including Canada, USA, Mexico and Chile. Its slogan, "open regionalism," tells all. Although its stated intention is not to perform like a trade bloc, it will be a vehicle for the easier expansion of capital by removing restrictions on markets, foreign investment and trade. It will operate through a cycle of annual ministerial meetings which are secretive, allowing observer access to a few chosen and powerful business-oriented organizations.

The Multilateral Agreement on Investment (MAI) is the newest and boldest attempt to serve the expansionary goals and needs of capital, regardless of the cost to people. Led by the rich nations' club of the Organization for Economic Development and Co-operation (OECD), this agreement gives power to the rich. It also provides tools for corporations to sue governments in Canada and elsewhere, at municipal, provincial and national levels, for protecting the rights of their people in the face of further pillage by the corporations. The rights to provide or protect local jobs, to demand just wages, to assure union protection and to provide a tax base for social programmes are now regarded as unfair competition by the corporations which have the tools and power to sue.

An indicator of the extent to which the neoliberal ideology dominates our consciousness can be seen in Canada's determination to continue its leadership role in the globalization process. The obscene behaviour of the 1997 Team Canada visit to Manila, one of the most crowded cities in the world, is new to Canadians. As the Team Canada entourage, equipped with new and expensive cars, moved throughout the city, they didn't wait in traffic lines like the Filipino people. Some traffic lanes were closed off to the public for the convenience of the Chrétien entourage. Canadians watching the news at home were embarrassed by the ugly, raw symbol of power as the prime minister, federal ministers, premiers and business representatives sped through Manila at 90 kilometres an hour, flexing their globalized muscles in this impoverished and struggling country. Such displays, which used to be reserved for dictatorships, indicate that our values and decency are forsaken. We have supposedly arrived on the global scene and can be as dirty as any other player in the imperial empire. The golden calf of commercial business transactions is now a priority. Canada believes that it can't afford to be invisible. If this means trampling on the poor abroad as well as at home, so be it. Furthermore, as our social programmes are slashed at home, our Overseas Development Assistance (ODA) keeps dropping even more rapidly. It is now down to less than 0.3 per cent of our Gross Domestic Product (GDP). This, in spite of the United Nations Development Report statistics (1995) illustrating that the richest 20 per cent of individuals around the world have sixty-one times more wealth than the poorest 20 per cent. Many of the richest, as we know, live here in Canada.

Seeds of Hope

Drastic as this picture may seem, it is not a time to despair. Instead, we need to create alternatives. As the authors of *The Road to Damascus: Kairos and Conversion* tell us, the alliance between politicians and private enterprise must be broken. The CEOs and directors of the transnational corporations will not voluntarily abandon their global domination unless they undergo a dramatic conversion similar to that of St. Paul. But an informed, prophetic people standing in opposition and armed with alternatives, like our own media, and a liberating system of education to denounce corporatism and announce the new alternatives, would kick-start a momentum and energize the creativity needed to transform this situation.

Where is the Church in relation to the royal household? Sadly, its members from the top down are on both sides. There are a number of Christians who enjoy very high positions in that household. Other members of our congregations are already reduced to serfdom. Many are unemployed or working in non-unionized jobs for wages that are below the poverty line and without the protection of adequate social benefits; many are caught in the race to the bottom, with decreasing wages in the face of increased neoliberal induced privatization and its accompanying "user pay" policies for such basic rights as health, education and other essentials. Women and single mothers are especially victimized and the removal of the Canada Assistance Plan as part of the cold-blooded passage of the Canadian Health and Services Transfer has a brutal effect.

Although there exists in this country a number of coalitions that dare to be vocal against corporatism, few are led by the Churches and Church participation is sparse compared to the 1970s and 1980s. Coalitions, institutes and organizations, such as the Alternative Federal Budget (AFB), are doing tremendous work in confronting societal numbness with facts, analysis and alternatives. The media often ignores them and sometimes even ridicules them but they plod on and the facts are there for anyone to see.

The process of creating alternatives to corporatism needs to be democratic in the truest sense. It is not enough that a few "experts" research the facts and figures and do the social analysis. Those most oppressed must break the silence and become more vocal. People of faith have a very powerful weapon in the preferential option for the poor. Properly understood, it could be our most powerful tool. We cannot analyse what is happening to our society without coming face to face with the way neoliberalism is impoverishing people. There are many ways to illustrate this, including the fact that the world's 358 billionaires own as much of the world's revenue ($760 billion US) as the 2.5 billion lowest income persons.

People in this country still care about other people; however, they accept the extreme inequalities by promoting Food Banks that take away what little dignity people have left. Such organized caring portrays good intentions, compassion and a desire to practise the Golden Rule. However, projects such as Food Banks are also co-opted by the imperial powers. They tend to delay the re-building of a society where all people have an opportunity to feed and clothe themselves.

Food Bank collections are rampant in many communities but they do not foster the very important concept of liberating the victims. To aim at overcoming poverty alone without attempting to transform structures constitutes only a first reading of the reality. While it is important to feed the hungry, we need to ask: why they are impoverished in the first place? If the amount of resources and energy that goes into Food Banks and soup kitchens could be turned into pressure on policy makers, and production and distribution of materials for educational purposes, our co-opted federal and provincial governments wouldn't be able to proceed with their war against those they continue to trap in poverty.

There are ways to involve people that keep them focused on the "race," as St. Paul would say, energizing the tired and restoring hope to those who are discouraged. The comfortable give up first. In their idolatry of money, they internalize the myths that scapegoat the impoverished.

The Relevance of Paulo Freire

The conscientizing methodology of Brazilian educator Paulo Freire is still one of the most effective means to energize and mobilize people for social justice. Born in Brazil, he already had a handle on the overpowering presence of the corporate world in the 1970s and 1980s.

Freire was a consistent believer in the bottom up approach to transformation. People must be given the possibility to enlighten themselves. Once they see themselves and the social situation for what it is, they themselves will decide to alter the conditions they find oppressive. These social actors/actresses challenge the existing system by developing their own way of action suited to their particular situation.

Our theology and faith response, Freire believed, should follow a sociology that assumes "the problem of dependence and liberation as the basic structure of analysis." [3] This replaces "the liberal meaning of liberty with the revolutionary meaning of liberation." [4] Once theology rearranges its categories and tools according to this new perspective, it discovers a new direction for its own reflection. The new sociological categories provide the scientific structure necessary to grasp, analyse and carry forward a phenomenon for which the theologian previously had no categories.

The conscientization method begins with action groups who want to bring about changes starting from their local community. The specialists play only a support role. The people themselves acquire the tools to research, analyse and do critical education for change. Participants start with their own "hot issues," which are stronger than felt needs. They make connections from the micro level to the macro level. They progress to the regional, national and international levels in a dialectical process of action/reflection which leads them to see the contradictions in society. Then, they mobilize in a democratic fashion.

The central focus of Freire's methodology is transformative action. He believes in the unity of theory and action. "If I think dialectically, I know that the real source of change is action but every action implies a theory. There is no dichotomy between theory and practice. There is unity." [5] It is essential that groups arrive at the problem of power. Those who feel their oppression most acutely will opt first for conscientization and for the transformation of structures in a relatively short time span.

Freire's process of conscientization is political education in its broadest sense. It is a process of social justice developing critical awareness and asking, "Where are we and in which time?" It starts with the concrete situations of the people. Its emphasis is collective action which demands that the coordinators live close to the people. Participants must be open to share experiences in order to build understanding among groups of how each one is oppressed, and to recognize what each has in common. This way they build solidarity.

Freire refers to the starting point as "the first reading of reality" or the "naive" level. The person submits to social change without understanding the real causes of problems and, therefore, grasps only the most immediate and external causes. There is a tendency to place too much value on the past, to accept mythical explanations, to debate. As they progress in the process, they transfer to a critical awareness that tackles problems, is open to new ideas, uses facts to find the real causes, lets go of magical explanations and is open to dialogue. The conscientized person throws off or rejects an internal oppressive consciousness, becomes less dependent, is no longer fearful and is freer. This person is able to commit to transformation and to the building of a new society.

Conscientization is not something that happens once and then remains forever with the person. It requires a permanent effort of action/reflection to keep up the struggle against dependence and domination. The person who becomes conscientized makes a clear option for and with the oppressed but also for his/her own liberation in the same society. The option is ethical and lends itself very well to faith-based groups who promote justice. It requires that the participants think politically and economically in today's corporate world. From a naive comprehension of reality, the person passes to a critical phase of probing the ambience of the reality which needs to be analysed, and makes a historical commitment or critical insertion into that history, including action with others. The acts of denouncing the old oppressive structure and announcing the new one will help people to know the dehumanizing structure in order to denounce it. Conscientization leads to alternatives which the people themselves propose.

In his pilot project, Freire enabled three hundred workers in the town of Angicas, Northern Rio Grande, Brazil, to become literate in forty-five days. In addition to being able to read and write, they were also politically literate. Later, as Director of a National Literacy Programme for the whole of Brazil, he planned a total of 20,000 circles of culture, each capable of educating thirty students in two months. His goal was to have 22 million people literate in the space of a few months. His programme, however, met severe opposition from the top. In Freire's case, it was overtaken by a *coup d'état* staged among other things against the Goulart government's "sympathy with experimenters on the left." Freire was arrested, jailed for seventy days and exiled. In Chile, where he worked on an Agrarian Reform project, he cut the illiteracy rate to five per cent in six years.

Freire divides education into Banking and Liberating Education. The Banking system which influences most of today's education, domesticates people, making them dependent. It accounts for much of the numbness and alienation in our society.

In 1970, Freire wrote that the oppressors need to keep the people passive. Therefore, they deposit myths in the media and educational system that are indispensable to preserving the status quo. These myths are still around:

> The myth that the oppressive order is a free society; the myth that all men [people] are free to work where they wish; that if they don't like their boss they can leave and look for another job; the myth that this order respects human rights and is therefore worthy of esteem; the myth that anyone who is industrious can be an entrepreneur; the myth of equality of all people, when the question: "Do you know who you're talking to?" is still current among us; the myth of the heroism of the oppressor classes as defenders of "western Christian civilization" against "materialist barbarism"; the myth of the charity and generosity of the elites when what they really do as a class is foster selective "good deeds," the myth of private property as fundamental to personal human development (so long as the oppressors are the only true human beings); the myth of the industriousness of the oppressors and the laziness and dishonesty of the oppressed as well as the myth of the natural inferiority of the latter and the superiority of the former. [6]

In Tony Clarke's days (1970s and 1980s) as Co-Director of the Social Affairs Commission of the Canadian Conference of Catholic Bishops (CCCB), the goal of building a broad social movement initially had a fair amount of support from church leaders. Six steps resembling Freire's methodology were outlined in the Canadian Conference of Catholic Bishops' 1976 Labour Day Message, *From the Words to Actions*: 1. Rediscover our prophetic faith; 2. Participate in people's struggles—listening to their problems, sharing in their struggles and listening to them in order to learn the various elements including the structural causes of human suffering and what can be done; 3. Develop a social analysis which is carried out whenever possible with the victims. (This requires several other sub-steps.) 4. Make moral judgements which denounce the injustice and announce the new society of justice. The Church's social teaching upholds the basic rights of people and the obligation of governments as caretakers of the common good to play their role by developing public policies which provide for basic needs. 5. Propose alternative directions. It is not enough to denounce. The alternatives, however, must be worked out with the participation of the people. 6. Take political action.

The bishops often said in those days, "Social justice is the goal . . . political action is the means." They also said many times in the 1970s and 1980s that we stand in the tradition of the prophets and Jesus Christ. One of the documents produced before the Pastoral letter *Justice in the World* (1971) was *Education for Justice,* which was influenced by the theory and methodology of Paulo Freire. It spells out a very exciting educational process. Unfortunately, like most of our social teaching, it is "one of our best kept secrets."

The Third World has been the bearer of some of the greatest and most recent signs of hope. Latin America gave us the theology of liberation and Paulo Freire's conscientization process. Southern Africa, particularly Zimbabwe, Mozambique, Angola, Namibia and South Africa, all overthrew the chains of colonialism. South African Blacks, after so many years of suffering under the system of Apartheid, finally triumphed—signs of victory and hope—and the Churches played a very important role.

The long hard battle to overthrow Apartheid had many phases and involved many actors—trade unions, women's groups, youth, churches, social movements, the African National Congress, Nelson Mandela and others in prison, international support and uprisings and various campaigns. David Abrahams, a South African authority on coalitions, participated in that struggle. He points to the contribution made by the "civics." These community-based resident's structures were formed mostly around struggles for better housing, but also around such specific struggles or concrete issues as increases in transportation costs and parent-student committees in support of school boycotts. At first, the civics were criticized as merely reformers. But they understood the relation between their concrete struggles and the bigger struggle against oppression and exploitation. They understood that they were "an integral part of the over-all national struggle." [7] The civics were the predominant organization in working-class areas. Their great contribution was putting the capacity for social change in the hands of ordinary people. Their struggles restored mobilization and mass organization to the forefront of the popular movement's tactics and strategies. Their emphasis on membership and developing the capacity of members was in line with the understanding that the revolutionary overthrow of Apartheid had to be a process in which the ordinary people participated.

The most powerful mark of the South African struggle was that participants never lost sight of the main goal of dismantling the oppressive Apartheid regime. All of the groups, from the civics to women, youth, churches, unions and the alternative party inspired by Nelson Mandela, kept that goal clearly in mind. The broader movement against Apartheid not only composed a *Freedom Charter*, but also had member groups borrow its lines as slogans which they put before the people at rallies, on posters and in publications.

In Canada, we have the potential to create change by mobilizing around issues that are linked with the greater challenge of transformation. As corporations push for privatization and control through the North American Free Trade Agreement and the Multilateral Agreement on Investment, they (and not the government) are calling the tune, while not even paying the piper. We are living in what Tony Clarke calls "the Corporate Security State." [8] From that stance, the federal government is a strong promoter of the MAI, the most powerful pro-corporate agreement yet. Led by the United States and backed by the other (twenty-eight) member countries of the OECD, it is relentless in its pursuit of "a profitable and predictable climate for transnational investment." [9]

Another hot issue is the safeguarding of our universal system of medicare in the midst of corporate attempts to destroy its universality by opening the door to a US style of privatized health care. The privatization threat to our public system uncovers one of the most heartless and shameful aspects of corporatism, that is, the making of profit from illness. Greedy US-based multinational for-profit health corporations, who are already making a killing off sick people in the US, are expanding to Canada and other countries. Critical minds in health care in the United States tell us, "Don't let these companies do this to you." The multinational drug companies have already gained twenty years of exclusive patent protection in this country for their new drugs. Brian Mulroney's Bill C-91 and NAFTA paved the way for this stranglehold on drugs by the US corporations.

Even NAFTA's twenty-year protection of patents could be overturned. The Canadian Health Coalition (CHC) mobilized thousands of Canadians in the spring of 1997 when Bill C-91 came up for review. The groups broadened the parameters of the review, challenging increasing corporate control of our health care by flooding the committee hearings with solid facts. Not only did they put a human and compassionate face on health care, they got in the face of both government and the corporations and called for alternatives to expensive drugs that now constitute the fastest growing part of health care. Their convincing arguments underlined the need for a national Pharmacare plan and the de-commodification of medically necessary drugs. The centre-piece of their campaign, a public education effort, produced some very valuable resource materials, including a twenty-page resource, *A Prescription for Plunder*, that uncovered the multi-billion dollar subsidy foreign drug companies receive in Canada. [10]

On Prince Edward Island, the former Social Action Commission of the Diocese of Charlottetown organized a research/action project based on Paulo Freire's conscientization methods. Seven local groups who either had below poverty-line incomes, or who were in solidarity with them, participated between 1982 and 1987. A publication entitled *From the Grass Roots* describes the stories of six of the participating groups and the methodology they used. The project, which generated tremendous energy for change and a critical analysis of neoliberal trends, continues to mobilize those who participated. This type of project requires a huge investment of time and should be backed by adequate resources for staff and materials. Its impact was evident in successful struggles around land and fisheries questions, especially Irish moss, a seaweed which grows offshore in parts of the Maritimes. It also proved to be a tremendous human development resource and a vehicle to reach the wider church constituency with educational programmes. Most of all, it instilled confidence in the participants who "found their own word" and remain effective leaders to this day. The heightened critical awareness and educational aspect of the project carried over into the 1988 "free trade" election. Politicians supporting the Free Trade Agreement (FTA) had no chance as various groups from the then Pro-Canada Network to Irish moss harvesters took the agreement to task.

The Alternative Federal Budget (AFB), produced by CHOICES, a Winnipeg-based social action group, and the Canadian Centre for Policy Alternatives, was released for the third year in a row. It is a made-in-Canada example of the kind of alternative that, with the participation of people, can help turn things around. It points out that the political and economic scene is not as hopeless as we are led to believe. The Minister of Finance and the Bank of Canada have choices. Thanks to the AFB, people can become literate about the finances of our country and how they are handled.

Working for Transformation at a Global Level

It goes without saying that change is more difficult to achieve on the global level. John Dillon of the Ecumenical Coalition on Economic Justice (ECEJ) writes in *Turning the Tide, Confronting the Money Traders* that, "Taken together, these phenomena—globalization, technological change, the abandonment of the local market, and increasing speculation—constitute a new stage of capitalism." [11] Finance has become the dominant force shaping peoples' lives. Dillon makes many suggestions to correct this problem including transforming the way we do economics. He believes that it is possible to establish a Tobin tax of .025 per cent on all foreign exchange transactions. It would be a means to renegotiate the destructive international financial system and curb short-term speculation. The tax alone would realize about $302 billion US per year that could be put towards alleviating the debts of the poorer countries ($1.29 trillion) and thus reducing one of the main reasons for their impoverishment. [12] A campaign mounted on a global level is one option which ECEJ is exploring as a means to get the tax implemented.

Is it a sign of hope that a few of the world's richest people are finally seeing through corporatism? One of these is George Soros, a billionaire of Hungarian ancestry, who is now publicly denouncing this system. He wrote in the February 1997 *Atlantic Monthly:*

> Although I have made a fortune in the financial markets, I fear that . . . the spread of market values into all areas of life is endangering our open and democratic society. The main enemy of the open society, I believe, is no longer the communist but the capitalist threat. [13]

Many of our church social teachings over the years have pointed out the unregulated "free market" as the root cause of poverty and injustice in our world. Does a billionaire pack more punch and moral authority when he addresses the limitations of capitalism? Hopefully not.

Soros has awakened to the threat of growing individualism at the expense of co-operation as people become unsure of what they stand for and rely more and more on money as their criterion of value. The "free market" mentality which sees government intervention as the enemy prevents both income and wealth distribution. According to Gwynne Dyer, for Soros, "Worshipping the free market is primitive nature worship, like adoring a sacred mountain or lightening." [14] The billionaire also states that blind faith in the open market is bad economics. Big business and government tell us another story, that of Adam Smith's theory that a "hidden hand" guides the economy. Although this is no longer the context today, we are being brainwashed by corporate interests into thinking that the unregulated market is the only economic system and the most moral one. If Soros and a handful of colleagues can recognize the difference, so can others.

John Saul writes in *The Unconscious Civilization* that Adam Smith's reference to the invisible hand is directed to the local and not the global market. According to Saul, "Smith saw the self-balancing market in a simple and limited circumstance where the options would be obvious to everyone." [15] Furthermore, Smith believed that growth and prosperity would come by paying high wages, not by forcing workers to price themselves into a low-paying job, as is the experience of today's workers.

The proponents of the globalized free market tell us that our own interests are not to be found within the boundaries of our own country but in the globalized economy. According to them, the nation state is obsolete. This is a clever trick to deprive citizens of any power to create change through their governments. Under the MAI and other expressions of neoliberalism, governments would no longer have power to fight for social justice for the people. Instead, they would be downsized and their responsibilities for the most part given over to the private sector. Neoliberalism is about *laisser-faire* economics where the state is not supposed to enter, except to open the door for proponents of neoliberalism to realize their goals.

John Saul describes us as "a civilization tightly held at this moment in the embrace of a dominant ideology: corporatism." [16] By accepting corporatism we "deny or undermine the legitimacy of the individual as citizen in a democracy." [17] This leads us to excessive self-interest and denial of the public good. "The overall effects on the individual are passivity and conformity in those areas which matter and non-conformity in those which don't." [18] Saul traces the problem to a mentality which holds that democracy was born of economics, beginning with the Industrial Revolution.

Walter Brueggemann, a biblical scholar, addresses the Church in a similar way. He believes that the "contemporary American church is so largely enculturated to the American ethos of consumerism that it has little power to believe or act." [19] This is true of the Church in most societies. We suffer from amnesia rather than rooting ourselves in energizing memories. As a result of our amnesia, "every form of serious authority for faith is in question, and we live unauthorized lives of faith and practice unauthorized memories." [20] He goes on to state that "the church has no business more pressing than the reappropriation of its memory in its full power and authenticity." [21]

Both Saul and Brueggemann point out the importance of language. Saul states that language has been divided into two parts—public language and corporatist language. The latter is characterized by narrowness and self-interest. Brueggemann argues that we need to develop a new language. We need a hope-filled language of amazement and grief to cut through despair and numbness. Jeremiah is the prophet who tries to penetrate the numbness, while Isaiah deals with despair.

Saul and Brueggemann converge in their view that we have been rendered unconscious or numb by the power structure which upholds the system of domination by the few. They both shed light on the obstacles this society presents to transformation towards a society of justice. Saul states, "certainly corporatism is creating a conformist society. It is a modern form of feudalism with none of the advantages of the early urban guild system, where obligation, responsibility and standards played a role." [22]

Brueggemann says similar things about the behaviour of the royal household in the time of Moses' radical social movement to counteract the royal power asserted from above. The royal consciousness precludes hope by stopping serious speech and nullifying the symbols of hope that reveal what is beyond royal administration. Moses is the prophet who evokes in Israel an alternative consciousness:

> Empires live by numbness. Empires, in their militarism, expect numbness about the human cost of war. Corporate economies expect blindness to the cost in terms of poverty and exploitation. Governments and societies of domination go to great lengths to keep the numbness intact. [23]

Israel drew strength and energy from inside its own experience and confession of faith, not from external factors. Moses dismantles the politics of oppression and exploitation by countering it with a politics of justice and compassion. In Brueggemann's words, "It is the marvel of prophetic faith that both imperial religion and imperial politics could be broken." [24] Yahweh is the genuine alternative who makes possible and requires an alternative theology and an alternative sociology. Grieving is an important part of liberation. Israel pleads in Exodus 2:23-25:

> And the people of Israel groaned under their bondage, and cried out for help, and their cry under bondage came up to God. And God heard their groaning, and God remembered the covenant. . . . And God saw the people of Israel, and God knew their condition.

Exodus is the primal scream against the empire that pretends that things are all right; this scream permits the beginning of history. Israel does not voice resignation, but instead expresses a militant sense of being wronged, with the powerful expectation that it will be heard and answered. This is the beginning of criticism. See Exodus 3:7-10.

In Egypt, the people's cry dismantles helplessness and Yahweh brings the empire to an end. This is not a comfortable, domesticated God who is well-fed by the dominators. This God takes sides. Moses has to dismantle the consciousness that undergirded and made such a regime possible in order to bring forth the new reality.

In his own time, Jesus penetrates the numbness. His compassion is the first step in making visible the abnormality that had become business as usual. Thus, compassion is criticism of the system, forces, and ideologies that produce the hurt. Brueggemann says that "If the church is to be faithful it must be formed and ordered from the inside of its experience and confession and not by borrowing from sources external to its own life." [25]

The February 1997 publication of the Canadian Union of Public Employees (CUPE), *Organize*, points out that for the past fifteen years or more big business has demanded the "reinvention" of government to suit the needs of Canada's largest corporations. Out of thirty countries Canada places twenty-second in the share of total market income. Canada is now at the bottom 20 per cent of households by giving only 5.7 per cent.

This country has jumped whole hog into neoliberalism by cutting back more drastically and quicker than any other industrialized country. As CUPE observes:

> For those who like to believe that Canada's "safety net" is superior to that of the US, the right wing Fraser Institute claims (arguing for further cuts!) that many US states have more generous benefits. BC places 16th in North America, Nova Scotia 30th, Quebec 38th, Alberta 39th, Manitoba 44th and Saskatchewan, 53rd. New Brunswick is the worst at 56th (out of 62 jurisdictions). [26]

The *kairos* document makes a problem of the way Christians are divided by class biases. We ignore or choose to remain ignorant of our social teaching based on our Judaeo-Christian tradition. We are consumers in the same way that others in society are consumers, including our participation in the destruction of mother earth and her creatures. In 1992, the United Nations Conference on the Environment held in Rio de Janeiro estimated that it would take 1.25 billion dollars per year to clean up the environment. While this goal is within our reach, we continue to remain aliens to God's plan and our call to be co-creators, instilling a new set of values of compassion, caring and equality, and building an agenda out of those values.

Women like Vitoria Corpuz call for unity and for close ties with groups at local, national and international levels to exert pressure on governments not to continue to sell people out to the transnationals and the World Trade Organization. She recognizes that people in the industrialized countries are also victimized by corporatism and neoliberal governments that slash and burn on a regular basis. From the Philippines, she sees the struggle against the mining corporations as a way to fight neoliberalism. She knows that one country can't do it alone.

Solidarity, that little known and even less practised aspect of faith, is a key component of change. We need to recapture it and replace its present hollowness by alternatives such as an economics and politics of solidarity.

As the end of the millennium approaches, the Church has declared a Jubilee year based on Leviticus 25 and the actions of Jesus. If we took this important event seriously, it would serve to ground us once again in solidarity and enable us to advance the task of creating strategic plans and new tools to uncover the corporate forces at work all around us. We need to replace the death-causing "corporate security state" and its top-down political structures that promote an elitist democracy. Creativity is essential for short and long term planning. The world is showing too many signs of strain from the impact of the corporate model. Industrial pollution causes an estimated three-quarters of the world's deaths each year. In approximately one-fifth of the countries of the world, war causes record numbers of refugees. Violence is also on the increase and culture is becoming more homogenized to the Western model.

As Christians, we are mandated to work for the common good, to assure that the community's basic needs are cared for. We are to work for all the conditions of life that assure people's growth and fulfilment. Politicians mandated to do this have failed miserably.

They are elected to care for societal needs and not to support divide-and-conquer tactics against helpless individuals. Their performance indicates the need for a transformed model of politics aligned not with the royal household, but with a citizen's agenda worked out in a democratic fashion and for the good of all.

Although it sometimes looks as if God sides with the rich and powerful because they succeed so well in life, we need only remember that God wished the freedom of the Israelites. Therefore, the days of Pharaoh were numbered. Jesus intended the church to be the nourisher of the Reign of God. We urgently need to reactivate that intention. We can trade the fatigue, the discouragement, the fear and feeling of powerlessness for the energy and creativity that is necessary to transform our world. To abandon that goal would be to forget Yahweh's deeds, the anguish of the prophets, and Jesus' ultimate triumph over death. Memories are our most powerful instruments. They lead us to a deeper understanding of God's plan and mighty deeds, to restoration of the values we need for a transformative agenda.

The thrust of the Jubilee Year will not be outdated in the year 2000. It is a continuation of the biblical themes of justice found in of both the Old and New Testaments. It is timely. Its emphasis on justice can help us to revisit and rediscover our history. It can help us to critique the present state of our world and mourn over what is happening in a hopeful way, knowing that there are alternatives. Maybe we can glimpse the Creator at work and marvel enough at that creativity to let it be cultivated, to let it take hold once again as the means to create a life-giving society. It won't be easy, but we have dramatic examples to strengthen us, in particular the Incarnation. We also gain strength from the most subversive of all of God's activities, Jesus' death and resurrection.

NOTES

1. Third Word Christians from El Salvador, Guatemala, Korea, Namibia, Nicaragua, Philippines, and South Africa, *The Road to Damascus: Kairos and Conversion* (Washington, DC: Centre of Concern, 1989), p. 27.

2. Vitoria Tauli Corpuz, Presentation to Women's Alternative Workshop on APEC, Manila, Tebtebba Foundation, November, 1996.

3. Paulo Freire, quoted by Jose Miguez Bonino, *Doing Theology in a Revolutionary Situation* (Fortress Press, 1969), p. 69.

4. *Ibid.*

5. Paulo Freire, Conscientization Workshop sponsored by the National Council of Churches (Stony Point, New York, 1973).

6. Paulo Freire, *Pedagogy of the Oppressed* (New York, NY: Herder and Herder, 1970), p. 135.

7. David Abrahams, "South Africa: Social Movement Coalitionist and the Struggle for Democracy," in *From Resistance to Transformation* (Ottawa: Canada-Philippines Human Resource Development Program, 1996).

8. Tony Clarke, *Catholic New Times,* Vol. 21, No. 11, 1997, p. 8. See also, Tony Clarke, *Silent Coup* (Toronto: Lorimer Press, 1997).

9. *Ibid.*

10. Canadian Health Coalition, *Medicare Monitor* (Ottawa), Summer, 1997.

11. John Dillon, *Turning the Tide, Confronting the Money Traders* (Toronto: Ecumenical Coalition for Economic Justice and Canadian Centre for Policy Alternatives, 1997), p. 1.

12. *Ibid.*, pp. 98-99.

13. George Soros, quoted in *The Atlantic Monthly,* February 1997.

14. Gwynne Dyer, *Guardian*, February 1997.

15. John Ralston Saul, *The Unconscious Civilization* (Toronto: Anansi Press, 1996), p. 141.

16. *Ibid.* p. 2.

17. *Ibid.*

18. *Ibid.*

19. Walter Brueggemann, *The Prophetic Imagination* (Fortress Press, 1978), p. 11.

20. *Ibid.*, p. 12.

21. *Ibid.*

22. John Ralston Saul, *op. cit.,* p. 90.

23. Walter Brueggemann, *op. cit.,* pp. 85-86.

24. *Ibid.*, p. 17.

25. *Ibid.*, p. 15.

26. Canadian Union of Public Employees, *Organize*, Ottawa (Feb. 1997).

THE TIME OF DISCERNMENT

Guy Paiement, sj

Guy Paiement received his PhD in Theology at the Institut catholique de Paris. At present, he is Research and Development Agent at the Centre Saint-Pierre *in Montreal and member of the editing staff of the* Relations *review. His most recent publications are* L'économie et son arrière-pays *(Fides, 1997) and* Pour faire le changement. Guide d'analyse sociale, second edition *(Novalis, 1991).*

I was eight or nine years old that winter. My father was unemployed and we no longer had money to buy coal or firewood. As the eldest of four children, it was my job to make the rounds of the alleys and collect discarded cardboard or newspapers. Afterwards, my sister and I would roll them into logs for the stove. On that particular day, I had already found a big armful of newspapers when suddenly I felt a muted anger welling up inside me. Back home, I screamed at my mother that this didn't make any sense, that I wouldn't go back to that alley again, that we would have to find some other way! I still remember how I remained the entire day in that state of anger, deaf to all the explanations that my mother tried to offer.

Later on, I attempted to understand what had taken place within me. Clearly, I had said NO to all that seemed to me to be unacceptable, unjust, fundamentally unjust. For years, I tried to discover what it was that I had said NO to, and why. As I considered my friends and neighbours, I noticed that some of them had said NO to similar situations. Others had not. I felt close to those who were on the side of the refusal.

Today, I am discovering that much of what I have studied, whether in social sciences or theology, has left me with a deeper understanding of this NO and that, in a way, it had provided a "foundation." I continue to feel like a brother to all those who, in our society and elsewhere, are likely to say NO to an injustice, to say NO to what appears fundamentaly unacceptable to them. For I know that such a NO opens a new path to explore and that an entire life even is too short to define little by little, to what, to Whom, we have said YES, a YES that escapes us, and yet attracts us.

Once upon a Time

All the Jesuit novices were assembled in the lecture hall. At the scheduled time, a member of the Committee for the Jesuit University introduced himself and began to explain the Committee's conclusions. Montreal needed a second Francophone university and the Jesuits had the colleges, manpower and the library resources to take this new institution in hand. Consequently, we were to seriously prepare ourselves both spiritually and academically to undertake this great project. We could bring to the project a decisive orientation consistent with our search for the greater glory of God that would certainly allow us to be a party to the new, effervescent Quebec. At question time, I was among those who had raised certain questions as to the place of the economically less favoured in such a project. We were told that scholarships would, of course, be available for some of the more destitute students. Other colleagues, already picturing themselves in the classroom, were requesting some indication of the disciplines which should receive preference. I left the room with a heavy heart. Something was not right I felt, but it needed clarification.

During the days that followed, there was a great deal of discussion and a number of us felt the same uneasiness. If a second university was necessary, did it have to be run by the Jesuits? Should we, as a social entity, continue the Church's hold on the field of education? Had the time not come to leave the terrain to others and to work more closely with those who would never be able to afford a university education? I remember that such questions were quickly swept aside, for the committee—we were reminded—included several experts who had studied every aspect of the situation.

Our uneasiness, however, was borne out, so to speak, a few years later when a strong opposition movement forced the government to refuse the Jesuits' offer. Furthermore, the new university was characterized as one intended for the masses and would seek to accommodate all adults wishing to return to university, regardless of their economic situation.

Did this shared sensitivity derive solely from the fact that we belonged to a new generation, more hesitant than our forefathers about the hold of religion on public institutions? Probably not, for the interests of various groups were also at stake. Some professors wanted power and were undoubtedly using the banner of secularism to take it. Conversely, it was very difficult to avoid seeing this same taste for power in certain Jesuits, drawn from their lengthy training in the best modern disciplines. In spite of everything, a change of consciousness was becoming apparent and we were witnessing it. But then, why did our predecessors not perceive this change taking place around them when they made their annual retreat? If the Spirit is at work and calling us, why had such important currents not been noticed and deciphered? Were we to be satisfied with finding a personal way to be faithful to the Gospel, as if the social milieu, political interests, the influence of the economy, did not weigh in the balance? These questions did not disappear. They lived in me. They directed my research and my experience of God as well.

On the Forehead and on the Hand

Years later, when I reread the Book of Revelation, I discovered that from the first century, my ancestors in faith, by the very fact of belonging to a well-defined and determining society, had become aware of this ambiguity in which we live. This memory from my youth and the ancient book thus strike me as a basic and unavoidable trail for reflection on our society and the space the economy occupies in that society.

For the Christians of the first century, a tiny minority lost in the Roman empire, being different must have been difficult. Nothing distinguished them from their neighbours, neither clothing, housing, nor work. The vast majority of Christians did not belong to the more influential or wealthier classes. This had not prevented them from distancing themselves interiorly from the pervading morality and going quietly about their business. No doubt they met occasionally, at the home of someone who had a larger house. Neighbours might have felt slighted. What could they be plotting, these people with such diverse occupations, often speaking foreign languages? But still, there was nothing much to make a fuss about.

These communities, however, if the author of the Book of Revelation is to be believed, were well ahead of their time. Admittedly more or less consistent in their faith, they were nonetheless aware of their ambiguity. In Chapter 13, the author reminds them that imperial propaganda has left its mark on everyone: "It compelled everyone—small and great alike, rich and poor, slave and citizen—to be branded on the right hand or on the forehead, and made it illegal for anyone to buy or sell anything unless he had been branded " (Rv. 13:16-17). Slaves were branded, as we brand cattle in our day. Therefore all are branded here, slaves more or less of the Empire and its legitimization. Each one is branded on the forehead, i.e., in a way of thinking, criteria, standards, a way of understanding desires and responding to them. Each one is also branded on the right hand, the one that is used for swearing a solemn oath, that supports authority and the system, that works as well, and contributes to maintaining the empire. The economy is at the service of the empire and no one can do business in it without accepting its laws. In this society, social groups take second place, for whether one is freeman or slave, all are programmed by the official method of understanding imperial power and supporting it. The dominant ideology occupies the entire symbolic field and has appropriated minds, if not hearts.

The Return of Fatalism

Why does the recalling of a bygone empire awaken so many echoes in us, the readers of today? How can we explain this complicity, save by the fact that a number of us realize how much we too are marked, programmed nowadays, by a society in which the economy appears to be all-pervasive?

Since the fall of the governments in Eastern Europe, events unfold as if some capitalist ideology had taken possession of our entire mental and symbolic space. The market-based economy seems to be the only reference. It tends, moreover, to corrode society more and more, so much so that everything—a bar of soap, an organ, a public service, an academic—appears to have a price. By the same token, propagandists of every stripe tell us that such market generalization will intensify, for we have entered the era of the globalization of trade. Boundaries and controls obviously lag behind in the face of such relentless pressure, but it is only a question of time! A growing number of those in power are discovering the good news and taking the necessary steps to adapt. Some even rush to transform themselves into travelling salesmen in order to pave the way for business.

In reflecting on the meaning of Rv. 13:16-17, we come face-to-face with the inescapable competitiveness of our era. The world has become a huge Monopoly game and woe betide the losers. We must make every effort to be counted among the players, and especially the winning players. It is essential to adjust continuously to the changes taking place. The permanent job is no more. Acquired experience is obsolete. The state, with its far-reaching tentacles, which endeavours to regulate and manage everything, is especially out of date. For that matter, are the bankers not doing governments a favour by reminding them of their debts and demanding more discipline and austerity from them and, consequently, more cuts in all these services that have made citizens dependent and querulous?

Those who try to erase the marks on their foreheads and their hands should not play the innocent. How many, in fact, have savings in an investment fund or a trust? How many wonder where their money is invested? Is it in a loan to a municipality? Or in a real-estate consortium that turns away those on low incomes? Perhaps it is in a factory making anti-personnel mines? How many of them object to their brokers seeking the highest short-term yields, even when doing so means investing outside the country? Obviously, there will be less money left over to revive a business here, but that is the law of the market! Each one benefits, or at least is expecting to receive benefits. From now on, each one will be a part of that great collective known as "consumers" and will wield power! This "annuitant economy" thus includes increasing numbers of people. It has a profound influence on the "clients" that we have become, and many Christians are a part of it. Even those with little money have entered into the whirlwind, as witnessed by lottery and bingo profits.

This triumphant economy also brands all those who work. There are many ways of working, but it is still work accompanied by a salary which seduces us. Profound transformations are in progress here. The person who is employed wonders about the possibility of joining the victims of "rationalizations." Others pursue jobs that end too quickly and no longer provide a living. As for all those who must fall back on government assistance or on the generosity of others, they discover the deep-rooted prejudice that stigmatizes those who are no longer needed to make the economy work and who are on their way to becoming irrelevant.

We are therefore witnessing a bizarre stratification of society, where the one who works looks with suspicion upon a person who has just recently become unemployed, for the latter can rapidly become a competitor for your job. The one who recently became unemployed feels superior to someone who has been without work for a longer period because of the perception that this person is unambitious or poorly trained. The latter scorns the disabled person who is still receiving a government allowance, whereas his own welfare cheque has been cut. Each person is therefore alone, facing the others, a prisoner of the vast game of *Monopoly*, forced to trample or be trampled, to defeat or be defeated, to outperform the others or be swept away by the iron law of wages in the great global game.

Let us not be mistaken here. The problem does not originate solely in reservations stemming from economic nationalism in the face of market globalization. Neither is it a type of moralism that is always ready to condemn the impoverished for the slightest spending on pleasure. It is rooted rather in this diffuse, widespread, valued "evidence" which leads us to believe that the situation is impossible to bypass. According to the new high priests, this is the price we must pay for market globalization and it appears that we have no choice but to adapt to the new reality. Each one must agree to play the game and interiorize those rules that will henceforth determine the global economy. The old "Fatality of the Ancients Greeks" is thus back in service and this nightmarish conviction that "no one has a choice any longer" reverberates from the top to the bottom of the social scale, from one level of government to another, creating a veritable culture of acceptance of the unacceptable. Is there at least a believer left in Nineveh?

In this respect, the author of the Book of Revelation is once again of great assistance to us. Having reminded his listeners of the widespread dependence on the empire's insidious propaganda, he emphasizes that "there is a need for shrewdness here." For there is neither divinity nor fatalism in this situation. The sign that has been imposed remains a human sign. We are rightly amused at the naivety of our ancestors who continued to be mesmerized by the official propaganda attempting to convince them of the Emperor's divinity. We in our day, however, are defenceless against the official discourse of the financial world and big business which persuades us of the inevitability of our situation. Again, I wish to make it clear that it is not the internationalization of trade that is in question here, even though it remains, for the moment, the work of a handful of large businesses and has not by any means integrated all the continents. Could any African, for example, be made to believe that the African continent is part of the current global game?

Instead, we should be referring to the globalization of capital, for it is the managers of capital who attempt to convince us to pursue their interests as though they were synonymous with the interests of all nations. The dedication of these great mercenaries is never in doubt for they are obliged to renounce their country, their health, their peace of mind and often their families. In exchange, they are not answerable to any government or local population. Just as they agree to surrender themselves, body and soul, to their companies, they demand an act of faith from governments and more or less reluctant populations. The interests of the multinationals become identified with the "happiness" that is just around the corner for everyone. Since Catholic sensibility readily thrills to this depiction of Planet Earth reduced to a global village, it also rapidly accepts the good news of promised happiness for all the impoverished masses in various parts of the world. But it is at this point that discernment becomes urgent! The reality has little to do with this promised utopia. On the contrary, utopian ideas are used to conceal economic interests.

There is nothing fateful or inescapable about it, because it is a human creation. By delving further, is it not possible to see, in such submission, the social consequences of the obliteration of traditional religious signs? For many of these managers, as for a great number of those who imitate them, the need for personal fulfilment is no longer written on some transcendent horizon. It is in the here and now that this fulfilment must take place. The resulting frenzy of individual accomplishment finds ample opportunity in a number of firms or in the senior public service. From that moment on, the only limits on individual performance are those imposed by competitiveness. In the past, excellence remained a quality of things and persons bound together for the duration. The pursuit of excellence enabled us to transcend all that was superficial, flashy, slapdash or cheap. From now on, it will be linked to what is ephemeral because tomorrow, another person can always be more outstanding than I am and cause me to lose my status of "winner." The result is a permanent struggle to stay in first place and a kind of intoxication induced by this continuous effort to surpass ourselves, even though we feel the threat of extinction or, even worse, the threat of becoming one of the "losers," who are banished to that contemporary hell that we have succeeded in creating.

Saving the Human Race

Whether it is a question of fatalism, exuded day after day, or this infatuation with unlimited achievement, we inevitably find ourselves facing a tragic conception of life. It is as if the fear of extinction and the fear of death cannot be accepted, and every effort must be made to erect stockades, fortifications, standards and an armoured social status in order to avoid seeing it. The code of the winner and loser seems to me to be imbued with just such a tragic sense. It includes a distinct relation to the old codes of the clean and the unclean which haunted the Pharisees during the time of the Galilean. We see that it invariably results in the marginalizing of thousands of non-achievers, the outcasts of the economic system, losers in every economic game, these reprobates, scum of the earth, the unclean of the twentieth century.

In order to be in a position to say NO to this infatuation with the tragic, it becomes urgent to affirm that the human, somewhere in us, is threatened. Before our existence as producers, consumers, managers, unemployed, or outcasts of the system, we are, first of all, human beings. Our fragile species is original in that it has enriched itself throughout the centuries by reflecting on its survival. At the outset, the taboo of murder allowed for the creation of new relationships, where pardon meant resuming life and recreating the social bond. Subsequently, the gradual evolution of the awareness of justice permitted alliances and social organization. Life came to be perceived as a gift that was to be shared and that could be improved through communal development. In spite of everything, conviviality, this fragile art of wanting to live together, developed so well throughout our history, that it is false to believe that we are nothing but economic puppets seeking no interests but our own. The slow development of human rights was accompanied by a proliferation of agreements, of alliances of all kinds, and this massive phenomenon demonstrates effectively that competitiveness is not the sole human reality but that collaboration, cooperation, solidarity are equally a part of it. We impoverish ourselves dangerously if we agree to relegate them to our private lives. For I cannot recognize in myself more humanity than I am prepared to acknowledge in others. This is the very boundary that must not be crossed. Underneath the jumble of policies, statistics, curves and economic projections, this stubborn ember of a shared humanity still burns. It is this that we must preserve; it is this that we must blow into flame so that it lights up all our efforts and all our dreams.

Saving the Spirit of God

If I seek to justify this urgency to save the human face that is common to us, it is of course because like many others, I see it becoming disfigured. I do not resign myself to being a mere consumer, still less an interchangeable unit which becomes part of a statistic. I refuse to accept being used to run the giant carousel of the economy as if I were at its service. In doing so, I do not accept either that it should be done to others. For when humanity is wounded in an individual, it is wounded in me also, and in others. We are of the same stock, of the same earth, and we have a shared responsibility to occupy it and to dwell in it.

But another incentive, more ambitious at first sight, nurtures my resistance. The bonds which are woven between us in our multiple networks of daily life, work, or commitments in the city, are charged with the Spirit of the Galilean. For this Spirit, [1] which was promised to us, joins forces with our own and gives us the energy to believe in the clay that we are, to have confidence in it, to love it in its brittle and mortal fragility. It is as if we ourselves are flutes, covered with holes, that we are, nonetheless, learning to play. Do not our awkward fingers eventually press on the holes of the flute and dance under the impulse of the breath going through it? It seems to me that the Spirit of Life is a little like this. But we must defend it, that is, let it be, allow it to go free. The performer does not create the music but is at its service. We surrender ourselves to its enchantment, but nevertheless use all our art so that the music passes through us and finds the proper notes. When it is over, even the most clever would be hard pressed to untangle what belongs to the flutist and what belongs to the music and the composer. Be that as it may, at the end of the recital, the flutist bows low to the audience which for a fleeting moment has been enchanted by this music, as if it had come back to life and continued on its way through the minds and ears of hundreds of other listeners. At this moment, is the flutist saluting the music? Or the public? Or the performance? And why is it necessary to choose or exclude?

It is for this reason that I can presume not only to believe in the Spirit of God, but to attempt to hear it through the layers of my commitments and the tangle of our encounters. The awesome challenge I face then is to know how to discern its passage and to provide myself with the indicators I need to do so. The entire spiritual tradition has attempted to propose such criteria and, for the Christian in me, the letter of Paul to his brothers in northern Galatia surely constitutes an indispensable starting point. Paul begins his epistle by voicing his astonishment that the Galatians had forgotten the liberation brought to them by the Gospel, a liberation he notes, that is not a universal licence but one that summons forth a desire to serve others. In Chapter 3, Paul specifies that it is the person of the Galilean, Christ crucified, who enables them to rise again and to reposition themselves. As they regain the awareness of being united to Christ as limbs to a body, the Galatians will be able to discern the passage of the Spirit and "let our behaviour be guided by the Spirit" (5:25). Therefore, before discussing the Spirit, we must start from this contemplation of Christ crucified.

The Galilean Crucified

Why does Paul insist so heavily on the contemplation of the Crucified to help the Galatians rediscover their interior freedom in face of the pressures of the traditionalists born of Judaism? The reason is simple. For him, it is no longer the Mosaic law that constitutes the heart of the religious universe but, indeed, the person of the Galilean, recognized as Christ and dead on a cross. Henceforth, it is this person who is the central axis of the faith and who organizes it from within. The believer is united to the Galilean who is affirmed as living. Thus refocused, believers can test their Spirit, their strength, their inspiration, and, in turn, rise again and again and seek new ways to serve others.

Admittedly, such discourse may seem a little too mystical for our modern ears. We like to be able to authenticate all things. In particular, we are distinctly uneasy with any discourse which appears too individual to nourish the current crisis of Christian roles and to breathe life into our particular situation which bears the stamp of the economy and global trade. Let us move on to two other writings dating to some fifty years after Paul's letter. By then, the Christian communities had time to verify the limits of such discourse. Even if Paul's proclamation of faith is inescapable, it nonetheless needs to be repositioned in the movement of the power struggles in society and even in the empire. This will be the role of the Gospels and, ultimately for us, of the Book of Revelation.

I shall begin with the book of John. In Chapter 13 John introduces, in the heart of Jesus' last meal, the story of the "washing of the feet." Let us forget for a moment this title added by the editors, and examine the scene. The disciples are seated at the table with Jesus. Sharing a meal already carries considerable significance, for one does not merely share the food on the table. One communes as well with the host, with his projects and his dreams. For Jesus, the meal is a kind of specific parable of the world to come: the world foreseen by God is similar to a group of people who gather around a table and, as brothers and sisters, share the goods that are in abundance and belong to all. At this table, no one is excluded, even those who had not been invited.

"But," the Galilean will say, "how can you preserve this great dream and above all, rekindle it continuously?" It is at that moment that Jesus rises from the table and goes to take the place of the one who is serving, who is not at the table, who is excluded from the meal. From this moment on, it becomes very easy to understand the change of perspective that will occur. As long as I stay at the table, I have a good view of what is on the table, the various kinds of food that I like, the people who are sharing it with me. But if I leave the table voluntarily to take the place of one who is not there, I immediately discover that a place and a plate are missing. And if the guests agree to make a place for me, will they not have to distribute the dishes differently?

In other words, putting myself in the shoes of the one who is not at the table allows me to discover that another place is needed for the meal to be complete. Similarly, if the meal becomes the table of a Board of Directors or, yet again, the table of the administration of a school or a government ministry, I discover that taking the place of the one who is excluded allows me to view the table differently and to propose the necessary changes. John's account thus goes far beyond the mere reminder of brotherly love. It implies removing oneself from the centre and choosing to show solidarity with the slave who was serving. By behaving thus, the disciple will not only have a better view of the entire road ahead, so that the dream of sharing and solidarity between us as brothers and sisters becomes even more of a reality, but the discipline will also know happiness: "Now that you know this, blessed are you," concludes the Galilean, "if you behave accordingly" (13:17).

Now let us go on to Chapter 18 of the Book of Revelation. The author has just evoked the fall of Babylon, a code name for Imperial Rome. He describes the surprise and despair of the merchants bringing the spoils siphoned off from all the conquered countries to the centre of the empire: "stocks of gold and silver, jewels and pearls, linen and purple and silks and scarlet; all the sandalwood, every piece in ivory or fine wood, in bronze or iron or marble; the cinnamon and spices, the myrrh and ointment and incense; wine, oil, flour and corn; their stocks of cattle, sheep, horses and chariots, their slaves and their human cargo." (18:12-13).

So why will this empire be destroyed? What sign is he giving to the believers for them to adhere to his prophecy and mentally forsake the fascination exerted by the empire? "Your traders were the princes of the earth, all the nations were led astray by your sorcery. In her was found the blood of prophets and saints, and all the blood that was ever shed on earth." (18:23-24). The all-powerful empire will thus collapse because it bears within itself the blood of the innocents who have been slain. It is another way of saying that any society that kills its innocents breeds its own contradictions and thus prepares its fall. We know, today, that this is what happened, but at the time, a large measure of fearlessness and audacity was needed to even think the unthinkable. This intuition of faith constitutes the other side of the beatitude promised at the meal in the cenacle. When a society and its members are incapable of putting themselves in the place of the one who cannot participate in the meal with the others, sooner or later, it breeds a violence which eventually causes it to self-destruct. The violence done to the innocent thus has a determining effect.

Rediscovering One's NO

I am not sure which is more moving, this mime of the Galilean which briefly summarizes the entire life of Jesus and is left to us as a promise of happiness, or the solidarity with the innocents slaughtered in the games of the empire and rediscovered in the persecuted communities of the first century. One thing is certain, we are in the presence of a conviction that is not always accepted. Despite the abuses of power, the inquisitions, and the stakes kindled in the name of orthodoxy, this conviction will live through two thousand years of history. In our time, we will rediscover it at the heart of various charters of human rights and in the countless movements of solidarity with those who are excluded. It will inspire the initiatives of Latin American Christians at the turning point of the Council and it continues to nourish the social interventions of ecclesiastical authorities in Quebec and elsewhere in Canada.

I think that it is up to each one of us to personally become a part of this movement. Obviously we are in the presence of what is more than merely a generous idea. We find ourselves again at the heart of a situation that will call us to reflect on our own experiences and prompt us to verify when, precisely, did we decide to take the side of the despised innocents rather than power, the outcast rather than the system which produces outcasts, the fragile truth rather than established falsehoods. I believe that each and every one of us can carry out a verification such as this. We need only ask when we said NO for the first time to a situation that we found intolerable. A considerable number of us have had such experiences. Whether it was contempt, violence, injustice done to us or to a loved one, we have been moved by the strength of our refusal, a kind of nausea in the presence of something that seemed to touch a living fibre of our being. We said NO then with all our soul, as if our dignity itself was exploding with the force and the rage of the disaster.

If the reader identifies with the foregoing, it will not be difficult to agree that such an experience is likely to be foundational. I can always come back to it, summon it forth, nourish it, support it, make it flesh of my flesh and a decisive orientation for my conscience. Subsequently, it will become easier to discover that a number of others around me have already said NO and that I feel an affinity with them. It is as if a kind of underground network linked us together and united us, as if our NOs had avoided precipices, rejected dead ends and opened before us a long route that is yet to be imagined and travelled.

I believe that it is on such a road that we can one day discover the Galilean suspended on a cross; the children abandoned on the steps of the Temple in the first century; the young Christian denounced by a neighbour and braving the beasts in the arena; the beggars and lepers who joined Francis and his friends in the Middle Ages; the women burned as witches because they disrupted the power of the doctors and priests; the Jewish families advancing toward the ovens while reciting a psalm; the young engaged couple falling under the bullets in Sarajevo; and the Rwandan women silently taking the road back with absurd baggage on their heads. The horde of witnesses is long and terrible. Little by little, however, we can discern the presence of the Galilean, stumbling forward, supported by a force, a Spirit, which makes it possible, along with the entire human caravan, to find new routes. It is at such crossroads that we can regain our breath and teach ourselves to discern the pathways that the Spirit of the Galilean helps us to open up. But not before.

The Spirit Restored

The preceding receptivity is not neutral. Rather, it is intended to remind us that there is no spiritual discernment without conditions. It is in my "body and conscience" that something important can happen. For this reason, I need to let myself be touched, in other words, reached, by the one who is not at the meal or, to return to the Gospel parable, by the one who lies wounded at the roadside. Accepting to have our itinerary disrupted, as the Samaritan did by introducing the other into our own journey, provides a setting which allows us to discover, in our conscience, new ways to continue along our own chosen path.

Thus, it is quite possible that we can henceforth more readily understand the decision of many "consumers" to change their buying habits. The most commonly held opinion consists in convincing us that *envy* is the most important motive of the consumer. The desire to have what the other possesses, or to procure it if the other does not wish to give it to us, constitutes the mechanism which turns the wheel of commerce and of consumerism. But other attitudes exist. If fraternity with, or proximity to, one who does not have enough to eat moves me, I quickly discover another attitude at the heart of this consumer society. It is *respect*, the glance brought to bear on others for what they are, without possessions of any kind, as if they were my brothers, my sisters, my fellow creatures in humanity. Respect for others is the opposite of envy. Subsequently, respect for those who have less than I have quickly becomes a gesture of sharing, of shared brotherhood, of the desire to travel the road together. If prejudice against the impoverished is still so deep-seated in our society, should we conclude that we have not left envy behind and that these others are still far from our field of vision? Out of sight, out of mind?

This way of allowing the other into my concerns also enables me to be on my guard against an individualistic solution that would quickly ease my conscience. Reducing one's lifestyle, cutting down on cake, candy, taking public transportation rather than the car, all are decisions which can promote a healthier life. But it is not necessarily an evangelical life if the other is not there. Such measures can obviously constitute a pedagogical exercise for regaining more interior freedom in the midst of consumption. It is the relationship with the other, however, which will give it another direction. This is, without doubt, the direction of the traditional Christian understanding which reminded us that *fasting* should make us open our hearts to *prayer* and this openness should find expression in *almsgiving*. It is a far cry from "Weight Watchers!"

But seriously reflecting on my position in social networks enables me to enter into another sort of discernment. This time, it is fringes of the population that I take into my line of vision. Instead of starting from the social scale which is presented to us as "normal," I may ask myself *who will truly benefit* from the decisions taken by various public decision-makers. A Master's degree in economics or sociology is not a prerequisite for attempting a reply. Whether it is the recent budget, increases in tuition fees, or cuts in public services, the question allows us to attempt a greater understanding of what is happening and to question the decisions that have been taken. Will they benefit the greatest number? Will they improve the lives of the most vulnerable? During the 1970s, when business taxes were being reduced and personal income tax increased, if more citizens had asked these questions, fewer members of today's middle class would be weighed down by the burden of taxes and perhaps fewer of these same individuals would be searching for the guilty among the most destitute members of our society.

Another way to better situate ourselves in the current economic dynamic summons up the traditional Christian perception of "social mortgage." This notion is rooted in the conviction of the Fathers of the Church in the fourth century who maintained that we all have the same human nature and that the goods of the earth belong to all. In their view, if the rich gave to the poor, it was not charity but justice. A rich person was merely the steward of the wealth which belonged to all and for that reason the poor were entitled to it. Belatedly, in the eighteenth and later in the nineteenth century, the right to property was understood to be inalienable, and responsibility for the poor fell within the province of charity rather than justice.

The notion of social mortgage ties in again with the universal purpose of goods by affirming that each property has a mortgage attached to it and that society, through the State, can reclaim it.

It is interesting to note that, in our time, an ecological conscience has enabled us to rediscover this *social mortgage* in relation to the environment. In future, businesses will no longer to be able to do as they please with the earth and the rivers, because they belong to all. There is no reason why we cannot demand such *social mortgage* from businesses, industrial or electronic, whether the property is material or, in the future, virtual. An entire field of intervention opens up before us, allowing us to switch from a "wall-to-wall" to a pluralistic economy, that is, one which makes room for the economy of giving, for services of closeness, personal development, art and spirituality. By doing so, on what is useful, the economy could regain its function of responding to needs rather than existing for the sole purpose of making money.

If I go a step further and acknowledge that I, also, am a party to my era and that my existence is outlined against a specific historical sequence, my discernment will once again undergo a change. Whether it is a question of the globalization of capital, the movement of millions of refugees, the communications revolution or global warming, I find myself involved in major currents that I must understand. To assist me in this understanding, the notion of "sign of the times" is a most relevant one. In this case, it is not merely a question of thinking about the leading trends in futurology. We know that the latter refers to long-lasting economic, social and political trends found in several areas. The "sign of the times" is more selective. It indicates important trends, of course, but trends that are in distinct harmony with what the Gospels call the Kingdom of God. It also has the characteristic of being a call to action, to change, to the transformation of those who talk about it. If, in fact, I believe that the Spirit of God animates our history, it can only be a *subversive* Spirit which prolongs the work and passion of the Galilean, who "makes straight what is twisted, warms what is cold, softens the rigid" as described by an old hymn to the Holy Spirit.

This reference to the passion of the Galilean and to my own responsibility will affect me all the more if I have been touched by specific events and real people. I am reminded here of two Quebec women who were moved by a report on hunger in Africa and the difficulties involved in distributing provisions. They talked about it to their friends, one of whom worked in a farming cooperative. He and his colleagues undertook to create a biscuit with a high nutritional value. In the meantime, they contacted international aid offices and some time later, boxes of biscuits were being parachuted into inaccessible areas in Africa. "The miracle of the loaves and the fishes," exclaimed an African catechist on witnessing the scene. Perhaps. What is certain is that such events take place here and there and if they are not numerous, the reason is that perhaps we are still marked on the forehead and on the hand by those who are in power. Letting ourselves be touched by "the ones who are not at the meal" becomes, here again, a condition for having a different view of what is happening, having an inkling of something new at work, something new attempting to chart its way ahead. Such solidarity would move us to thrill to the action of the Korean workers who, at the risk of their lives, demanded better working conditions in their factories. Or else, move us to support Development and Peace which has allowed Canadian students to discover the slavery of young people their own age making famous brand-name running shoes on the other side of the globe.

Thousands of people everywhere throughout our world are fighting for more justice, dignity, and genuine development: many more of us, therefore, could discover such *signs of the times* as foreign workers, from the West Indies and from Mexico; or those crammed together here as seasonal workers and treated like animals; accountants attempting to persuade the international community to tax the movement of capital; groups of ecologists reminding leaders of the resolutions on the environment adopted in Rio; and all those assisting local populations to become self-supporting and to regain control over a part of their agricultural economy. They beckon to us. Something of the Spirit of God comes through them. Discovering it opens our hearts to new paths and to a joy which could be shared a little more. How can our faith not be strengthened by it? How can we not be convinced that the Spirit of Life is at work and continuously liberating a desire for creativity within us? The new century before us need not necessarily be the century of wall-to-wall economy. It may very well be the century of solidarity, of citizenship and conviviality, that is, the art, so fragile and difficult, of knowing how to live together without losers and without outcasts.

* * *

As I arrive at the end of this route, in spite of the weight of problems and the erosion of hope, I feel like distributing the following advertisement everywhere: *"New emerging society seeks midwives. Anyone, man or woman, may apply. Good ability to discern required."*

NOTE

1. In this text, the words "Spirit" and "Breath" are used interchangeably to refer to the Spirit of God.

CONCLUSION

The Bread of God and Stone Soup

The story of stone soup illustrates how we can create a rich and nourishing meal by sharing what we have with one another. A turnip here, a potato there, some salt, pepper, onions, carrots . . . and, although no one ingredient alone can sustain us, together—as community soup—they provide us with all the necessary vitamins and minerals we need to survive and be healthy. Vivian Labrie tells us a real-life story of how an idea became a plan and mushroomed into a significant social action, "Relay Fast for the Rejection of Poverty," in the manner of stone soup.

We need spiritual sustenance as much as bodily nourishment. We must feed our spirits with divine manna—the bread of life: "For the Bread of God is the one who comes down from heaven and gives life to the world" (John 6:33).

Christians believe Jesus, the son of Man and the Son of God, born in Bethlehem (literal meaning, "house of bread"), is the bread of life and the bread of understanding. God plants the Word in the ground of our heart as seed—it is up to us to see that it grows into wheat and contributes to making bread of understanding. This bread enables us to discern the signs of the times and detect the movement of God in our world. This is how Brother Anthony (a Carmelite hermit living in the woods of Eastern Canada) describes the transformation the Spirit of God works in us:

We are the dough
Humility rests in knowing we are dust;
Flour which the waters of Baptism through the Holy
Spirit forms into dough.
Meekness is letting ourselves be handled by Him,

By His hands that knead and press the mass to be
shaped into the Mould he desires:
Christ Jesus—His Son.
It does not matter if He places us into the oven next
Because by the Leaven of His Word we know that He is making Bread out of us.
When the loaf is done He takes it out awhile
For it has risen and is almost bursting with the generosity that seeks to give itself.
He then takes it in His hands, breaks it, and gives it to the rest to eat,
This Bread which is us
That through us others may partake of His Goodness.
This is the daily Bread that He gives to the world.
Yesterday, today and tomorrow
God works.
He is always making Bread. [1]

The editorial committee for this book asked each author to consider what it means to be faithful to God in today's world of neoliberalism and globalism, a world where 358 billionaires own as much of the world's revenue ($760 billion US) as the 2.5 billion lowest income persons—as Mary Boyd informs us. A world where, as Leonard Desroches tells us, "between 1962 and 1982, there were at least 10,700,000 people killed in 65 wars in 49 countries, an average of 1,465 people killed every day." A world where, according to 1995 figures, 51 of the top economies in the world were transnational corporations. Wal-mart, for example, had an economy bigger than 161 of the 191 countries in the world!

What is an appropriate understanding and faith response to economic social change in such a world? Each writer has provided a personal reflection in response to this basic question. Notwithstanding the unique features of each viewpoint, taken together the writers share a common understanding. They complement one another, and together offer us a comprehensive ethical and theological understanding of economic social change in today's world in the light of faith.

Neoliberalism: The Predominant Force Driving Local Social Change

The authors agree that the dynamic of social change at the local level is best understood in terms of the predominant and determining force of global economics. This is the framework and horizon of each writer's analysis in this book. The authors frequently use terms like globalization, globalism, corporatism, the international unregulated market, world capitalism, and, of course, neoliberalism. Their logical and spontaneous impulse is to discuss social change in terms of global economics.

Neoliberalism is the term used most often to explain the nature of the global economic system of today's world. Each person has a unique view of neoliberalism. Vivian Labrie points out that the meaning of this esoteric sounding term "neoliberalism" is often not clear to the people suffering the most from its impact: "How long they are, these words that describe what eats away at us," she says in exasperation, "when the words get too long, we should perhaps make a point of relating the deeds as well. . . . " The discourse of professional sociologists and economists can sometimes confuse more than enlighten. With a careful examination of the "deeds" of neoliberalism we gain a correct understanding. The previous chapters have already told us much about the deeds.

Mary Boyd gives us one of the more graphic descriptions of the deeds of neoliberalism as she outlines the changes and transformations brought about from Structural Adjustment Programmes (SAPs) in the Philippines. Everywhere, workers are being transformed into slaves, and the earth is being abused, polluted and destroyed. Technology makes this possible. Competitive capitalism on a global scale and new information technologies now makes the most remote village proximate to the urban hubs of economic activity in the downtown financial districts of major cities.

With globalism comes the end of Keynesian economics, the triumph of the notion of the self-regulating market. This is the lifeblood of neoliberal policies, to remove impediments to the free movement of capital throughout the world. The human and social costs are immense.

Michel Beaudin describes neoliberalism as a "project that destroys our common house." He adds, "Our global economic system represents the first social order in history to base the social bond on economic opposition or competition among the members. Anti-solidarity is therefore engraved in the very fibre of the economy and society, thus concealing the responsibility for exclusions in a mechanism that coincides with the normal 'course' of a society redefined as market."

Neoliberalism: A New Era for the World

Global neoliberalism is not only the driving force in the world; it truly represents the passage from one era to another: from the liberal era of multinational political and economic relations to the neoliberal era of transnational corporate empires. Gregory Baum and Michel Beaudin point to the end of the era of capitalism under Keynesian economics, which recognized that economic growth was linked to the welfare of nations. The welfare state has since drowned in the rising tide of transnational corporations controlled by "new feudal lords" (Boyd and Beaudin) that take populations hostage and pit them against one another. The authors share the notion that accumulated private wealth has a social mortgage—capital has fundamental moral obligations to contribute to the common good. But the owners of capital continue to become fewer and far more wealthy and powerful as more and more of the world's population suffers in poverty.

The authors offer a critical social and cultural analysis of the emerging neoliberal, global economic system. Gregory Baum points to the loss of the cultural optimism that was based on the idea that " . . . economic expansion could be extended to the whole world." In this new phase of history, people are now "excluded from work and the necessities of life." According to Keynes, the task of national governments was to protect their citizens from destructive forces and to create a region of security and social peace. This interventionist understanding of economics rejected Adam Smith's belief that the self-regulating market was steered by a 'hidden hand' to serve the well-being of society. Mary Boyd believes "we are being brainwashed by corporate interests into thinking that the unregulated market is the only economic system and the most moral one." Several authors point to the sheer power of consolidated international capital, and the accompanying cultural belief that "there is no alternative to neoliberalism," as further evidence of the establishment of a new social era—where the ruling idea is that "we have no choice but to adjust." National governments have relinquished their power and bestowed it on international finance. Gregory Baum believes: "The important decisions affecting society and its citizens are made today by transnational corporations and international financial institutions such as the World Bank and the International Monetary Fund." Mary Boyd tells us about the Multinational Agreement on Investment (MAI) which "gives power to the rich and tools to the corporations to sue governments in Canada and elsewhere at municipal, provincial and national levels for protecting the rights of their people in the face of further pillage by the corporations." If this is true, what can we possibly do but adjust?

Some authors offer a historical analysis of this shift from liberalism to neoliberalism. They agree that neoliberalism is both an economic, political and cultural project whereby economic activity becomes increasingly owned and controlled by transnational corporations operating globally, no longer subject to national government taxation and regulation. This means that transnational corporations can operate without sufficient consideration for the human, social and environmental costs which are produced by or result from their "deeds". The emergence of transnational corporate rule has taken on such magnitude, and constitutes such a fundamental threat to democracy, that the authors have each described the new era in terms of empire.

Neoliberalism is not simply the return to the self-regulating market of the nineteenth century. It is the return to the self-regulating market *with a vengeance.* In today's world, a couple of hundred transnational corporations unimpeded by national governments essentially direct and drive the world's economy. Operating on their own authority, they are extremely efficient in the task of excluding more and more people from sharing in the benefits of economic activity. They operate as empires.

Neoliberalism and the Rise of Global Economic Empires

The economic deeds of domination, exploitation and exclusion are the deeds of empires. Empires function by usurping power and control, by exploiting workers and resources, always striving to own and control more and more. These are the deeds which the authors ascribe to the owners of transnational capital here in Canada and throughout the world.

Neoliberalism is far more than an economic system. It is a global and totalitarian project which touches all areas of life. The authors all use the image and language of empire to describe the dominant belief in our culture that there is no alternative to global corporatism and neoliberal economics. Like forced submission to the empire, we feel we have no choice but to surrender to neoliberal policy changes and adjust to the new world.

Guy Paiement asks: "Why does recalling a bygone empire awaken so many echoes in us, readers of today? How can we explain this complicity save by the fact that a number of us realize how much we too are marked, programmed nowadays, by a society in which the neoliberal economy appears to be all pervasive?" He goes on to say that we are marked—as the subjects in the Roman Empire in its day—on the forehead and on the hand: "Each one is branded on the forehead, i.e., in his way of thinking, criteria, standards, his way of understanding his desires and responding to them. He is also branded on the right hand, the one that is used for swearing a solemn oath, that supports authority and the system, that works as well, and contributes to maintaining the Empire. The economy is at the service of the Empire and no one can do business in it without accepting its laws."

Michel Beaudin believes that neoliberalism has transformed the economy into a project "with totalitarian pretensions, into a perverse infinitude that undermines the social terrain." For Guy Paiement, it is a fatal submission to the death-dealing system of neoliberal economics which has ascribed a value to everything in life: "The market-based economy seems to be the only reference. It tends, moreover, to corrode society more and more, so much so that everything, a bar of soap, an organ, a public service, an academic appears to have a price." Several authors describe it as a return to "the utopia of the old, supposedly self-regulating market of the nineteenth century." Gregory Baum too describes neoliberalism as both a "socio-economic project and cultural enterprise." He believes that neoliberalism "is grounded in a social philosophy, an updated version of the nineteenth-century Social Darwinism, and is supported by an appropriate culture that legitimates the public indifference to solidarity." He adds that, "The success of the socio-economic project depends on the ability to gain the approval of the majority of the population. Serving this interest is a public culture that fosters success-oriented individualism, short-term utilitarianism, ethical relativism and indifference to the suffering of others."

The authors agree: neoliberalism is cruel—it ignores or forgets vast numbers of people by deliberately ascribing no value to them. As Michel Beaudin puts it, in former days people "felt secure despite a poverty that although common at the time, was unaccompanied by the pain of social exclusion." And the forces which are doing the excluding are transnational corporations.

Mary Boyd speaks of the return to feudalism on a global scale, "with its royal households of transnational empires." Guy Paiement likens neoliberalism to the return of the old "fatalism of the ancients" where the refrain "*no one has a choice any longer*, reverberates from the top to the bottom of the social scale, from one level of government to another, creating a veritable culture of acceptance of the unacceptable." Michel Beaudin tells us that "current capitalism has decreed the end of utopias [. . .]. It has thus tried to block the imaginary and to destroy the hope of any other." As André Myre notes, "Today, the role of the Romans, of Herod and the high priests in the time of Jesus is played by this empire of neoliberalism. It smothers the people and the least among us who are waiting for the good news of liberation."

The Transformative Impact of Neoliberalism

Because neoliberalism is so all pervasive, it is having a major transformative impact on people and communities everywhere. The dynamic of competition breeds isolation and suspicion between people, especially when there is a large surplus of labourers to manipulate. The new technology has created an entire sector of excluded people, "a third sector," where the market is oriented toward maximizing profit. Because the economic system is based on certain principles and objectives which condition our understanding and behaviour, they do not transform our society in some abstract sense, they transform society by transforming us, forcing compliance with new social rules and practices.

Baum once wrote that the essence of social change lies in the transformation of consciousness which occurs from our participation in economic social change—we may or may not be aware of this transformation: "For a while people may nourish their ideals of life from a great religious tradition, but by participating in economic life, they acquire a new self-understanding, and, even without realizing it, they are transformed in accordance with the public ideals of profit and competition." This can happen where people live with a split in their world view which categorizes life as "secular" or "religious," as separate domains in an abstract conceptualization of the world, rather than a single dynamic process integrating the two. Len Desroches captures how we lapse in moral awareness with his subheading: "I just make wires." Vast numbers of people can excuse their contribution to the most heinous crimes against humanity by refusing to take any responsibility for the indirect contributions they make—contributions without which the crime would not have been possible. There is need for transformative actions rather than acts of blind obedience giving in to the negative dynamics of conformity to neoliberalism.

Submission to Economic Empires and Idolatry

It is the all-pervasive influence and power of neoliberalism to make us believe it is impossible to live without supporting the empire. Mary Boyd believes that neoliberal economics creates a sense of inevitability. It "dominates our consciousness"; we have, she tells us, become "worshippers of money, power, privilege and pleasure. . . . Living with an oppressed consciousness and lacking a critical awareness of our situation can leave us 'living in a dream world', sleeping through our daily routines of work, television and entertainment while failing to see the world is becoming ruled by the global marketplace." Meanwhile, we see the law of competition becoming more and more established and the economically powerful continue to be rewarded for their exploitation.

Mary Boyd's notion of "sleepwalking" is similar to the state of moral consciousness Leonard Desroches refers to when he talks of the "spiritual numbness that has poisoned our souls." How can we fathom what it means that 100 million "anti-personnel" land mines kill at least 800 children, women and men each month simply to keep 75 manufactures of between 5-10 million land mines annually in 65 countries profitably in business? These statistics should bring a moral outrage, but they don't. As Gregory Baum notes, fictional violence in films and on television "hardens our moral sensibilities and reinforces our indifference to the suffering of others."

All the authors talk about a corruption of moral culture because of the new neoliberal phase of global capitalism. As Priscilla Solomon puts it, the dominant culture fosters a "separation of belief and the practice of virtue or goodness that makes it possible for neoliberalism to flourish. In other words it becomes very easy for some of the best values of a culture to be co-opted and corrupted." She is thinking especially of the attitude of man's domination over the earth and other living creatures, saying that it will take massive attitudinal and cultural changes to develop the level of awareness that will lead to changes to protect Mother Earth.

The dynamic practice of our faith is lost in a dualistic course of action which renders our belief in God an abstraction, a pipe-dream happening in our minds only. What is required is the establishment of justice in our relationships, our communities, and the organizations which constitute what we call society at the local, national and international levels. The authors see exactly the opposite happening in what they call neoliberal ideology and social practice which is currently transforming the entire world. Their strongly felt beliefs fit together to make for a remarkably unified analysis.

Priscilla Solomon says that capitalism "seems to have taken on a life of its own like that of a huge monster [. . .] trampling to death anyone and everyone who does not and cannot hold its reins." Christians should not reconcile themselves to neoliberalism because it destroys life and ruptures the moral fabric of the human family. We are called to reject this new ideology, an ideology which takes the shape of "idolatry" for believers. We must say no to worship of the empire.

The Incarnation and the Kingdom of God

There is an unmistakable tendency in our society to view religion as a solely private affair, with its own domain of interest, to be considered once a week on the Sabbath or Holy Day of worship. This mode of consciousness is categorically rejected by the authors of this book. They oppose this dualistic world view which presents human nature as split between material and spiritual, body and soul, and which severs faith and economics, heaven and earth into separate domains. Priscilla Solomon believes that "an active personal engagement in the ongoing process of the transformation of one's cultural values is intimate in as much as one actually knows what the true values are in the culture and how those values are lived out in one's daily life. It is a process of actualizing, or incarnating, what one believes." The secular world would like to keep religion concerned only with the hereafter. André Myre reminds us how the mainstream media and business sector regarded the Bishops' ethical commentary on economics as incredible and without legitimacy—church people should only talk about the "hereafter and the eternal truths of God," not the application of the ethical implications of these eternal truths in the "here and now." We are told that the "here and now" belongs to so-called secular powers—those who control economics and set the direction for the ongoing transformation of society.

For believers, these economic and cultural trends have moral and spiritual significance. We need to take note of the transformation they bring about in our lives. The "here and now" are of central importance to Christians. We are called to evangelize, and as André Myre tells us, that means we are " . . . to bring to the people and to the poor, the good news that inevitably clashes head on with the powers of this world and religions more interested in the 'eternal truths'. That is why it is quite in line with the Galilean and the Jesus of the Gospel to struggle against the empire of neoliberalism. . . . "

All of the authors show the intrinsic connection between eternal truths on the one hand and a legitimate ethical and spiritual response to social injustice and evil in today's world on the other hand. They portray the task of following Jesus as, in part, a rejection of this evil social system, an evil which is economic in nature, where everything in life has been given a value in money, where "price" is determined by trade or sale. It is essential that we align ourselves with the Galilean who put himself in the place of one who was not at the table, the place of the excluded. Guy Paiement tells us that "When a society and its members are incapable of putting themselves in the place of the one who cannot participate in the meal with the others, sooner or later, it breeds a violence which eventually causes it to self-destruct." This is what always happen with empire. Michel Beaudin asks, "And why will the Empire fall? Because 'in her you will find the blood of prophets and saints, and all the blood that was ever shed upon the Earth'" (Rv. 18:23-24). Guy Paiement says almost the same thing: "The all-powerful Empire will thus collapse because it bears within itself the blood of the innocents who have been slain. It is another way of saying that any society that kills its innocents breeds its own contradictions and thus prepares its fall."

Seeking Alternatives in Solidarity with the Excluded

Guy Paiement describes neoliberalism as "a huge *Monopoly* game and woe betide the losers." We live in a harsh age when people are routinely excluded, forgotten and ignored. The belief that there is no option besides international competition in an unregulated global market creates great insecurity and violence in human relationships, and generates distrust and ill will among people. Workers look with suspicion on those who have become unemployed recently and see potential competitors for their jobs. "Each one must agree to play the game and interiorize those rules that will henceforth determine the global economy." We are reminded that God sides with the poor, with those who do not have a seat at the table. We too must find ways to say "NO" to intolerable situations.

Mary Boyd tells us, "We can trade the fatigue, the discouragement, the fear and feeling of powerlessness for the energy and creativity that is necessary to transform the world. To abandon that goal would be to forget Yahweh's deeds, the anguish of the prophets and Jesus' ultimate triumph over death." Indeed, all the authors share a hopeful long-term outlook with faith in the resurrection of Jesus from the dead. The victory has ultimately been accomplished as

Christians await the second coming of Jesus and the resurrection. Until then, there is much to do in the world.

Michel Beaudin says that the reader should let the "words of this book in its entirety be read as an act of resistance, of summoning, and rebuilding of hope." The power of this book lies in its proclamation that Christian hope is more powerful than neoliberalism. And we find echoes of this power everywhere. Despite the gloomy situation we face at the end of the millennium, Baum tells us "the collapse of optimism does not mean that Christians give up hope. Believing that God is graciously at work in the world, Christians scan society to detect 'the stirrings of parturition' occurring in it. The drama of redemption, revealed in Jesus Christ, continues to be operative in the history of nations."

Governments must be accountable to the people; they must not invoke "necessity" as the reason to abdicate democracy, Baum continues, "as if the market were a natural force, like forces in chemistry or biology that simply follow the law of nature." We are free human beings; we can not evade our personal and collective moral responsibility to others, to the common good, to the preservation of the earth. Baum suggests that we must contribute to building a culture of cooperation and solidarity by aligning ourselves with "currents in the social movements, old and new, such as the labour movement, the women's movement, the ecological movement, the peace movement, the cooperative movement and the movement against free trade." Likewise, Guy Paiement encourages us to look for signs of the times, some of which he sees as "foreign workers, from the West Indies, from Mexico, or those crammed together here as seasonal workers and treated like animals, accountants attempting to persuade the international community to tax the movement of capital, groups of ecologists reminding leaders of the resolutions on the environment adopted in Rio, all those assisting local populations to become self-supporting and to regain control over a part of their agricultural economy, in a word, thousands of people everywhere throughout our world fighting for more justice, dignity and genuine development."

Some authors see neoliberalism as vulnerable in its blatant disrespect for life. "In its frenzy, it has touched what is vital to us and is in the process of rousing the populations against it." Gregory

Baum cites Karl Polanyi's view that "when society has been threatened by economic forces, social movements emerge among ordinary people that try to protect the community and its environment from disintegration." Guy Paiement tells us to look for "trends [. . .] that are in distinct harmony with what the Gospels call the kingdom of God." He adds that "It also has the characteristic of being a call to action, to change, to the transformation of those who talk about it."

Both Vivian Labrie and Priscilla Solomon refer to the criteria for the final judgement in Matthew 25: "I was hungry, did you give me food? I was thirsty, did you give me drink? I was alone, did you visit me?" Vivian Labrie suggests that "The fight against exclusion entails preparing the place for those who will come. It implies making it possible for them to stay, to notice a place, to take it and live there, to be at home." Or to be a "restorer of ruined houses," as Michel Beaudin suggests. It is at all times the aim of the cultural struggle to create a majority of people who recognize the social disintegration and the human suffering caused by neoliberalism. Self-help groups and community economic development are of central importance to win back democratic control of our lives. Though international political changes are required ultimately to hold transnational corporations socially responsible, local struggles against neoliberalism serve important spiritual and social ends. "They create community, rescue people from isolation and passivity, and offer them active participation. They create a culture of cooperation and solidarity, at odds with the dominant culture." They give us opportunity to share our gifts with others, to contribute to building the kingdom of God.

Kevin Arsenault

Kevin Arsenault, a long-time social activist, has a PhD from McGill University in theology and social ethics. He served as the executive secretary for the National Farmers Union and the executive director of the Jesuit Centre for Social Faith and Justice and remains the president of Rural Dignity of Canada. His study Ethics and Awareness *will be published by Sheed & Ward in 1998.*

Note

1. Brother Anthony, *The Bread of God* (New York, NY: Vantage Press Inc., 1975).

Glossary

Alternative Federal Budget (AFB)

A project of the Canadian Centre for Policy Alternatives (Ottawa) and Choices, a Coalition for Social Justice (Winnipeg), to prepare an alternative to the official budget each year with the input of grassroots groups across the country who supply the priorities. A group of policy analysts and researchers then prepare a budget based on those priorities and an independent firm is hired to audit the result. It is presented to the Minister of Finance just prior to the publication of the official Federal Budget.

Asia Pacific Economic Cooperation (APEC)

This is a series of negotiations taking place between countries on the Pacific Rim to establish a Free Trade Zone for that region of the world. The project is advancing rapidly. Canada participates actively.

Business Council on National Issues (BCNI)

This is a lobbying organization established by the major corporations operating in Canada and, at this point, is so powerful as to practically constitute a "shadow cabinet."

Canada Assistance Plan (CAP)

The overarching structure of the Federal Government to provide funding and assure national standards in the provision of welfare. Until it was abolished in 1996, it had the ability to regulate the policies governing the application of social assistance programmes nationally.

Civilian-Based Defence (CBD)

A plan for national defence that is based in the participation of civilians rather than military. It is already operative in Costa Rica, which has no military.

Community Economic Development (CED)

A movement for development of local economic initiatives at the grassroots. It usually involves locally administered services or local production by economically marginal groups.

Canada Health and Social Transfer (CHST)

The overarching structure for economic sharing among the provinces regarding social programmes. Administered by the Federal Government, it is designed to provide funding to the provinces for health, post-secondary education and welfare as well as equalizing the disparities between provinces. Introduction of the transfer included significant and severe reductions in transfer payments. The CHST replaced CAP and a number of other funding mechanisms.

Free Trade Agreement (FTA)

An agreement between Canada and the US regarding trade and other economic issues.

International Monetary Fund (IMF)

A fund established at the same time as the World Bank (at the Bretton Woods conference in 1944) to assure economic equalization between rich and poor countries. Not subject to the United Nations, it is governed by a panel of countries dominated by the rich nations, especially the United States. It provides loans to poor countries in times of economic stress but places strong conditions on management of the economy, usually called SAPs (Social Adjustment Programmes). As a profit-making organization, the IMF charges interest on its loans.

Multilateral Agreement on Investment (MAI)

A treaty on foreign investment currently being negotiated within the Organization for Economic Cooperation and Development (an organization of 29 leading developed countries). The treaty would require local and foreign investors to be treated exactly the same.

Neoliberalism

A term used widely today to refer to the contemporary economic system by which a free-market operates with an absolute minimum of outside regulation and every aspect of life is incorporated into the market. In the past it has sometimes been called neo-conservatism because of the role of M. Thatcher and R. Reagan in its contemporary implementation.

North American Free Trade Agreement (NAFTA)

The first free trade agreement entered into by the United States, Canada and Mexico. It has now been extended to Chile in the FTA. (See above.)

World Bank (WB)

Established at the same time as the IMF, its official title is the International Bank for Reconstruction and Development. It encourages capital investment for reconstruction either by channelling private funds or by making loans from its own funds in two ways: directly to governments or to others with the government as guarantor.

Printed in Canada